The DEAD SEA SCROLLS

AND

THE CHRISTIAN FAITH

By

WILLIAM SANFORD LASOR

MOODY PRESS
CHICAGO

By the same author
GREAT PERSONALITIES OF THE OLD TESTAMENT
GREAT PERSONALITIES OF THE NEW TESTAMENT
BIBLIOGRAPHY OF THE DEAD SEA SCROLLS 1948-1957
THE DEAD SEA SCROLLS AND THE NEW TESTAMENT

ORIGINALLY PUBLISHED AS
Amazing Dead Sea Scrolls

Dedicated

to

The Chapel Bible Class

of

The Glendale Presbyterian Church

Glendale, California

Foreword

IT IS CUSTOMARY to offer to the reader a few words explaining why the author felt constrained to write the particular book. I must not ignore the custom—although I believe the answer will be readily apparent. The Dead Sea Scrolls are news, and people want to know about them. I have had some rather intimate contact with the subject, and perhaps I can pass along some of the things I have learned.

Of course, many others have written on the same subject. The number of books and articles in a ten-year span is phenomenal. Why add one more? Some of the books are too sensational, or too technical, or not sufficiently documented for the person who wants to read further in the subject. Or they are in some foreign language which too few American readers can read easily. Or perhaps they fail to have a purpose that appeals to the devout Christian. I would not even seem to suggest that this is negative criticism. My obligation to other scholars will be all too apparent on every page. It is simply that I believe there are many readers who want a book on the subject that is trustworthy and yet not too technical, that is sufficiently documented to engender confidence and open other areas of study, that is in their own language, and above all, that is definitely related to the implications of the Dead Sea discoveries for our Christian faith.

The name "Dead Sea Scrolls" is not a good one. Much of the material is no longer in the form of scrolls, but only fragments. The discoveries were not made in or on the Dead Sea. To say that it was "near" the Dead Sea is not sufficiently accurate. "Qumran Manuscripts" is a better term, but still not accurate. But in the mind of the average man, the term "Dead Sea Scrolls" is easier to say and easier to remember. So I have yielded to popular usage at this point.

I have tried to err on the side of understatement rather than overstatement, caution rather than sensationalism. (Those who may happen to quote my work will remedy that, I have no doubt!) In the original work, from which the present book was largely drawn, every statement was documented, requiring more than 1,600 footnotes. In the present work this documentation has frequently been omitted, both out of deference to the reader and in the interest of economy. The reader, however, can be assured that the same rigid discipline underlies the present work. It is my conviction that the Christian has nothing whatsoever to fear from the truth. We can accept every true fact and every valid inference made therefrom. At times, it may require some readjustment of our convictions, or our prejudices. But in the end, we shall find that we have lost nothing eternal from our faith.

Sitting here in the Austrian Alps, away from my friends and loved ones, I get a unique sense of pleasure in recalling the many favors that should be acknowledged here. My colleagues and students at Fuller Theological Seminary contributed to this work in a way of which they were probably not aware, by indulging my eccentricities and shortcomings during the period of research and writing of the original work. Two of my good students have particularly put me in their debt: Haskell Stone, who has checked the numerous references and thus reduced the quantity of error that inevitably gets into a manuscript; and Gerald

Swaim, who has prepared the index that will, I trust, make this work of greater usefulness. One of the faithful secretaries, Louise Hoffman, has contributed a vast amount of time and interest, not only in typing the original drafts, but more especially in helping me check hundreds of bibliographical items. The results of these efforts, requiring of her linguistic ability as well as meticulous accuracy, will, I trust, appear in a bibliography to be published later. Nor would I neglect to mention my Graduate Committee, particularly Prof. Eric L. Titus, of the School of Religion, the University of Southern California, under whose supervision the original work was written. Lastly, I am indebted to Kenneth Taylor, of the Moody Press, who encouraged me to put the results of my research into the present form.

Strobl-am-Wolfgangsee   WILLIAM SANFORD LASOR
Salzkammergut, Austria.
August 1, 1956

TO THE SECOND EDITION

An author is always pleased when a second edition is required, and I am no exception. Due no doubt to my conservative nature, I find little cause to make a major revision of my work, but there were numerous errors that needed correction, and several points that needed clarification. New discoveries have made it advisable to add to certain chapters. I am grateful to Dr. Howard F. Vos, of the Moody Press, for the suggestion that a revision rather than a reprinting should be effected.

Jerusalem, 4 July 1962   WILLIAM SANFORD LASOR

Acknowledgments

The author hereby gratefully acknowledges the kindness of the following publishers in giving permissions for the use of copyrighted portions:

The Catholic Biblical Quarterly, for quotation from "The Qumran Scrolls and the Johannine Gospel and Epistles"; (1955) 17:412; and *art. cit.*, 17:415; 559-574.

Harper & Bros., for quotation from *History of New Testament Times*, by R. H. Pfeiffer (1949) page 227.

Hebrew Union College Annual, for the tabular form of Calendar by Morgenstern, pages 130, 131.

Illustrated London News, for paragraph on page 208 from *Where Christ Himself May Have Studied:* An Essene Monastery at Khirbet Qumran, 227 (Sept. 3, 1955), pages 379-381.

The Macmillan Company, for paragraph from *Encyclopaedia Biblica*, IV, 5428; and quotation by Dupont-Sommer, *Dead Sea Scrolls*, original French, translated by E. Margaret Rowley, page 98.

Oxford University Press, London, for quotation by H. H. Rowley, *The Zadokite Fragments and the Dead Sea Scrolls* (Basil Blackwell, 1952), page 41.

Charles Scribner's Sons, for sentence from J. H. Moulton, "Zoroastrianism" in *Hasting's Dictionary of the Bible* (1919) IV:988.

Viking Press, Inc., for quotations by M. Burrows, *The Dead Sea Scrolls*, pages 294, 405.

Introduction

Y OU AND I are living in a fascinating age. This is particularly true in the area of Biblical studies. Not too many years ago, young men were being advised against work in the Old Testament or New Testament fields, "because everything worth while has been done." Today there is a rush of young scholars into these fields; and the task to be done is so great that there are still not enough men for the work.

The reason for this change of affairs is largely the result of archaeological discoveries of the past century. Those who have not worked in the subject are sometimes unaware of the fact that the modern science of archaeology is only about one hundred years old. Some of the most important discoveries have been made only in the past thirty years. And one of the most important discoveries was made less than ten years ago. The great Assyriological discoveries of a century ago gave Biblical scholars their first contact with the Babylonian "creation" and "flood" stories. The Nuzu tablets shed a great deal of light on the Patriarchal period and its customs. The discoveries at Ras Shamra, or the Ugaritic materials, opened up the study of Canaanite religion approximately contemporary with Moses. But it is the discovery of the Dead Sea Scrolls, or the Qumrân Literature, that has most recently fired the enthusiasm of Old and New Testament scholars, because this literature comes from about the time and place of the beginnings of Christianity.

Many have written on the subject of the Qumrân finds; and many more will do so. I do not apologize for adding to the number, for it is only by much work that the results of an archaeological discovery can be understood. The layman is often unaware of the fact that discovery is only the first step in the process of interpreting and evaluating what has been discovered. I remember returning from the Bible world a few years ago, to be greeted by an enthusiastic preacher with the words, "What's the latest news from the field—what's the latest discovery?" As a matter of fact, it takes twenty-five to fifty years to evaluate a discovery. Layard and Botta made their great discoveries in the middle of the nineteenth century, and scholars are still working at the problem of integrating the results of their work. Hammurapi's Law Code was discovered at the beginning of the twentieth century, and books are still being written about it. Ninety-five per cent of the Nuzu tablets have not yet been translated after thirty years; and the same can be said of the Mari tablets. Gordon's *Ugaritic Grammar, Ugaritic Handbook,* and *Ugaritic Manual,* spread across fifteen years, amply demonstrate the fact that what seems remarkably rapid to the scholarly world crawls but a weary pace in the eyes of the layman. I predict with all assurance that the year 2000 (if the world holds on that long!) will still see scholars working at the Qumrân materials.

At the same time, the person who is not a professional scholar wants to know, and, indeed, is entitled to know, the facts of the discoveries as well as their interpretation. Many claims have been made about the Dead Sea Scrolls. One scholar writes that they will revolutionize our ideas of Christianity. Another claims that Christ may have studied in the

Qumrân monastery, and John the Baptist almost certainly did. Still another claims that the Bible text is affected by the discoveries. What is the minister in the pulpit to say to his people who read these statements not in the scholarly context, but rather in the popularized form of a newspaper or magazine—or even worse, the pulp or cheap paperback account?

It is for this group that I am writing the present work. I shall try to the best of my ability to be as nontechnical as an author can be when writing of technical matters. I shall try to limit my documentation to the necessary footnotes. Once in a while I shall be forced to use a Hebrew word—but for the large part, I shall try to keep the unskilled reader in mind. *You* want to know what all this talk of the Dead Sea Scrolls is about; I shall try to tell you. Questions that ministers and laymen have asked me repeatedly, as I have spoken or lectured, or just chatted, on the subject, have formed the outline of this study. I shall simply try to answer them in turn. If at times I seem to be less positive in my conclusions than some of you might wish, please remember that I have dedicated my life to scholarship, and therefore I try to keep within the limits of that which can be proved beyond reasonable doubt or which seems highly probable. When I was a minister in the pulpit, I confess that I often spoke "with authority," in matters that would have taken years of research to substantiate. This is, I believe, a common trait (I was going to say, fault) of men of the cloth. But the professional scholar is required by his fellows to support every claim by valid documentation. In this book, the documentation will usually be omitted—but I assure you that it has not been omitted in the work on which this book is based. If at times I seem to be overcautious, then it is because the facts, as I see them, will not at present permit me to say more.

And this leads me to add one other thought. There are some Christians, it seems, who long for stronger supports for their faith. Frequently when lecturing on archaeology, I have found that they want a more dogmatic answer than I was willing to give. But tell me, what did Christians do before the discovery of archaeology? How is it that only in the last 100 years we have suddenly required props for our faith? I am grateful for every discovery that has helped me understand the Bible better. I realize that human beings need to have their faith strengthened. I, too, have felt this need. But long before the Dead Sea Scrolls were discovered, men believed their Bibles and trusted their Lord. Surely we can afford to wait patiently while the scholars work through the maze of complexities, without damage to our faith! The Bible is the same, and the Lord is the same. Is our faith in archaeology—or in Him?

Table of Contents

Contents

CHAPTER ONE

What Are the Dead Sea Scrolls?

IT MAY SEEM INCREDIBLE that there are some who still ask the question, "What are the Dead Sea Scrolls?" However, since I was asked this question very recently, and since I have set myself to answer the questions you are asking, perhaps I should risk taking the time to tell the story that has already been told hundreds of times.

THE NAME

First, let me say that the most common name, "The Dead Sea Scrolls," is actually the least satisfactory. The scrolls came from a place near the Dead Sea—but it is also near Jericho. They have been called "Scrolls from the Wilderness of Judea," "Scrolls from a Jericho Cave," "the Jerusalem Scrolls," "the 'Ain Feshkha Scrolls," and several other names. The nearest location on the Palestine map is a seasonal river known as Wadi Qumrân, and a ruins known as Khirbet Qumrân, hence the name "Qumrân Scrolls" is appropriately descriptive. But only a fraction of the material discovered is still in the form of scrolls. The balance consists of thousands of fragments of scrolls, plus other archaeological remains. The written material is therefore more accurately called, "Qumran Literature" (abbreviated QL).[1]

---

[1]Qumran is pronounced approximately, *koom-ráhn*. For typographical reasons, I shall henceforth omit the circumflex accent on the â, since it merely indicates a long vowel in the Arabic word.

13

THE DISCOVERY

Two shepherds of the Ta'âmira tribe—Bedouin who live
in the desert region west of the Dead Sea—were searching
for a goat that had strayed in the craggy hills which rise
suddenly from the plain forming the western shore of the
sea. The cliff is pocked with caves in that region, and the
rock is friable. It is with considerable risk that a person
climbs the hills or enters a cave. I know, for the rock
crumbled under me as I was setting up a camera, and I slid
a considerable distance, trying to save the camera, and gain-
ing a few bruises in the process. The Bedouin tossed a rock
into one of the caves and heard a crashing sound. Entering
the cave, Mohammed edh-Dhib and Ahmed Mohammed
found eight large jars. From one of these they drew out
three leather scrolls, which they took to an antiquities dealer
in Bethlehem. The dealer declared the scrolls to be worth-
less.

Next, the Bedouin took the scrolls to a shopkeeper who
thought the writing on a fragment broken from one of the
scrolls was Syriac. He took the scrolls to the St. Mark's
Syrian Orthodox Convent in Old Jerusalem. The time was
spring or early summer, 1947.[2]

On Wednesday, February 18, 1948, Father Butros Sowmy,
of St. Mark's Convent, telephoned the American School of
Oriental Research in Jerusalem, and talked with Prof. John
C. Trever, acting director *pro tempore* of the school. The
director of the school, Prof. Millar Burrows, was at the time
on a trip to Baghdad. Prof. William H. Brownlee, an Annual
Fellow of the school (as was Trever), was away from the
school temporarily. Trever arranged for Sowmy to bring

---

[2]Cf. *Discoveries in the Judean Desert*, Vol. I, ed. D. Barthélemy
and J. T. Milik (Oxford: Clarendon Press, 1955), p. 5.

the scrolls to the school. He did so, accompanied by his brother Karim Sowmy.[3]

It is fortunate, if not providential, that Trever was not only somewhat skilled in paleography (the study of ancient writing) but also expert in photography. He recognized the writing as similar to that of the Nash papyrus, and immediately sensed the possibility of an important discovery. With outdated film, that was never intended for copy work, and with fluctuating electric current, he managed to get quite satisfactory photographs of the scrolls. In fact, it was these photographs that were subsequently published, when permission to rephotograph the scrolls could not be obtained. A 35-mm negative was sent off by air mail to Prof. William F. Albright, the dean of American archaeologists and expert paleographer, who confirmed Trever's judgment, and announced a tentative date of about 150 B.C. for the manuscript. Trever had meanwhile identified the largest of the scrolls as a complete manuscript of Isaiah.[4]

Meanwhile, Prof. Eleazar L. Sukenik, expert in Palestinian Archaeology at the Hebrew University, Jerusalem, had come into the story. According to his account, Mar Athanasius Y. Samuel, Syrian Archbishop-Metropolitan of Jerusalem, had purchased some of the scrolls. Samuel had shown his purchase to a number of persons, including members of the École Biblique, a Dominican college of Biblical and Archaeological studies in Jerusalem, all of whom declared them to be late. Then he took the scrolls to a Jewish physician, Dr. Maurice Brown, who in turn relayed the news to Dr. Judah L. Magnes, then president of Hebrew University. Magnes

---

[3]For Trever's account, see "The Discovery of the Scrolls," *BA*, 11 (1948): 46-57.

[4]Cf. W. F. Albright, "The Dead Sea Scrolls of St. Mark's Monastery," in *BASOR*, 118 (Apr. 1950): 5-6; and M. Burrows, *The Dead Sea Scrolls* (New York: Viking Press, 1955), pp. 3-7.

referred the matter to the university librarian, who sent two representatives to the monastery to examine the scrolls. They did not feel qualified to pronounce upon them. Sukenik was at the time in America, and by the time he had returned to Jerusalem, the bishop had departed for Syria, taking the scrolls with him.

Sukenik continues: "Then one day—it was the 25th of November, 1947—a dealer in antiquities showed me in Jerusalem a fragment of a scroll, written in the old square writing."[5] On November 29, Sukenik met with the antiquities dealer and bought several bundles of parchment and two clay vessels. That same day the United Nations Commission partitioned the land, and the Arab-Israel hostilities began.

Sukenik tells of clandestine meetings in Jerusalem, of his examination of the scrolls, and of the promise of President Magnes to provide funds for their purchase. Sukenik came to know of the visit of the Syrians to the American School, and of the subsequent removal of the scrolls to the United States "for safekeeping." The story at times reads with all the intrigue and mystery of a novel, and not a few articles have appeared labeling the whole affair a hoax. This charge will be considered later in our work.

Reports of the find began to filter through to the outside world. Albright declared it to be "the greatest manuscript discovery of modern times."[6] Prof. G. Ernest Wright reported it in an article entitled, "A Phenomenal Discovery," beginning with the words, *"The most important discovery ever made* in Old Testament manuscripts."[7] Accounts appeared in the public press in many countries and many languages. Because of the confusion in Palestine and the

---

[5]Sukenik, *'osar ha-megillôt ha-genûzôt* (Jerusalem: Bialik Foundation and Hebrew University, 1954), p. 13. This work is now available in English translation.

[6]In *BA*, 11 (1948): 55.

[7]Cf. G. E. Wright, "A Phenomenal Discovery," *BA*, 11 (1948): 21.

impossibility of getting the principals together, many contradictions appeared, and many false accusations were made. Scholars were accused of "smuggling" the documents out of the country,[8] of failing to notify the Department of Antiquities as the law required.[9] Burrows answers these points, as does Trever.[10] And they are almost the only persons in a position to know the facts. In normal times, doubtless the whole matter would have been handled differently; but the times were not normal.[10a]

PUBLICATION

Just what was "discovered" in these scrolls that passed from hand to hand? The world was not satisfied with vague announcements, regardless of the superlatives that were used; nor was the scholarly world satisfied with the verdict of a handful of scholars about something that could not be examined and verified. Fortunately, editions of the scrolls were published with what was, for normal times and even more so for a time of warfare and confusion, remarkable dispatch.

The scrolls purchased by Sukenik and the Hebrew University were published in Hebrew by the Bialik Foundation and the Hebrew University, first in partial form, and later in full.[11] They include the following works:

---

[8]G. Lankester Harding, "The Dead Sea Scrolls," *PEQ*, 81 (1949): pp. 115-116.

[9]*Discoveries in the Judean Desert*, I: p. 5.

[10]Cf. Burrows, *op. cit.*, p. 14.

[10a]Sukenik's story has now been well told by his son; cf. Y. Yadin, *The Message of the Scrolls* (New York: Simon and Schuster, 1957), pp. 15-30. A thorough account is given by John M. Allegro, *The Dead Sea Scrolls* (Pelican A376; Baltimore: Penguin Books, 1956), pp. 15-40; I cannot agree with all of Allegro's work, however. For the story by one of the first to see the scrolls only to reject them, cf. J. van der Ploeg, *The Excavations at Qumran* (New York: Longmans, Green and Co., 1958), pp. 1-28.

[11]E. L. Sukenik, *The Dead Sea Scrolls of the Hebrew University* (Jerusalem: Magnes Press, 1955), 103 pp., 58 pls. For the Hebrew edition, see p. 8, n. 5, above.

The *Hebrew University Isaiah Scroll* (1QIs[b]), a partial scroll of Isaiah, containing portions of chapters 10, 13, 16, 19–30, 35–66; from chapter 38 to the end, it is a single piece, with gaps;

The *Order of Warfare* (1QM), also known as the *War of the Sons of Light against the Sons of Darkness*, comprising nineteen columns of text describing a war (real or spiritual) between the tribes of Levi, Judah, and Benjamin, on the one hand, and the Ammonites, Moabites, Edomites, and others, on the other hand;

The *Thanksgiving Hymns* (1QH), originally four pieces, containing twelve columns of psalms, or about twenty psalms.

The scrolls originally purchased by the Syrian archbishop were published with his permission (except for one scroll[12]) by the American Schools of Oriental Research.[13] They include the following works:

The *St. Mark's Monastery Isaiah Scroll* (1QIs[a]), a complete scroll of Isaiah;

The *Habakkuk Commentary* (1QpHab.), the text of chapters 1-2 of Habakkuk with a running interpretation;

The *Manual of Discipline* (1QS), a document containing rules for the members of the religious community.

TRANSLATIONS

Translations of these works began to appear almost at once, and since translation of previously unknown documents is difficult, corrections, revisions, and improved trans-

---

[12]The so-called Lamech Scroll, which could not be unrolled at the time due to its state of decomposition. It has since been unrolled, and identified as the *Scroll of the Patriarchs*, or *A Genesis Apocryphon*.

[13]*The Dead Sea Scrolls of St. Mark's Monastery*, eds. M. Burrows, J. C. Trever, and W. H. Brownlee, Vol. I, *The Isaiah Manuscript and the Habakkuk Commentary*, Vol. II, *Plates and Transcription of the Manual of Discipline* (New Haven: American Schools of Oriental Research, 1950-1951).

lations have continued to appear. For scholarly study, annotated translations in English, French, German, and several other modern languages, can be found in several scholarly journals as well as in a number of books that have appeared. For the reader for whom the present work is intended, the most convenient translation is included in Burrows' book.[14] Unfortunately, Burrows has not seen fit to include all of the texts (he has omitted chiefly the fragmentary portions, it is true, but some of these contain significant material), nor has he indicated his own additions, emendations, or conjectures. However, I have found little occasion to be critical of his work, and have no hesitation recommending it with this minor warning. The man who wishes to make a serious study of the Qumran Literature should, of course, use several scholars' translations—or, better still, work in the Hebrew text.

EXCAVATIONS

All that has been described thus far is not indeed scientific archaeology. A priest bringing to the archaeologist something that he claims he obtained from a merchant who claims he bought it from a Bedouin who claimed he found it in a cave—surely this is flimsy evidence! Prof. Solomon Zeitlin, editor of the *Jewish Quarterly Review,* took the lead in challenging such a "discovery," and his criticisms were at first not ill-founded.[15] As soon as conditions would permit, scholars undertook systematic archaeological investigation.

Through the interest of Capt. Philippe Lippens, a Belgian

---

[14]Burrows, *The Dead Sea Scrolls,* pp. 349-415, *More Light on the Dead Sea Scrolls* (New York: Viking Press, 1958), pp. 387-404.

[15]Zeitlin has published a volume which is chiefly composed of previously published articles, *The Dead Sea Scrolls and Modern Scholarship* (Jewish Quarterly Review Monograph Series, 3; Philadelphia: The Dropsie College for Hebrew and Cognate Learning, 1956), 154 pp. It must be recorded, however, that Zeitlin has failed to adjust his objections in the light of the more recent evidence.

army officer serving as an observer for the United Nations, who in turn interested General Lash, British commander of the Arab Legion, Colonel Ashton, archaeological adviser to the Legion, and G. Lankester Harding, Director General of the Department of Antiquities of the Hashemite Kingdom of the Jordan, an expedition was arranged, and a detachment of legionnaires under Capt. Akkash el-Zeben was able to locate the cave where the Bedouin had found the manuscripts.[16] That was January 28, 1949—nearly two years after the original find. There was evidence that the cave had been visited in the meantime.

The question has been raised as to whether it was the same cave. Systematic excavation was undertaken by Harding and Père Roland de Vaux of the *Ecole Biblique,* from February 8 to March 5, 1949. The floor of the cave was carefully sifted, and thousands of manuscript fragments were recovered, as well as fragments of jars, other pottery remains, and fragments of the cloth that had wrapped the scrolls. The first reports that fragments had been discovered that actually fit holes in the previously discovered manuscripts turned out to be false. However, there can be no doubt that the writing, the writing material, the pottery, and the cloth, which had been found in the cave, were of precisely the same kind as that brought by the Bedouin to Bethlehem. It would take an extraordinarily perverse mind, it seems to me, to refuse to be convinced by the baskets full of evidence that have been produced.[17]

---

[16]Cf. G. Lambert, "La grotte aux manuscrits du désert de Juda," *Revue Générale Belge,* 51 (1949-50): 405-424, for Lippens' account; and for Harding's account, "The Dead Sea Scrolls," *PEQ,* 81 (1949): 112, and *Discoveries in the Judean Desert,* I, pp. 5-6.

[17]Cf. R. de Vaux, "La cachette des manuscrits hébreux," *RB,* 56 (1949): 234-237, and "La grotte des manuscrits hébreux," *ibid.,* 56: 586-609. Cf. also, O. R. Sellers, "Excavation of 'Manuscript Cave' at 'Ain Fashkha," *BASOR,* 114 (Apr. 1949): 5-9.

WHERE IS THE CAVE?

Lankester Harding locates the cave at the co-ordinates 1934.1287 of the Palestine survey map.[18] This can be more easily understood by most of us if we say that the cave is 2½ miles north of the spring 'Ain Feshkha, and 7½ miles south of Jericho, in the rocks west of the Dead Sea, about a mile from the shore, and about 1,000 feet above the surface of the sea.

Subsequently other caves have been explored, and some of them have yielded other manuscript finds. The first cave is therefore identified as 1Q—the first Qumran cave. All finds taken from it are identified with the *siglum* 1Q.

These are the Dead Sea Scrolls. But there is much more. Other excavations have been made; other materials have been found. In order to understand fully what is meant by the expression, we shall have to cover each phase of discovery, and then attempt to explain the entire picture as we reconstruct it.

---

[18]F. M. Cross gives it as 1933. 1289 (correcting *Discoveries in the Judean Desert, I*); cf. *The Ancient Library of Qumran* (Garden City, N. Y.: Doubleday & Co., 1958), p. 8, n. 9. The difference is relatively unimportant for our purpose.

CHAPTER TWO

Other Caves and Other Finds

To judge from some of the statements that have been published by certain scholars, you might suppose that only the original eleven scrolls (representing six compositions)[1] had been found. They were, we are told, originally in a synagogue in Hebron, were spirited away from there during a pogrom in 1929 and hidden in Jerusalem, and were taken from a chest in the monastery in 1948. This naïve presentation completely overlooks the fact that tens of thousands of manuscript fragments, all in similar script, were recovered from at least eleven Qumran caves. Are we to suppose that some clever antiquities dealers managed to have manuscripts forged by the hundreds, all properly aged and paleographically correct, that these manuscripts then were torn into fragments (why?—complete manuscripts would be worth more!), the fragments carefully deposited in several caves, broken pottery of the correct style and age placed with the fragments, and all this so cleverly done that expert archaeologists were completely fooled? But we are running ahead of our story. First, we must answer a few questions.

WHAT OTHER CAVES WERE DISCOVERED?

In the Qumran area, probably the region where John the Baptist stayed until the days of his baptizing, and where Jesus went to be tempted of Satan, the Judean desert southeast of Jerusalem rolls gradually from 2,000 feet or more

---

[1]See p. 18.

above sea level to sea level, then drops precipitously to the shore of the Dead Sea more than 1,200 feet below sea level. A valley coming from Bethlehem cuts down through this wilderness and empties into the Dead Sea. This valley has different names at different points: near Bethlehem it is Wadi[2] Ta'amrê; where it empties into the sea it is Wadi Darajeh; where our interest is centered it is called Wadi Murabba'at.

North of Wadi Murabba'at a few miles is Wadi en-Nâr, which is the same valley as the Kidron Valley at Jerusalem. And north of Wadi en-Nâr another few miles is Wadi Qumran. The cliff that faces on the Dead Sea will of course conform to these (and other) valleys that cut down through it. In a geological age past, the cliff was greatly eroded at Wadi Qumran, and a plateau was formed from the alluvial deposit; the plateau is about 300 feet above the surrounding shore. Wadi Qumran has since worn a canyon in this plateau. There are hundreds of caves in the face of the cliff, and several others in the steep sides of the plateau facing on the canyon. About 230 caves were explored by archaeologists, after the original finds, of which about 40 contained pottery and other objects, 25 contained pottery of the same type as that found in the first cave (1Q), and a dozen or more contained manuscript fragments.[3]

Eleven of the caves in the area of Wadi Qumran have thus far yielded manuscript fragments that can be compared with the original scrolls from cave 1Q. The most important discoveries, next to those of cave 1Q, were made in caves 4Q and 11 Q—which we shall discuss later. Some fragments were recovered, together with other archaeological mate-

---

[2]Wadi is an Arabic word, now Anglicized, for a seasonal river, dry except in the rainy season. The word is pronounced *waa'dee*, with *a* as in hat.

[3]Cf. R. de Vaux, "Fouille au Khirbet Qumrân, rapport préliminaire," *RB*, 60 (1953): 83-86.

rials, from caves in Wadi Murabba'at. Still other fragments were discovered in a ruins known as Khirbet Mird, which may be more familiar to some if we identify it as the site of Hyrcania. Not all of these caves can be dated at the same period, and, as we shall see, we must be careful not to confuse the evidence produced.

THE "MONASTERY"

In 1873, the French Orientalist, Canon Clermont-Ganneau, noted and described a ruin near Qumran, called by the obvious name Khirbet Qumran (i.e., ruin of Qumran). Albert Vincent had been there in 1906, and Gustav Dalman in 1914. Dalman identified the ruins as a Roman fort. The ruin is located on the alluvial plateau.

Harding and de Vaux had visited the ruins in 1949, but the first systematic excavation was made late in 1951. Since then, four other campaigns have been conducted, in 1953, 1954, 1955, and 1956. These have been reported in "preliminary" reports—as archaeologists call them; actually the reports are sufficiently full for basing sound conclusions on them—published chiefly in *Revue Biblique*.[4]

There was one main structure at Khirbet Qumran, about 100×122 feet, with secondary buildings at the northeast, west, and south. In archaeological excavation it is necessary to work from the top down, and the latest levels are uncovered first. However, after the archaeologists have reached the "bottom," and there is no evidence of any further occupation beneath that level, they number the levels from the bottom up. At Khirbet Qumran there were three levels. Level I showed signs of having been seriously de-

---

[4] Cf. de Vaux, *art. cit.*, *RB*, 60 (1953): 83-106; "Fouilles de Khirbet Qumrân rapport préliminaire sur la deuxième campagne," *RB*, 61 (1954): 206-236; "Chronique archéologique: Khirbet Qumrân," *RB*, 63 (1956): 73-74; "fouilles de Khirbet Qumrân. Rapport préliminaire sur les 3ᵉ, 4ᵉ, et 5ᵉ campagnes," *RB*, 63 (1956): 533-577.

stroyed by an earthquake. Level II gave evidence of having been occupied by the same persons or the same general type of inhabitants as Level I. It was destroyed by fire. Level III was occupied by an entirely different sort of inhabitants.

Those not familiar with archaeology may wonder how such statements can be made. If the occupants move out of a house, they will take everything of value with them. However, they may overlook a few coins in dark corners, especially with dirt floors, and they will leave behind pieces of broken pottery, etc. On the other hand, if there is a catastrophe, much more will be left behind. An earthquake will preserve some objects in the fallen ruins that would have been consumed by fire. Fire leaves a distinctive layer of ashes. Rebuilt and patched-up walls can easily be distinguished, as can rubbish piles from the clean-up. Objects left behind by a religious community will be quite different from those left behind by a garrison of soldiers. The archaeologist who has spent years in his science can interpret these details with amazing accuracy.

It was evident to the archaeologists that Levels I and II were equipped for feeding a large number of persons, but were not equipped for housing purposes. For example, there was one large room in the southwest corner of Level I with a bench running around all the walls. It could have been used for a large dining hall or large meetings. In the northeast corner there was a suite of rooms with several indications that they formed a kitchen and pantry. The remains of a large number of ceramic vessels were found, obviously left in orderly arrangement, totaling nearly 1,100 pieces, chiefly plates and bowls. At the south of the central court a room contained several basins, and in the southeast corner, there were two cisterns or tanks which appeared to have been used for bathing or baptizing. One of these had 14 steps leading down to it. Water had obviously been brought from natural basins in the Buqê'ah, or wilderness drained by Wadi Qumran above the cliffs, where it accumulated during the rainy season, by an aqueduct still traceable across the nearby countryside, to a large cistern discovered south of the building. This large cistern in turn fed the smaller cisterns or tanks in the building.

In the vicinity of the interior cisterns were a lavatory, a sink, and a latrine. The last item had a pavement around it, a ring of pottery, then pebbles, and under them the natural marl of the region—all of which formed a well-designed septic tank.

In Level II, fragments of a brick structure which had been plastered over were found on the upper floor. They were taken to the Archaeological Museum in Jerusalem and reconstructed, forming a narrow table about 16½ feet long and 20 inches high. The distance from the kitchen suggested that the table was not for dining purposes. The discovery of two inkwells in the same level, one bronze and one terra cotta (one with dried ink still in it), furnished the clue that led archaeologists to call the room a *scriptorium,* or the place where the scribes produced the manuscripts.

Other items were found, of which we shall mention only a pottery factory, including pits for tempering the clay and two ovens for firing it, described by de Vaux as "the most complete and best preserved in Palestine."[5] It is obvious that the inhabitants of the Community not only ate at the refectory but also engaged in productive work.

THE CEMETERY

East of the Khirbeh,[6] separated from it by an esplanade,

---

[5]*Art. cit., RB,* 61 (1954): 567.
[6]The word should only be pronounced Khirbet when it is joined to the following word, as Khirbet Qumran.

there is a large cemetery which extends over the plateau and the four small hills to the east. The cemetery contains more than 1,000 graves, placed in three groups with lanes between them. In the plateau portion of the cemetery, the graves are oriented north-south, with the heads toward the south (one was toward the north). On the hills, east-west caves were more common, with the heads toward the east. A number of the graves were opened, and important facts were revealed.

The bodies had been laid on their backs, with hands either folded across the pelvic region or placed straight at the sides. No objects of value were found in the graves, suggesting either poverty or lack of interest in items of value. The skeletons were extremely fragile, but it was possible to preserve nine of them with paraffin and ship them to Prof. H. V. Vallois, Director of *Le Musée de l'Homme* in Paris. He identified them as Alpine, or better Armenoid (even today the dominant element of the indigenous population of Palestine), two between 20 and 25 years of age, four about 40, two over 50; several were female. While this report is extremely important, de Vaux rightly cautions us to remember that less than 1 percent of the cemetery was tested, which is insufficient for statistical purposes.[7]

POTTERY

As is usual in Palestinian archaeology, large quantities of pottery were found. Fragments of at least 50 jars were recovered from cave 1Q. Some of these were pieced together, like giant three-dimensional jig-saw puzzles, and they proved to be unlike any previously discovered. Later, two whole jars were purchased by Sukenik, and are published

---

[7]*Art. cit., RB,* 60 (1958): 95-103.

in his posthumous work.[8] Several scholars promptly concluded that the jars had been manufactured expressly to
contain the manuscripts. Later, when similar jars were
discovered at the "monastery"[9] of Khirbet Qumran, one of
them sunken in the ground in a corner of the kitchen, it was
concluded that the jars had been manufactured and used
for the storage of grain, oil, and other foodstuffs.[10] The use
of the jars to store the manuscripts in the caves was then
thought to have been an emergency measure in the face of
grave danger. (Personally, I think the former explanation
is still very much a live option.)

To the untrained, pottery chronology is often subject to
suspicion. How can you tell the age of a piece of a dish?
But if you ever have the opportunity to study pottery, you
will see that there is quite a science connected with it.
Pottery is cheap, fragile, and almost imperishable as fragments. If a woman drops a cheap jar or bowl and it breaks,
she does not try to salvage it. She kicks the pieces in the
corner of the room or tosses them on the rubbish heap.
Robbers did not steal clay jugs from an abandoned village.
And clay, once it has been fired, is as imperishable as the
rocks of the hillside. Pottery fragments do not melt or
dissolve. Walking on them will not break them beyond a

---

[8]Cf. *'ôṣar ha-megillôt ha-genûzôt* (Jerusalem: Bialik Press and
Hebrew University, 1954), Fig. 4. I had the opportunity of buying
similar jars, perhaps the same jars, in Bethlehem in 1952. Two factors hindered me: my incompetence to determine authenticity of
such objects, and the antiquities law of the country.

[9]I put the word in quotes, since the Community, as we shall see,
included women and children—hence this was not in the true sense a
monastery.

[10]The burying of large jars in the ground to serve as storage for
foodstuffs, particularly grain, is a common practice. I have seen it in
the villages of northwest China. Rats, etc., cannot get through fired
pottery. Temperature extremes are avoided. Space is saved. However, a somewhat dry climate is rather a prerequisite for this method.

certain point (depending on the curvature of the fragment). Millions of pieces can be found anywhere in the Middle East.

Moreover, women are closely connected with pottery, and women like changes of style. Enterprising potters have always known this, and new styles were sure to encourage new purchases. Variations of shape, of coloring, of decoration, and the like, can be traced, just as we can identify styles of architecture, clothing, and even dinner glassware. Archaeologists who specialize in pottery chronology have classified thousands upon thousands of fragments, and have reached the point where they can date a piece of a jug they happen to kick on the ground.

Of course, pottery chronology is relative. I mean by that, the archaeologists have first arranged the styles in the correct order (controlled by other data, coins, letters on clay tablets giving names of rulers, scarabs, and many other items), and then assigned to a particular style a name, such as "Hellenistic," or "Obeid." That style can be dated approximately—but not absolutely. The experts dated the Qumran jars "Hellenistic," which is in the period 323–63 B.C. If the experts did not specifically say so, it was because they thought everyone would realize that these dates are only close approximations. Styles may hang on in one region longer than in another. Or they may originate in one region before they are carried to another (they usually do!) The dates were only approximate—but it would be most unusual if they were not within a few decades or at most a century of the actual date.

Several objections were raised against the dating of the Qumran scrolls from Qumran pottery.

It was argued that there was nothing to guarantee the contemporaneity of the two classes of material. This sounds reasonable. The drinking glasses in a library (if they still use glasses) are not necessarily of the same date as the books. Only if it could be proved that the jars were made for the manuscripts would the date of the jars be relevant. Actually, this is going too far, for it is also possible that the same group produced the jars and the manuscripts, without intending the one for the other. It would be enough to demonstrate this latter fact. The *scriptorium* in the Khirbeh, the pottery factory, and the presence of the same type of jars in the ruin as in the caves, is reasonably conclusive, although not positively so.

It was also argued that the archaeologists could not agree on the date of the pottery, and it was inferred therefrom that pottery chronology was not reliable. Zeitlin was particularly vociferous,[11] although not alone. Actually, the chronologists were changing their estimates, but only to narrow down their figures. To shift from "Hellenistic" to "Maccabean," or "pre-Herodian," is only to narrow the dates 323–63 B.C. to 165–63 B.C. and then to perhaps 63–37 B.C. The revision to "early Roman" did not substantially alter these dates. What was happening was simply this: the archaeologists, of themselves, were correcting their observations in the light of further observations. This is scientific methodology at its best! To dismiss it cavalierly and to say that the only criterion of dating the manuscripts is internal evidence[12] is, in my opinion, unwarranted, and comes close to a repudiation of the whole scientific method.

CLOTH WRAPPINGS

When the original scrolls were brought to light, there

---

[11] Cf. "The Hebrew Scrolls Once More and Finally," *JQR*, 41 (1950-51): 10-14; "The Propaganda of the Hebrew Scrolls and the Falsification of History," *ibid.*, 46 (1955-56): 164.

[12] Cf. Zeitlin, *art. cit.*, *JQR* 46 (1955-56): 165.

were fragments of cloth attached to some of them. The cloth was badly decomposed, but portions were sent to experts for examination. Later, fragments of the same kind of cloth were recovered from the dirt floor of cave 1Q.[13]

Harding took some of the cloth to England in 1949, and asked Mrs. G. M. Crowfoot, an expert in textiles, to examine it. Her report was published in 1951, and a fuller report by her is included in *Discoveries in the Judean Desert*.[14] Major G. O. Searle of His Majesty's Norfolk Flax Establishment also made a study of the cloth. It was definitely of flax, some of it of fine quality. Some pieces had a design woven into them with blue cloth. Others were plain. Still others had fringes. Some of the fragments were of coarse material, and from the wadded shape of them it was obvious that they had been used as jar covers. Mrs. Crowfoot was satisfied that the linen was native Palestinian, probably woven locally. Miss Louisa Bellinger, of the staff of the Textile Museum at Washington, D.C., who had been requested to examine a fragment of the cloth brought to America by Prof. Ovid R. Sellers, was in agreement with this conclusion.[15] Mrs. Crowfoot concluded that the cloths had been woven especially for the purposes of covering the scrolls and serving as jar covers, in the light of the designs woven in the cloth, for the designs made it possible to calculate the size and shape of the original pieces of cloth. That such wrappings were used for covering manuscripts is known from rabbinic literature.[16]

Four ounces of this cloth were sent to Dr. W. F. Libby of the Institute for Nuclear Studies, the University of

[13]For descriptions and photographs, cf. *Discoveries in the Judean Desert*, 1: 18 and Plate I, Nos. 8-10.
[14]*Ibid.*, 1: 18-38. Cf. also, *PEQ*, 83 (1951): 5-31.
[15]Cf. report in *BASOR*, 118 (Apr. 1950): 9-11.
[16]Cf. *Shabbat* 9. 6.

Chicago, for a radioactive carbon (Carbon-14) test. At that time, the accuracy of radiocarbon dating was within limits of error of ±10% (it has since been improved to within ±5%). Dr. Libby reported that the cloth was to be dated A.D. 33, with limits of error ranging from 167 B.C. to A.D. 233.[17] Some scholars, with obvious misunderstanding of the science of radiocarbon dating,[18] have criticized dates of the cloth based on this test. Organic material, i.e., material which lives, replenishes the minute traces of radioactive carbon as long as the life process continues. However, when it dies, there is no further replenishment of this isotope. Since it is radioactive, it breaks down at a known rate (known as the "half-life," since it is a geometric progression of half quantities). By measuring the amount of Carbon-14 remaining, the scientist can tell when the life process ceased. Since the formula is a geometric progression, it becomes less accurate as the time period becomes greater. Some have objected that, since wood from the glacial age cannot be measured with great accuracy, therefore we cannot trust the dates of the cloth from the Qumran cave. But this is sheer nonsense. The limits of error are a *percentage*. If the object being tested is only 100 years old, the test is accurate to within 10 years on either side. If the object is 10,000 years old, the test is accurate to within ±1,000 years. The limits on the cloth are not to be measured by the limits of a test on glacial-age wood. Moreover, to argue that only one piece of cloth was tested, and it is conceivable that its date is at the low end of the limits of error (i.e., A.D. 233), and then to imply that the error should

---

[17]To quibble over 167 or 168 is nonsense, since 10 per cent of 1917 years is only 191.7 anyway. The 200 years is itself a round number.
[18]G. R. Driver, for example, explains it as depending on the length of time light has been kept from the object; cf. *The Hebrew Scrolls* (London: Oxford University Press, 1951), pp. 46-47.

be figured from that date is to miss the significance of limits of error. It is granted that a single test is not as precise as several tests would be. But that is why such latitude is allowed in establishing limits of error.

More important is the relationship of the cloth to the scrolls. The cloth, we can be reasonably certain, was made (at least the flax was cut, so that the life process stopped) within the time limits set by the Carbon-14 test. Mrs. Crowfoot's studies are, in my opinion, convincing. The cloth was made to cover manuscript scrolls. It may have been a few years old when the manuscripts were written—but it is hardly likely that this time interval could have been more than a few years. Or the manuscripts may have been quite old when wrapped in the new cloth. We shall have to use other lines of evidence to determine this point. But we cannot ignore the cloth or the radiocarbon dating of it.[19]

The Copper Scrolls

In the spring of 1952, two badly oxidized copper scrolls were found in cave 3Q. They are approximately 12 inches high, and appear to have been originally formed of three sheets, each about 32 inches long, riveted together to form a continuous strip. Roll "A" has about 6½ turns of the copper, with the joint coming 2¼ turns from the outer edge. Roll "B" has 3½ turns. The end of "A" has rivets which are spaced identically with holes in the end of "B" indicating that they were once joined.

According to a report of Prof. H. Wright Baker in the *Manchester Guardian* of June 1, 1956, the specialists have

---

[19]The question is sometimes raised, why not test the manuscript material? The answer is simple: it takes considerable material to make a test, and no responsible person has been willing to sacrifice the necessary quantity of valuable manuscripts. But who would be convinced by radiocarbon dating of the manuscripts, if he is not convinced by radiocarbon dating of the cloth?

succeeded in unrolling and deciphering these copper scrolls. The decipherment confirms in part the provisional conclusion of Prof. Kuhn which had been made on the basis of the embossing of the reverse of the outer layer of the scroll, namely that the scrolls contained a description of hidden treasures.

The details that might lead unauthorized persons to the sites of the hoards have been suppressed, according to Lankester Harding (as reported by Baker). There are sixty hoards of treasure listed in the copper scrolls, comprising nearly 200 tons of gold and silver, buried at depths of from 16 to 18 feet, in a line between Hebron and Nablus (the ancient Shechem). We must now wait until the archaeologists are able to determine whether the sites of these hoards can be identified, and if so, whether the hoards have been already discovered. It is of course possible that the records are untrue at the outset: in other words, there may never have been such treasures buried by the Qumran group.[20]

COINS

One of the most important discoveries in the excavation of the Khirbeh was a large quantity of coins. The first excavation uncovered about 250 coins in nearly all places and in all levels of Khirbet Qumran. Later campaigns added several hundred more. None were found in the Qumran caves. The coins were badly oxidized, but could be read after receiving long chemical treatment. Because of the im-

---

[20]The question has already been raised, according to Baker's report, why an Essene sect should have shown such interest in wealth of this amount. The answer, of course, will not be immediately forthcoming. We would suggest, however, that it might possibly be that the Qumran sect showed such interest in wealth *because it was not an Essene sect at all.* Some scholars seem to have ruled out this possibility entirely. In our opinion, it is unrealistic to formulate conclusions until all evidence is taken into consideration.

portance of the finds for the dating of the Community, I shall include the complete list of the coins found in the first campaign, as published by de Vaux. The coins of later campaigns have not been published in tabular form (to my knowledge), but de Vaux tells us that they "appear to confirm the dates proposed in the last report for the three periods of the buildings.[21] The list follows:

Description of Coins	Number
Antiochus VII, 136, 130, 129 B.C.	3
John Hyrcanus, 135-104 B.C.	14
Alexander Jannaeus, 103-76 B.C.	38
Hasmoneans, uncertain	15
Antigonus (Mattathias), 40-37 B.C.	2
Herod the Great, 37-4 B.C.	1
Tyre, 29 B.C.	1
Herod Archelaus, 4 B.C–A.D. 6	6
Procurators under Augustus	3
Procurators under Tiberius	7
Agrippa I, A.D. 37-44	23
Procurators under Claudius	5
Procurators under Nero	15
First Revolt, Year 2, A.D. 67-68	11
Caesarea under Nero, A.D. 67-68	8
Dora under Nero, A.D. 67-68	1
Dora, same type, date missing	1
Vespasian, A.D. 70	1
Ashkalon, A.D. 72-73	1
Same type, date effaced, surcharged "X"	1
Judaea capta under Titus, after A.D. 79	3
Agrippa II, about A.D. 86	1
Second Revolt, A.D. 132-135	13
Byzantine (two coins on the surface)	3
Arab (one coin on the surface)	2

Certain facts should be noted, as de Vaux points out.

---

[21] *Art. cit., RB,* 61: 567-568.

There is almost complete absence of coins during the long reign of Herod the Great.

There are no coins between the time of Agrippa II and the Second Revolt.

Coins from the second century B.C. were found in Level I and the portion of Level I used again as part of Level II.

Coins from the first century A.D. were found in Level II, except those marked "Caesarea under Nero" and later, all of which were found in Level III.

From the rubbish heap about 100 feet north of the building, about 30 coins were taken from a trial trench: one of Antiochus II, another similar but illegible, three of John Hyrcanus, eleven of Alexander Jannaeus, nine of uncertain Hasmoneans, one of Archelaus.

De Vaux comes to the following conclusions:

1. Level I and the rubbish pile are to be dated in the Hellenistic period, from about 135 B.C. to a time just before or soon after the beginning of the reign of Herod the Great.

2. Level II was occupied from about the beginning of the Christian era to about A.D. 67-68.

3. Level III was occupied from A.D. 70 to the end of the first century A.D., and then briefly in the time of the Second Revolt (A.D. 132-135).[22]

This fits very nicely with the archaeological evidence of the levels and the building damage. Level I ended with an earthquake in 31 B.C. (although it is possible that the occupation of the building may have ended before that by persecution or other cause). Level II ended in conflagration, possibly by war (to judge by arrowheads, etc., found in the ruins).

---

[22] de Vaux, *art. cit.*, RB, 61: 230.

In a later chapter, when we are considering the date of the Qumran Community, we shall find these facts most helpful.

'Ain Feshkha

We have mentioned a spring south of Khirbet Qumran, known as 'Ain Feshkha (p. 21, above). In 1956 the remains of buildings were noticed and exploration was begun by Père de Vaux. The excavation was resumed early in 1958. According to de Vaux's report, the building was an agricultural center, with a paved enclosure adjoining that was possibly used for drying dates. Another courtyard on the northern side, with water tanks and aqueducts, may have been used for the tanning of leather for sandals, straps, and tools. The untanned skins used for the manuscripts may have been made here as well.[23]

---

[23]Cf. de Vaux, "'Ain Feshkha," *RB* 65 (1958): 406-408.

CHAPTER THREE

Manuscripts and Fragments

WHILE THERE IS COMMON KNOWLEDGE about the Dead Sea Scrolls, in a general way, I have found, when lecturing on the subject, that specific knowledge is unusual, and whereas knowledge of the manuscripts or scrolls is widespread, knowledge of the fragments of manuscripts is severely limited. Therefore I would like to set forth in considerable detail just what has been found. It must be acknowledged at the start that even as this is being written, other fragments are being pieced together, and other manuscripts are being identified from the results. Therefore, this list is not complete.

THE MANUSCRIPTS

Chapter One includes a description of the manuscripts that were found. Some of these are fairly complete, but others are to a greater or lesser degree damaged. Pieces which had been broken off may be identified among the fragments, and will in that case help us where readings are at present conjectural. We must not, therefore, conclude that the manuscript-find is now closed.

Moreover, there are rumors that another manuscript (or possibly manuscripts) will one day turn up when the unauthorized person (or persons) holding it is convinced that it is safe and profitable to make it known. This may be in the nature of unfounded gossip,[1] but the possibility should not be overlooked. Further, other caves in other areas may still disclose unsuspected treasures. I mention these points to forestall the conclusion that our source of material is exhausted and our knowledge is now complete.[1a]

The Fragments

Tens of thousands of fragments were gathered from the floors of the caves, and are gradually being sorted and classified in the Archaeological Museum in Jerusalem. The exact number is probably not known, and would be of no great value. Dr. Frank Cross says that 382 different manuscripts are represented by the fragments so far identified from just cave 4Q alone.[2] Add to this number the different manuscripts represented by the fragments in each of the other caves (none of which yielded as much as cave 4Q), and it is possible that the total number of manuscripts was between 600 and 800. Some of the fragments are so small that they contain a single letter of the alphabet. These are of little value. Other fragments contain just a few words, and still other fragments contain two or more columns (or portions of columns) of text. With a good eye, a scholar can match fragments to make larger pieces. For example, when the first publication of 4QSam[a] [that means the *a* or first manuscript of the books of Samuel from cave 4Q] was made, 27 fragments had been pieced together to form parts

[1]One of the original intermediaries, faced with an unexpected question, "Where are the other two manuscripts?", told me in 1952, "One is lost; the other will turn up any day now." It has not yet turned up. I admit that he may have been shrewder in his answer than he appeared to be.

[1a]Discoveries from cave 11Q, not yet fully published, serve to underscore this paragraph.

[2]Cf. F. M. Cross, Jr., *The Ancient Library of Qumran and Modern Biblical Studies* (Garden City, N. Y.: Doubleday & Co., 1958), pp. 19-36.

of two columns. Two years later this particular manuscript had grown to 47 columns (out of the original 57), including 23 of the 33 columns of I Samuel and 24 of the 24 columns of II Samuel. How many pieces had been joined to form this patchwork is not recorded.[3] Once several words are identified, it is usually possible to identify the passage from a concordance. In some cases, however, no concordance is available (for previously unknown works, or Hebrew texts of works previously known only in another language, for example), and scholars are forced to do the best they can. For this reason you will sometimes read an article identifying an "unknown" fragment as part of a certain work, and later read that it is part of an entirely different work. This does not mean that the scholars do not know what they are doing. It means simply that they are honest men, doing the best they can, and correcting their mistakes when they recognize them. To date, the mistakes have been few indeed!

As in the case of the scrolls, the fragments represent several types of literature, and not just Biblical writings.

The Biblical Texts

Of the 382 manuscripts represented by the fragments of cave 4Q, about 100 are Biblical manuscripts. Every book of the Hebrew Bible, with the exception of Esther, is represented. To the best of my knowledge, no fragment of Esther has been identified among the finds from other caves. The following description is not intended to be a complete catalogue of the texts thus far identified. Rather I present it as an indication of what has actually been found. It is too early to attempt a complete catalogue, for each new identification would make it out of date.

Genesis. Fragments of five different MSS from 4Q, fol-

---

[3]Cf. Cross, "A Report on the Biblical Fragments of Cave Four in Wâdī Qumran," *BASOR*, 141 (Feb., 1956): 10-11; *The Ancient Library of Qumran*, p. 31.

lowing the Massoretic Text [hereafter, MT]. Fragments from other caves.

Exodus. Fragments of six MSS from 4Q, following the Old Greek text (cf. Acts 7:14 and Exod. 1:5 LXX). A "superb specimen of Exodus" was found, in the Samaritan recension.[4] Other fragments were recovered from 2Q and Wadi Murabba'at [hereafter, Mur].

Leviticus. Three fragments from 4Q; mixed text types. Two different MSS in Paleo-Hebrew script were represented in 1Q, 2Q, another in 6Q. Papyrus fragments in Greek from 4Q. An almost complete scroll of Lev. in Paleo-Hebrew script from 11Q has been reported.

Numbers. Four MSS from 2Q, two from 4Q, one of which has a text between the Old Samaritan and Old Greek..

Deuteronomy. One of the favorite books; 14 different MSS in 4Q, two or three in 2Q, and others.

Joshua. Two MSS in 4Q, representing the Hebrew text from which the Septuagint (Greek translation; hereafter LXX) was made, fragments in Syro-Palestinian in Khirbet Mird.

Judges. Two MSS in 4Q, another in 1Q.

Samuel. Three MSS in 4Q, all representing LXX text. One is the oldest MS yet identified, at the end of the third century B.C.[5]

Kings. One MS in 4Q, another MS (not MT) in 6Q on papyrus.

Isaiah. Another of the favorite works. In addition to the scrolls 1QIs[a] and 1QIs[b] described in Chapter One, 12 MSS of Isaiah were found to be represented in the fragments of 4Q, and other fragments in other caves, including 1Q and Mur.

---

[4]Cf. P. W. Skehan, "Exodus in the Samaritan Recension from Qumran," *JBL*, 74 (1955): 182-187.

[5]*Ibid.*, 182.

Jeremiah. Three MSS in 4Q, another in 2Q, 4Q Jer[b] follows the shorter text found in LXX.

Ezekiel. Two MSS in 4Q, another in 1Q.

The Twelve. Eight MSS in 4Q. 4QXII[c] indicates Hosea, Joel, Amos, Zephaniah, and Malachi, 4QXII[d] Hosea, 4QXII[e] Zechariah, and 4QXII[f] Jonah, in the contents. Cross says: "None is complete. We cannot always be sure that all twelve Minor Prophets were copied on a given scroll."[6] Portions of Micah, Jonah, Nahum, Habakkuk, Zephaniah, and Zechariah, in Greek, were among the fragments brought to light by the Bedouin in August, 1952, but their provenance is unknown.

Psalms. The third of the favorite works. Ten MSS are represented in 4Q, and others in 1Q, 2Q, and the materials of unknown provenance. An almost complete scroll of Psalms has been found in 11Q.

Job. Fragments in 4Q in Paleo-Hebrew, also in 2Q.

Ruth. Two MSS in 2Q and two in 4Q.

Canticles (Song of Solomon). Two MSS in 4Q, one in 6Q.

Ecclesiastes (Qoheleth). Two MSS in 4Q.

Lamentations. One MS in 3Q and one in 4Q.

Esther. None identified thus far.

Daniel. Fragments in 1Q, four MSS in 4Q, one on papyrus in 6Q, written in semicursive script. It is interesting to note that 1QDan contains the portion where the language changes from Hebrew to Aramaic (Dan. 2:4), and 4QDan[a, b] contain the portion where the language changes back from Aramaic to Hebrew (Dan. 7:28—8:1), demonstrating that the two languages were used, at precisely the points where they are found in the Daniel text today, in the time when the Qumran texts were produced.

Ezra-Nehemiah. One MS in 4Q.

---

[6]Cross, *art. cit.*, BASOR, 141: 11.

Chronicles.[7] One MS in 4Q on a strip of leather and badly deteriorated.[7a]

Once again, it should be emphasized that this is not intended to be a complete list. It serves to bring out certain important points.

The books most commonly found are precisely those books most frequently quoted in the New Testament, namely, Deuteronomy, Isaiah, and Psalms.

Three text types are found: the ancestor of the Massoretic Text (our present Hebrew Bible), one similar to the Septuagint Greek (or LXX), and a third text differing from both of these. It is possible that this third text could be further subdivided. The New Testament likewise witnesses to three Hebrew texts in its quotations from the Old Testament, for sometimes it follows the Hebrew Bible (the MT), sometimes the Greek (the LXX), and sometimes neither.

The Book of Samuel, which is textually difficult in MT, and which often has a superior reading in LXX, is shown by the Qumran discoveries to have had a Hebrew text like LXX. We should be willing to accept improvements in Samuel as readings of an older text (4QSam), and no longer as conjectural.

The Book of Daniel, which, according to the critics, was composed no earlier than 168 B.C., and which, according to some critics, was written by two authors (ch. 1 to 6 in Aramaic, ch. 7 to 12 in Hebrew; subsequently edited, 1:1–2:4a being translated into Hebrew, and ch. 7 being translated into Aramaic "to give the book unity"), existed in several manuscripts and in the Hebrew-Aramaic-Hebrew arrangement precisely as in the Hebrew Bible today, at the time

---

[7]The order of the books in the Hebrew Bible has been used.

[7a]For a complete catalogue to the time of publication, cf. C. Burchard, *Bibliographie zu den Handschriften vom Toten Meer* (Berlin: Töpelmann, 1957), pp. 114-118.

the Qumran materials were written. This does not allow much time for the steps required by critical theories! In fact, Driver has pointed out, in arguing for a *later* date for the Qumran scrolls, that the early date would force an earlier dating of the composition of Daniel.[8]

Also in connection with Daniel the text of the MSS in 4Q agrees with MT, which is interesting in view of the conflicting evidence of the Greek texts of Daniel. Again, the apocryphal additions to Daniel (the Prayer of the Three Children, Dan. 3:24-91; Susanna and the Two Elders, Dan. 13; and Bel and the Dragon, Dan. 14), are not found in the Qumran fragments. These additions are in the Roman Catholic Bible, taken from the Greek and Latin versions.[9]

The matter of Paleo-Hebrew script will need further study. When the Qumran discoveries were in the early stage of interpretation, fragments of Leviticus in Paleo-Hebrew were pronounced to be from about the fourth century B.C. As more and more fragments turned up, in nearly every cave yielding literary remains, the matter of date was reviewed. Cross says: "There can no longer be doubt that the Paleo-Hebrew MSS date roughly from the same period as MSS in formal Jewish, or cursive script."[10]

DEUTEROCANONICAL WRITINGS

The Roman Catholic Bible contains seven books, in addition to additions to Daniel, Esther, and Jeremiah, which are not in the Hebrew Bible (or the canonical Bible of the Protestants). These writings are called "deuterocanon-

---

[8]Driver, *The Hebrew Scrolls*, p. 9, n. 5. Driver has since accepted an early date for the DSS; I have not, however, seen any further statement by him relevant to the date of Daniel.

[9]It must be recognized, however, that this is an argument from silence. Fragments of these additions may be identified in the baskets of fragments still unsorted.

[10]Cross, *art. cit., BASOR,* 141: 11.

ical" (i.e., the second canon) by some scholars, and "apoc-ryphal" by others, which has led to some confusion, since other writings are considered "apocryphal" by both Protes-tants and Catholics. The seven in question are Tobit, Judith, Wisdom of Solomon, Ecclesiasticus (not to be confused with Ecclesiastes), Baruch, I and II Maccabees.

The fragments discovered at Qumran represent the fol-lowing books:

Tobit. Three MSS in 4Q, one Hebrew, two Aramaic, one of which was on papyrus.

Judith. Not identified.

Wisdom of Solomon. Fragments in Greek from Khirbet Mird.

Ecclesiasticus. Fragments from 2Q.

Epistle of Jeremy. Fragments on papyrus from 7Q.

Baruch, I and II Maccabees. Not identified.

New Testament Writings

Fragments of Mark, John, and Acts, in Greek, and frag-ments of Matthew, Luke, Acts, and Colossians, in Syro-Pal-estinian, were found in Khirbet Mird.

These fragments have been dated from the fifth to the eighth centuries A.D., and hence have no relationship to the Qumran Community. They are important, however, for other purposes.

I have often been asked why no New Testament writings have been found at Qumran—the question sometimes im-plying that this is an argument against the authenticity of the New Testament. The reason is simply the date: it was too early for any writing of the New Testament to have been circulated sufficiently for copies to get to Qumran. Moreover, there was no reason why they should.

Apocryphal Writings

There are a number of important writings, not accepted as canonical (authoritative for matters of faith) by either Protestant or Roman Catholic, which have been used by scholars to help us understand the development of religious ideas in the last pre-Christian centuries and the early Christian centuries. Some of these have been found in the Qumran fragments. Other writings of a similar *genre*, previously unknown, have also been found.

Jubilees (or the Little Genesis). Five MSS in 4Q, one on papyrus. The Latin and Ethiopic texts are faithfully reproduced. Two MSS are also known from 2Q and two from 1Q.

Enoch. Fragments from 1Q were identified as part of Enoch. Ten MSS of Enoch are represented in the fragments from 4Q, all in Aramaic. Four of them are textually close to the Greek and Ethiopic text. The "Similitudes" are notably lacking.

Book of Noah (mentioned in Jub. 10:13; 21:10, and the Aramaic Testament of Levi). Fragments from 1Q.

Testament of Levi. Fragments from 4Q and 1Q. The text is markedly longer than the previously known Greek text.

Testament of Naphtali. Fragments [from 4Q?] with text longer than the corresponding Greek text.

Sayings of Moses (or "Little Deuteronomy"), previously unknown. Fragments of four columns from 1Q.

Scroll of the Patriarchs, originally called (provisionally) the Lamech Scroll (1QLamech). This was one of the original scrolls from 1Q, and is included here for reference purposes. Fragments broken from it are in the collection of fragments from 1Q now in the Museum in Arab Jerusalem. The scroll, in Israeli Jerusalem, has been published as *A Genesis Apocryphon.*

Unknown. Fragments of one apocryphal work in Hebrew, and two apocryphal works in Aramaic have been identified among the material from 1Q. A work, originally identified as a commentary on Psalm 107, is now identified as another apocryphal writing, similar to a *genre* represented by two examples from 4Q. Other works that might be mentioned are: *Psalms of Joshua, A Vision of Amram, The Prayer of Nabonidus,* and a pseudo-Jeremiahic work.

Book of Mysteries, a tentative identification of the work originally called the "de Vaux fragment" from 1Q. Two, and possibly four, MSS of this work have been identified in 4Q.

It is still too early to do more than record these fragments and point out that such writings apparently held an important place in the life of the Qumran Community. Whether that group distinguished between "canonical" and "noncanonical," we cannot say with assurance. There is some indication that they did, as we shall see.

COMMENTARIES

The *Habakkuk Commentary* is one of the original scrolls found by the Bedouin in cave 1Q. Other commentaries, similar in nature, have been identified among the fragments. Fragments in 1Q represented commentaries on Micah, Zephaniah, and Psalms 57 (?) and 68.

Fragments in 3Q were identified as a commentary on Isaiah.

Fragments in 4Q represented three MSS of commentaries on Isaiah, one MS of a commentary on Genesis 49, one MS of a commentary on Hosea, one on Nahum, and one on Psalms 37 and 45.

It is characteristic of these commentaries to quote a passage of Scripture, and then give "its interpretation" (*pišrô*, from *pešer*, interpretation). Since these commentaries are thus far limited to canonical writings, it would seem to indicate that the Qumran group held those writings to be authoritative and worthy of interpretation.

Closely related to the Commentaries are the *Testamonia* (4QTest), a collection of passages relating to the Messiah (Deut. 18:18ff; 5:28 ff; Num. 24:15-17; Deut. 33:8-11) followed by a quotation from the *Psalms of Joshua;* and *Florilegium* (4QFlor), a similar collection of Messianic texts with commentaries.

SECTARIAN WRITINGS

Among the scrolls of the original find were three which seem to belong to the Qumran group particularly, and therefore have at times been called sectarian writings. These are the *Manual of Discipline* (1QS, the S for *sérek*, Hebrew for "rule" or "order"); the *Order of Warfare* (1QM, the M for *milḥāmāh*, Hebrew for "war"); and the *Thanksgiving Hymns* (1QH, the H for *hôdāyôt*, Hebrew for "thanksgivings.")[11] These documents, we shall see, are extremely important for the reconstruction of the Community, its life and its thought.

In a sense, the commentaries just described are also sectarian in character, for their "interpretations" of Scripture are not expositions which bring out what the authors intended, but rather they are an effort to read elements of the history of the sect back into the Scriptures. This will quickly become apparent to anyone who will take the trouble to read the *Habakkuk Commentary.* Consider, for example, the following passage:

"For the violence done to Lebanon will overwhelm

---

[11] In the system of *sigla* now generally adopted, it is customary to use the Hebrew names of sectarian documents in order to designate them as such. Cf. *Discoveries in the Judean Desert,* 1: 47.

you; the destruction of the beasts will terrify you, for the
blood of men and violence to a land, to a city and all
who dwell in it." Its interpretation: the wicked priest, to
repay him for his recompense which he recompensed the
poor. For Lebanon is the Council of the Community, and
the beasts are the simple ones of Judah, the doer of the
Law. . . ."[12]

Note in passing that the *p* in 1QpHab. is also chosen in accordance with the principle of using the Hebrew word for
the sectarian writing.

In 1897 in a Genizah[13] in Old Cairo, a quantity of old
manuscripts were discovered and taken to the library of
Cambridge University. President Solomon Schechter of the
Jewish Theological Seminary, New York, identified a number of fragments as similar in character and content, and
published them in 1910 as *Fragments of a Zadokite Work*.[14]
The work created an immediate sensation, and a survey of
the bibliography of the subject will show that periodically
articles and books were published dealing with the *Zadokite
Fragments* even down to 1946—the year before the Qumran
materials were discovered.[15] The palaeography was that
of the Middle Ages, but the language and content were
identified as much earlier. There were many arguments
about the date, the relationship to Judaism, and the relationship to Christianity, just as there have been in the
case of the Qumran discoveries.

As soon as the *Manual of Discipline* was edited, scholars
began to point out its close relationship to the *Zadokite
Fragments* (or *Damascus Document*, as it was frequently

---

[12] 1QpHab. 12:1-5, based on Hab. 2:17.
[13] A Genizah is a storage place for old manuscripts of the Scripture,
which are no longer fit for use, but too sacred to be destroyed.
[14] S. Schechter, *Documents of Jewish Sectaries*, Vol. I, *Fragments of
a Zadokite Work* (Cambridge: University Press, 1910), lxiv, 20 pp.
[15] For bibliography before 1947, see L. Rost, *Die Damaskusschrift*
(Berlin: Töpelmann, 1933), and H. H. Rowley, *The Zadokite Fragments and the Dead Sea Scrolls* (Oxford: Basil Blackwell, 1952);
since then, W. S. LaSor, *Bibliography of the Dead Sea Scrolls 1948-
1957 (Fuller Library Bulletin*, 31 [Fall 1958]), §§ 2650-2667.

called, because the group described in it had migrated to
Damascus). Prof. Brownlee, among others, set forth a
comparison of the two documents that not only included
words and terms, such as "Teacher of Righteousness," "Man
of Lies," "New Covenant," "Community," "those who repent
of transgression," "sons of Zadok," "men of the Community,"
and many others, but even closely parallel passages. Compare, for example, just these two:

Manual of Discipline	*Damascus Document*
So that there should be no remnant, nor any to escape of them (4:14).	So that there should be no remnant, nor any to escape of them (2:6).
And to love all that He chooseth, And to hate all that He rejecteth. . . .	And to choose what He approveth, And to reject what He hateth;
And to walk no more in the stubbornness of an evil heart and eyes of fornication (1:3-6).	To walk uprightly in all his ways, And not to go about in the thoughts of an evil imagination And eyes of fornication (2:14-16).[16]

Other points of comparison to be noted are the unusual
terms, "The Book of the Hagu," unknown elsewhere, but
mentioned in the *Damascus Document*[17] and the *Manual
of Discipline*,[18] and *sérek* used in the peculiar sense of
"rules" or "order."[19]

If there was any doubt remaining concerning the connection of the *Damascus Document* with the Qumran Community, it was removed when fragments of the same document were found in the Qumran caves. Fragments were

---

[16]Cf. W. H. Brownlee, "A Comparison of the Covenanters of the
Dead Sea Scrolls with Pre-Christian Jewish Sects," *BA*, 13 (1950):
50-56, "I. Comparison with the Covenanters of Damascus."
[17]CD 10:6; 13:2.
[18]1QSa 1:6.
[19]Cf. CD 7:6, etc., and 1QS 1:16, etc., 1QM 4:9, etc.

found in 6Q equivalent to CD 5:18–6:2, and in 4Q fragments of no less than seven MSS of Text A of the *Damascus Document* were found, one of them on papyrus.

Fragments of eleven MSS of the *Manual of Discipline*, two on papyrus, were found in 4Q. Even more important was the discovery of large portions of the first part of the *Manual of Discipline* (which was missing from the scroll 1QS), in 1Q, now identified as 1QSa and 1QSb.

Five MSS of the *Thanksgiving Hymns* were represented in the fragments of 4Q, one on papyrus. These are important in that they complete the gaps in 1QH. The order of the Hymns was variable. Four or five other MSS in 4Q resemble 1QH, but are not the text of that work. It is not yet clear whether there were several collections of Hymns, or what the explanation of these other MSS will be.

Four MSS of the *Order of Warfare* were identified in 4Q, likewise important for filling in the gaps of the original scroll (1QM). Different textual recensions are represented in these MSS.

There are other writings which might be described in the category of sectarian writings. Four MSS of a Wisdom composition were found in 4Q which are to be related to 1Q26, and five other Wisdom-type MSS were identified in 4Q. A description of New Jerusalem is among the fragments of 1Q, 4Q, and 5Q, but insufficient information has been published to know whether a single composition is represented. And there are other items.[20]

---

[20] The above information has been assembled from many sources, chiefly articles in *Revue Biblique* reporting the expeditions and reports in *Biblical Archaeologist* and *BASOR*. But by far the most useful synthesis of this material is a report on the present status of publication, by several scholars who are active in sorting and identifying the fragments, in *Revue Biblique* 63 (1956): 49-67. For detailed bibliography, cf. W. S. LaSor, *Bibliography of the Dead Sea Scrolls 1948-1957*, §§ 2001-2667.

OTHER MATERIALS

We do not know what the future has in store for us in this fascinating field of study. Caves 7Q, 8Q, 9Q, and 10Q, excavated in the spring of 1955, have yielded inscribed potsherds and MS fragments, some of which are in Greek. Cave 11Q was found in 1956, over a mile north of Khirbet Qumran. Two almost complete scrolls were found (11QPsa, 11QLev) and significant fragments of five or more other scrolls. At last report, they were still unedited.

Of two things, however, we can be certain: until all the fragments are identified and published, we can anticipate interesting reports from the specialists engaged in this work; and again, it is much too early to be dogmatic in the conclusions we reach—in fact, it is too early to reach "conclusions." Ministers, Bible teachers, and other educators who are nonspecialists, should be alert to check and sift news about the Dead Sea Scrolls. But the technical decisions should be left to the specialists. There is a remarkable number of scholars at work on the Dead Sea Scrolls—of many nations, and of various religious beliefs. Protestants, Catholics, Jews; Conservatives, Liberals, and Moderates—all are represented. In my lifetime I have never seen so many engaged in a project of this type. We can confidently expect unusual results.

CHAPTER FOUR

The Date of the Qumran Materials

THERE HAS BEEN MUCH DISCUSSION about the date of the Qumran discoveries. At first, the scholars were entirely unaware that the Dead Sea Scrolls were to be associated with a religious community. The main interest lay in the fact that a scroll of Isaiah had been found which, according to some, was to be dated c. 150 B.C., whereas before that the oldest Hebrew manuscript was no older than the tenth century A.D. Then, when the *Manual of Discipline* was translated it became apparent that a religious group was described. Meanwhile, on the basis of palaeography (the study of ancient writing) scholars were dating the scrolls anywhere from the second century B.C. to the sixth century A.D. At times the discussion descended below the level of scholarship.

It was Burrows I think who pointed out most clearly the complexity of the problem. First, there is the date of the composition of the writings used by the Community. The Qumran group could not have existed prior to the time of the composition of the latest writing—but on the other hand, the composition could have been in existence for centuries before the Community. Isaiah would be an example.

Again, the date of the manuscripts and the date of the jars are not necessarily the same. The pottery experts could date the jars in the Hellenistic period, but that did not of itself date either the composition of the writings or the copying of them.

Third, the date of the manuscripts and the date of the occupation of the caves are not necessarily the same. The manuscripts in the cave could not be dated "Hellenistic" by the jars, or "Roman" by the lamp (later redated), or for that matter, "modern" by the cigarette roller found in the cave. Scholars who were debating the date of the scrolls on the basis of the jars and the lamp seemed to have overlooked this obvious fact.

On the other hand, it is ridiculously obvious that the manuscripts could not have been written *after* they were put in the caves, and they could not have been put in the caves *after* the caves and the Community were abandoned. Therefore the starting point in determining the *terminus ante quem* (or latest possible date) of the manuscripts should be the destruction of the Qumran Community.[1]

Date of Abandonment of Community

Two lines of evidence help to establish the date when the Community was abandoned. Pottery chronology for a while oscillated between "late Hellenistic" and "early Roman," and finally narrowed to the latter on the basis of the discovery of sherds in a location where coins dating from Augustus (31 B.C.–A.D. 14) to the First Jewish Revolt (A.D. 66-70) were also found.

At the same time archaeologists responsible for the excavation of Khirbet Qumran were convinced that the occupation of Level II was by the same or a similar group as the occupants of Level I, but Level III was occupied by an entirely different group. Level II, as we have seen from the

---

[1] Cf. Burrows, *Dead Sea Scrolls*, pp. 73-74.

evidence of the coins, ended in about A.D. 68, with destruction by fire following a military conquest. Géza Vermès concludes that the manuscripts were placed in the caves, "likely when, pressed by the Roman armies, the inhabitants of Qumran prepared to quit the region."[2]

The Jewish historian Josephus describes an action that may have included the end of the Qumran Community, although he does not give the name or specific details. In the *War of the Jews* he tells us that Vespasian led the greatest part of his army from Caesarea to Antipatris, Lydda, Emmaus, Samaria, and finally, in June, 68, to Jericho. The inhabitants of Jericho put up resistance and finally fled into the mountains that "lay over against Jerusalem."[3] About that time Emperor Nero died, and in a short while Vespasian was made emperor and Titus took command of the Roman forces which were to besiege Jerusalem. Titus brought the Tenth Legion against Jerusalem from Jericho, and it would seem from Josephus that this included the garrison which Vespasian had left at Jericho.[4]

One of the coins found in Level II of Khirbet Qumran is stamped with an "X"—taken by some to indicate the Tenth Legion—, and three are stamped *Judaea Capta*. It is not unreasonable to conclude that these coins represent the time of the destruction of Jerusalem. If so, then we can reconstruct the closing events of the Qumran Community.

At the time Vespasian's army drove the inhabitants of Jericho into the mountains, it became apparent to those who inhabited the region that the Roman commander would likely attempt to wipe out all who lived in the hills and who

---

[2]*Les manuscrits du désert de Juda* (Tournai: Desclée, 1953), p. 36. This work is now available in an English translation (revised and enlarged). *Discovery in the Judean Desert* (New York: Desclée, 1956).

[3]Josephus, *War of the Jews*, 4: 8.1-2.

[4]*Ibid.*, 5: 1.1, 2.3.

were therefore a threat to the forces that must form one arm of a pincers-movement on Jerusalem. From the hills about Qumran it is possible to look down on the plains about Jericho, although, as I recall, Jericho cannot be seen from cave 1Q. However, news travels rapidly "by the grapevine" in the Middle East. Moreover, scouts of the army would doubtless be seen from vantage points in the hills. The Community probably removed its scrolls and any other valuables it possessed to the caves. The delay occasioned by Nero's death may have been the factor that made the preservation of the scrolls possible. Soon after that, Titus cleaned the Jewish resistance out of the hills, burned the Qumran buildings, and moved against Jerusalem.

With the destruction of Jerusalem, it was necessary to guard the approaches to the city—and Wadi Qumran and Wadi en-Nâr lead to Jerusalem by the Kidron Valley. We know that Roman forces were stationed at other points in the Judean Wilderness; we now are reasonably certain that a garrison was stationed at Khirbet Qumran. That would have been what the archaeologists now identify as Level III, and the few coins found in Level III, all dated between A.D. 67 and A.D. 86, could have been dropped by the soldiers.

As for the coins of the Second Revolt, we may suppose that revolutionists used the ruins as a dwelling. The Qumran Community had ceased to exist, or had fled elsewhere, nearly 60 years before that time.

WHEN WERE THE SCROLLS PRODUCED?

Having established the *terminus ante quem* of the scrolls beyond reasonable doubt, the scholars were anxious to fix the earliest time (the *terminus a quo*) of the scrolls.

The Community at Qumran, or more precisely, the buildings of the Community, should be placed within the limits established by the coins found in the excavations. As we have seen, this would be after c. 135 B.C. Of course, it is possible that the Community was there before that date, and just did not happen to drop any coins (or have any) prior to that of Antiochus VII. But scientists must work from the data in hand, not from possible speculations.

Someone will probably ask, "Why do you say that the beginning of the Community is dated from the time of the first coins? Today, we may have coins in our pocket dating from 1930, or even 1920." True. Take all the coins out of your various pockets and pocketbooks, and examine them. Most of them will be within the past 10 or 15 years, especially those of lower value. Quarters and half dollars will have a longer span. But you are forgetting something. Since our presidents do not mint their own money, there is no propaganda value in our coinage. You would probably not find coins of Hitler, or Mussolini, or Chiang Kai-shek in their respective countries, even a few years after their reigns ended. The tendency in an autocracy is to call in the money as quickly as possible and remint it with the likeness of the new ruler. It is reasonable to hold that the coins found in the lowest level of Khirbet Qumran are not greatly separated in time from the limits of its existence.

But could the scrolls not have been produced some time prior to the establishment of the Qumran Community, and have been brought there by the members who founded the Community? The answer is, of course, affirmative. Other evidence must be considered.

One line of evidence is the *scriptorium*, which indicates that the Community produced some manuscripts. We are safe in concluding that some of the manuscripts recovered from the caves were produced in the Community.

The evidence of the cloth contributes also to the solution of the problem. However, the nature of the hiding places of the scrolls must be determined, for if the caves were in the nature of a Genizah, and if the Community was simply covering old, but still sacred, scrolls out of a sense of reverence, then the age of the cloth does not help us. A number of experts in this area have written on the matter, and they have concluded that the nature of the documents found in the caves precludes the identification of the caves as a Genizah.[5] But if the caves were not a Genizah, and if the view already presented, namely, that the scrolls were hidden at a time of emergency, is valid, then the age of the cloth, which in that case must have served to protect the scrolls even before they were hidden (for that was no time to weave special cloth!), must definitely be related to the age of the scrolls. And the age of the cloth, as determined by radiocarbon dating, must be placed within the limits 167 B.C.–A.D. 233.

Determining the Age of a Manuscript

There are several contributing studies to help the experts determine the age of a manuscript, among which may be mentioned the material on which it is written, the kind of writing (palaeography), the spelling (orthography), words used, ideas included, and various other subjects.

The ink of the manuscripts and the ink of the inkwells in the *scriptorium* have been subjected to tests. Both are nonmetallic. Metallic ink was introduced at some time after A.D. 100, but its use for sacred writings was forbidden, and nonmetallic ink was used for scrolls of the Law down into

---

[5]Cf. P. Kahle, "The Age of the Scrolls," *VT*, 1 (1951): 38.

the Middle Ages. Obviously this line of evidence does not help us.[6]

The Qumran manuscripts were written on parchment and papyrus, as well as ostraca (broken pottery) and the copper scrolls. Leather was used as a writing material certainly from the twentieth century B.C. down to the time of the invention of printing from movable type. Papyrus was used in Egypt as early as the Fifth Dynasty (2500-2350 B.C.), and continued to be used down to Arab times.[7] Ostraca were used as writing material certainly from the time of the Gezer fragments (nineteenth to seventeenth centuries B.C.) down to the Hellenistic period or later. We have no parallel for the copper scrolls. Again, it is clear that this line of evidence will not help us with the present problem.

Arrangement on the "page" sometimes helps to date a manuscript. At certain periods, horizontal lines were ruled (or scratched) on the writing surface, to aid in aligning the writing, and vertical lines were ruled to control the width of the columns as well as their spacing. The Talmud, by prescribing horizontal ruling for Esther as well as for the Torah, suggests that such ruling had come into use before A.D. 500.[8] Ruling with a lead plummet, which leaves a mark similar to that of a lead pencil, did not come into use in Hebrew MSS before the ninth century A.D. Ruling with ink did not come into practice before the thirteenth century. The Qumran scrolls exhibit various practices. One

---

[6] See the report of Plenderleith in F. F. Bruce, "Recent Discoveries in Biblical Manuscripts," *Journal of the Transactions of the Victoria Institute* 82 (1950): 146-147.

[7] G. R. Driver, *Semitic Writing from Pictograph to Alphabet* (London: Oxford University Press, 1948), pp. 81-82.

[8] *Megillah* 16b.

Isaiah scroll (1QIs^a^) is unruled. The *Habakkuk Commentary* is ruled both vertically and horizontally. Colored ruling is not found. Driver therefore concluded that the scrolls must be post-Christian. However, the Talmud preserves a story that Moses invented the ruling of manuscripts.[9] This probably means nothing more than a hint that the ruling of manuscripts was already so old that its origin was forgotten. Once again, however, we have no help in the problem of dating the Qumran scrolls.

The general neatness and regularity of writing is known technically as *expertise*.[10] Older writing, whether in ancient inscriptions or in documents, generally tends to be less neat and regular than more recent writing. The Qumran manuscripts are very neat, and Driver therefore concludes that the *expertise* indicates a date between the Mishnah and the Talmud (i.e., third to fifth centuries A.D.). However, *expertise* is a somewhat indefinite quantity. There has been a tendency in recent printing to make use of type faces that resemble hand-lettering or that fail to line up the letters. On the other hand, some of the neatest inscriptional lettering is to be found in Old South Arabic, dating several centuries before the Qumran materials. To argue from *expertise* alone would give a completely distorted picture of these two examples.

The study of ancient writing, or palaeography, belongs to those who have made a careful study of it. Like pottery chronology, it yields relative dates. Yet in the hands of an expert it gives remarkable results. The best palaeographers do not trust their eye and their hand. They enlarge photographs of various manuscripts to be studied, then cut out individual letters, representing the various letters of the

---

[9]*Megillah* 71d.
[10]Pronounced *ex-pair-teez'*.

alphabet and the various styles of each letter. These enlargements are pasted on a large cardboard, and studies and published charts are made from the paste-up. Sometimes letters will be superimposed on a grid, which quickly shows details of proportion, overhang of certain lines, etc. Color slides often show more than can be seen in black-and-white photographs, and certainly more than printed reproductions. Better still is the examination of the actual manuscript with a magnifying glass. Infrared photography is always used when the manuscript is in poor condition, when the writing is obliterated, or when it has to be written over (a "palimpsest").

Since I am not a palaeographer, I do not think it is out of place for me to say that the scholar who has not made serious study of palaeography is not in a position to dismiss the evidence of palaeography summarily or to devalue the work of scholars devoted to its study.

If datable documents can be included in a palaeographic study, then controls are imposed upon it. Some manuscripts have the name of a governor or some other historic person or event included in the content. Among the Qumran materials, a few letters from the Second Revolt furnish a probable control.[11] And in the general study, other datable materials from other places (such as the Aramaic papyri, from Elephantinē, the Lachish ostraca, etc.) can be used. When a comparative chart is made up, it is quite obvious that the Qumran materials fit very nicely in the period prior to the end of the pre-Christian era.[12] Some of the scrolls, particu-

---

[11]These are not from the Qumran caves, but since they were discovered in Wadi Murabba'at as part of the Qumran expeditions, they are generally discussed with the Qumran materials. Certainly no objection can be raised against including them in a palaeographic study!

[12]Cf. S. A. Birnbaum, *The Qumrân (Dead Sea Scrolls) and Palaeography* (*BASOR*, Supplementary Studies, 13-14; 1952), 52 pp.

larly those in Paleo-Hebrew script, may be two or three centuries earlier, although recent statements indicate that both
styles of writing are, in the Qumran materials, approximately contemporary.[13]

Orthography furnishes evidence of date, although this is
not always apparent to the English-speaking person who
has not thought much about it. In countries that have had
spelling reforms in recent years, it is obvious that the new
spelling will be found only after the time of the reform.
Even the King James Version has passed through a spelling
reform in English, of which most of us are unaware. G. R.
Driver argues that the spelling found in the Dead Sea
Scrolls is too late for the dates assigned. The use of "vowel
letters" (*matres lectionis*), peculiar suffixial forms, "Ara-
maizing" forms, etc., indicate a date in the Mishnaic period,
or shortly thereafter, according to Driver and a few other
scholars.[14]

However, in the case of the Hebrew language, we have no
record of a "spelling reform." It is a known fact that the
use of *matres lectionis* developed after the eighth century
B.C., and that they were more commonly used in post-Christian times than in the Persian period. However, to say that
these peculiar orthographical forms are not found until
Mishnaic times is to argue from silence, for up until the
discovery of the Qumran writings, there was no evidence
for the period. In fact, even this building of theories on the
evidence of Mishnaic Hebrew should have been questioned,
and was questioned by a few, before the Qumran discoveries. M. H. Segal had clearly stated the case for a con-

---

[13]Cf. p. 44, above.
[14]Driver, *The Hebrew Scrolls*, pp. 36, 96-100. Cf. Zeitlin, "The
Hebrew Scrolls: Once More and Finally," *JQR*, 41 (1950-51): 28,
et passim.

tinuation of Hebrew and a development leading quite naturally into Mishnaic Hebrew, as long ago as 1926.[15] Rather than force the well-established dates of Qumran to fit an outmoded theory, the grammarians must remember that grammars never determine the facts of an ancient language: they only describe them. And when new evidence is produced, the grammars must be revised. It is time for a restudy of Hebrew and Aramaic in the light of the Qumran finds.

Similarly, the use of such internal evidence as vocabulary, ideas, etc., to establish the date of a manuscript is only valid as long as objective evidence is present. For example, we might say that the reference to airplanes in literature is internal evidence that the literature was produced since the days of the Wright brothers. If a literary fragment is discovered, datable prior to the time of the Wrights, mentioning aircraft, we would be right in suspecting its date. But if the date is established objectively, then we must look for evidence of aircraft prior to the time of the Wrights. Many times, and in many areas of the history of ideas, scholars have been forced to do something similar to this, and many times they have had to push the dates back. The Dead Sea Scrolls are now objective evidence, and the history of theological ideas in Judaism must reckon with them —it has no right to ignore the evidence.

I am not minimizing the value of internal evidence. Both internal evidence and external evidence must be given full consideration. For example, the *Damascus Document* is openly critical of the Jerusalem priesthood, and speaks as if the Temple was still standing.[16] This is internal evidence

---

[15]*Grammar of Mishnaic Hebrew* (Oxford: Clarendon, 1927), pp. 1-20. The work was written in 1926, published in 1927.
[16]CD 4:13–5:17; note 5:6, in particular.

for a date prior to A.D. 70, which the proponents of a later
date on the basis of internal evidence seem to have overlooked. Moreover, it is my opinion that the development of
certain theological ideas is not as far advanced in the
Qumran literature as in the Mishnah—but this is a matter
for experts in Judaism to discuss.

CONCLUSION

In the light of all the evidence, most scholars are convinced that the Qumran materials are to be dated in the
period between 175 B.C. and A.D. 68, probably several
decades within these outside limits in each case. From my
own consideration of all the evidence to which I have had
access, I think these dates are established beyond reasonable doubt. Archaeological excavation of Khirbet Qumran,
the evidence of the coins, palaeography, the evidence of
radiocarbon dating, and pottery all point to these dates,
and there is no external evidence, and in my opinion no
internal evidence, that is incompatible with these dates. It
is difficult for me to imagine what kind of evidence could
possibly be produced that would substantially alter these
conclusions.[17]

---

[17]In this respect, I must mention my regret that a journal that claims
to be a voice for Evangelical Protestantism once published the
extreme views of Zeitlin without any critical comment. The publication of his views is news; and I would insist that Zeitlin be given the
same freedom to publish his conclusions as that which he so gracious-
ly gives even to his opponents in the pages of the journal which he
edits. At the same time, an editor owes it to his readers to present the
complete story; and certainly the almost unanimous verdict of many
scholars in many fields, contrary to Zeitlin's conclusions, should be
included in careful news reporting.

CHAPTER FIVE

The Qumran Community

WORKING WITH ARCHAEOLOGICAL MATERIALS can be as much fun as trying to solve a jig-saw puzzle or reading a mystery novel. Unfortunately, teachers of ancient history often fail to use this approach, and instead of helping the student develop his imagination, they drive him from the subject by imposing upon him a mass of meaningless memory material. At least someone did that to me in high school, and it took years for me to learn to enjoy delving into the past.

From the materials uncovered in an archaeological excavation it is actually possible to reconstruct the past. As a matter of fact, there are some communities (for example, Nuzu) about which we have more complete knowledge than we have of American cities and towns in Colonial days. This is due to several facts: for one thing, clay tablets are far more permanent than paper; again, the custom in some ancient civilizations included the keeping of detailed records about nearly everything. In the case of Qumran, we do not have clay tablets, and we do not have detailed records of business transactions, lawsuits, etc. But we do have some of their hymns, their rules for the conduct of the Community, and other materials including the nonliterary items which also constitute important evidence.

Biblical Materials

The vast quantities of Biblical materials discovered in the Qumran region testify that the Community was in some way linked with the Jewish religion. The presence of other religious writings, plus the fact that non-Biblical books are quoted in the Qumran writings, suggests that we are dealing with an offshoot of Judaism rather than a pure form. But these suggestions need confirmation.

The relatively larger number of manuscripts of Deuteronomy, Isaiah, and Psalms, suggests that these writings were favorite with the members of the Community. On the other hand, the presence of commentaries on several of the Minor Prophets indicates that the Community attached considerable importance to these works. In Rabin's edition of the *Damascus Document,* he finds quotations from, or allusions to, every Old Testament book except: Joshua, Joel, Jonah, Haggai, Ruth, and Lamentations.[1] Some of these references seem far-fetched. But we still get the picture of a Community that was devoted to the same Old Testament that we know today.

Non-Biblical Materials

Our best information concerning the aims and organization of the Community comes from the *Manual of Discipline* (1QS) and the *Damascus Document* (CD). Other details can be filled in from the *Habakkuk Commentary* (1QpHab.), the *Thanksgiving Hymns* (1QH), and the *Order of Warfare* (1QM).

The best way to learn about the Qumran Community, of course, is to read these documents over and over again. Students should be encouraged to read the source materials,

---

[1]Chaim Rabin, *The Zadokite Documents* (Oxford: Clarendon, 1954), 78-80; 2d ed., pp. 81-83.

rather than just books about the source materials. The process is slower. But, properly done, it stimulates interest, develops the imagination, trains the student to observe details, and ultimately gives a far more intimate and accurate picture. I shall try to lead you through the results of my own studies in these Qumran documents; but I urge you to read the materials for yourself.

THE NAMES USED

A great deal can be learned about a group from the names they use for themselves and the names they use for others.

The Qumran writings make repeated use of the term *yáhad*,[2] which is perhaps best translated "community." The word is related to the words for "one," "together," "only," etc., and stresses the oneness of the group, and perhaps also the unique character of the group. Several scholars have pointed out the similarity of this word, in meaning, to the word *koinōnia* in the New Testament, which can mean "fellowship," "communion," and other similar ideas.

The rules of the Community are known as "The Order of the Community" (1QS 1:16). In fact, this could well have been the title of the work we call the *Manual of Discipline*. The members are "The men of the Community" (1QS 5:1-2) or "The Council of the Community" (1QpHab. 12:4).[3] They practiced truth "in common"[4] (1QS 5:3), they circumcised "in common" (1QS 5:5), ate, blessed, and took counsel "in common" (1QS 6:2-3). They spoke of the "wealth of

---

[2]Cf. 1QS 1:1 and often, 1QpHab. 12:4; 1QH 3:23; 1QM 2:9; and in slightly different form in CD 20:32. The word is pronounced *yach'ed*, with the *yach* similar to German *ach*.

[3]It is possible that "the Council" was a particular part of the Community.

[4]The expression is *be-yáhad*, the word "common" being the same as the word we have translated "community."

the Community"—or perhaps we should translate it, wealth of the commonness (1QS 7:6-7). It is possible that one expression can be translated "the teacher of the Community" (CD 20:1).

They called themselves "the Community of God" (1QS 2:23), "the Community of His counsel" (1QS 3:6), "His true Community" (1QS 2:26), and "a Community in the Torah (Law)" (1QS 5:2).

Another term they used is "covenant," which is the same as the word commonly used in the Old Testament (*berît*). They were "the members of the New Covenant" (CD 6:19), or "the men who had entered into the New Covenant" (CD 8:21). The covenant was "a covenant of loyalty (or covenant love, *ḥésed*)" (1QS 1:8).

The Community was "the House of Truth in Israel" (1QS 5:6), "a holy Congregation" (1QS 5:20), "the Council of God" (1QS 1:10),[5] and "a Council of Community (or commonness)" (1QS 3:2). In some cases we cannot be sure whether we are dealing with a proper name for the group or simply a common term. Perhaps it is misleading to use capital letters, for Hebrew does not have such things. But the idea is approximately the same.

The members had certain expressions which they used for themselves. They were "sons of light" (1QS 1:9), "sons of righteousness" (1QS 3:20), "sons of truth" (1QS 4:6), "the men of God's lot" (1QS 2:2). They were "the volunteers (or dedicated ones)" (1QS 5:8), "sons of an eternal council (or possibly, eternal secret)" (1QS 2:25), and "the men of the Community who hold firmly to the Covenant" (1QS 5:2-3). They called themselves "the many (or majority) of Israel" (1QS 5:22), "men of truth" (1QpHab 7:11), "men of perfection" (1QS 8:20), "the perfect of way"

---

[5]In this passage, perhaps it should be "the counsel of God."

(1QS 4:22), and "those who are upright in the way" (1QH 2:10). In the *Damascus Document* they are referred to as "the members of the New Covenant in the Land of Damascus" (CD 6:19), but whether "Damascus" is to be taken literally or figuratively we are not certain.

Some of these names would not be too significant if they were used rather generally. But when we place alongside them the names which were used for nonmembers, we get a better idea of what the names were intended to imply.

The nonmembers were "sons of darkness" (1QS 1:10; 1QM 1:1), "sons of perversion" (1QS 3:21), and "men of the pit" (1QS 9:22). They were "treacherous men" (1QH 2:10), "the men of Belial's lot" (1QS 2:4-5), "the dominion of Belial" (1QS 1:18). They were "unclean" (1QS 3:6). Their priests were "priests of Jerusalem" (1QpHab. 9:4), their prophets "prophesied falsehood" (CD 6:1), and their preacher was "the preacher of the lie" (1QpHab. 10:9). We should keep in mind that it was official Judaism in Jerusalem to whom the Qumranians were referring. It was official Judaism that they branded as "men of scoffing" (CD 20:11), "in the army of Belial" (1QM 1:1), and "messengers of his dominion" (1QM 1:15); they were "in the band of Edom and Moab and the Ammonites" (1QM 1:1). If we recall what Israel thought of Edom and Moab and the Ammonites (Jer. 25:21; Ps. 83:7; Ezra 9:1, etc.), we get a better idea of the awful reproach intended by this expression!

It is my opinion that there can be no doubt that we are dealing with a separatist group, a group that had repudiated official Judaism. Other points I believe will confirm this judgment.[6]

---

[6]On the other hand, P. Kahle, "Die hebraischen Handschriften," *VT*, 1 (1951), 234, says the group was not sectarian.

THE ORGANIZATION OF THE COMMUNITY

In the *Manual of Discipline*, the following statement is included in the ritual:

> The priests shall pass over first in the order according to their spirits, one after another, then the Levites shall pass over after them, then all the people shall pass over in the third place in order, one after another, by thousands, and hundreds, and fifties, and tens, for every man to know his appointed place [literally, the house of his appointment] in the Community of God, for an eternal council (1QS 2:19-23).

This same division of Priests, Levites, and People is found in the *Order of Warfare:* "Israel and Levi and Aaron" (1QM 5:1). It is reasonable to suppose that a distinction between "priesthood" and "laity" is intended, and that the expression "Aaron and Israel" (1QS 5:6; CD 1:7, etc.) is just another way of saying "priest and layman."

The priests are described as "sons of Aaron (1QS 5:21), and "sons of Zadoq" (1QS 5:2). This latter term is of primary significance, it seems to me, in understanding the origin of the Qumran sect, as we shall see in a later chapter.

The "sons of Zadoq" are distinguished from "the majority of the men of the Community" (1QS 5:2-9). The *Damascus Document* specifies that "the priest that is appointed [at the head] of the Many shall be from thirty to sixty years old" (CD 14:6-7). One priest was necessary whenever there were ten males in the council of the Community (1QS 6: 3-4), but it is not clear whether the "council of the Community" is another term for the "Community," or a subdivision of the Community. The *Damascus Document* states that there shall be "groups of ten men as the minimum" (CD 13:1). I understand this to imply that small communities, of which Qumran was one, could be established in various places, much as synagogues (which also had the requirement of a minimum of ten males) were established by Diaspora Judaism.

It was the duty of the priests to pronounce blessings on "the men of God's lot" (1QS 2:1), to invoke the blessing at the common meal (1QS 6:5), to recount God's righteousness (1QS 1:21), and to participate in the military activities described in the *Order of Warfare* (1QM 13:1). On this last point we cannot be certain whether actual warfare or spiritual warfare is intended—I incline to the latter interpretation. Only the sons of Aaron had authority "in matters that concern law and property" (1QS 9:7).

Twelve "chiefs of the priests" are mentioned in the *Order of Warfare*, ranked after "the chief priest and his second" (1QM 2:1-2); their duty was to offer before God the perpetual oblation. The same work mentions also certain "princes," including a "prince of the ten" (1QM 4:15), as well as "princes of the thousands" (1QM 4:1), "princes of the hundreds" (1QM 4:3), and "princes of the fifties" (1QM 4:4). There has been some question whether these "princes" were to be identified with the "chiefs of the priests," and the matter is not yet entirely clear. However, in the light of the *Rule of the Congregation* (1QSa), I am inclined to distinguish between them.[7]

The Levites are mentioned several times as a group dis-

---

[7]D. Barthélemy has proposed that the *Two Columns* (1QSa) be called the *Rule of the Congregation*, and the *Manual of Discipline* (1QS) be called the *Rule of the Community*, in the light of the terms occurring in each. The suggestion is good, but the term *Manual of Discipline* seems to be too firmly entrenched in the literature by now to change it. J. T. Milik proposes the name *Benedictions* for 1QSb. *Discoveries in the Judean Desert*, I: 108.

tinct from the priests, and they participated with the priests in the ritual of the Community. The priests seem to have had charge of the positive work of the priesthood, whereas the Levites had the task of pronouncing curses.[8]

Fifty-two "fathers of the Congregation" (1QM 2:1) and 26 heads of the "courses" (1QM 2:2; cf. Luke 1:15) are mentioned, but the relationship of these offices to the Community is not yet clear.

The balance of the Community was apparently the laity. How many members there were, it is difficult to say with certainty. The number of dishes found in the refectory, together with the number of graves in the cemetery, do not substantiate the references in the literature to "thousands and hundreds and fifties and tens." W. R. Farmer suggests that the Qumran Community included possibly several hundred members.[9] Burrows supposes that the references to thousands can "hardly be anything more than a rather wistful echo of scriptural language."[10] This to me is less reasonable than to suppose that a larger, perhaps ideal, group was in view, of which Qumran was but a part.

The terms *Community* and *Congregation* are used, perhaps synonymously—although scholars seem to incline more to the view that they are not the same. The Congregation was under an officer designated as "the president of all the Congregation" (1QSb 5:20; cf. CD 7:20); the Community was under an officer designated as the "Supervisor" (1QS 6:12; CD 9:18-22). The duties of the former are indicated in the following passage:

> Let no imbecile enter into the lot to exercise authority over the Congregation of Israel, to defend a cause, to

[8]1QS 1:21-2:5.
[9]"The Economic Basis of the Qumran Community," *TZ*, 11 (1955): 296.
[10]Burrows, *The Dead Sea Scrolls*, p. 231. The expression is found in Exod. 18:25 and I Macc. 3:55.

take up the responsibility of the Congregation, or to exercise authority in war (1QSa 1:19-21).

The last clause, "to exercise authority in war," is difficult to interpret in the light of almost-pacifist statements in the *Manual of Discipline*.[11] The "Supervisor" was to be from 30 to 50 years of age, "master in every secret of men and in every language according to their families" (CD 14:9).

The Congregation included men, women, and children, and there were regulations concerning the education of the children of all ages (1QSa 1:4, 6-16). The Community has generally been considered by scholars as a closed, quasi-monastic group.[12] However, we should remember that when Brownlee first published his translation of the *Manual of Discipline,* he thought he saw the second part of the word for "women" at the beginning of the document.[13] Nothing found in all the rest of the literature is incompatible with that suggestion. It may be that some scholars, in their anxiety to link the Qumran group with the Essenes, have too quickly jumped to the conclusion that the Community was monastic. The passage in 1QSa should, in my opinion, carry more weight than arguments from silence.

In the "council of the Community" there was a group consisting of twelve laymen and three priests (1QS 8:1). There was also a "conclave of the Community" (1QS 6:16). Whether the two groups are the same is not clear, but Brownlee's suggestion that the fifteen men of 1QS 8:1 formed the "conclave" within the "council" has merit.[14] Likewise, in the *Damascus Document* there is an inner group of "ten judges," four of whom are "from the tribe of

---

[11] Cf. 1QS 9:16, 22-23; 10:18.
[12] Cf. *Discoveries in the Judean Desert*, I:108, citing 1QS 6:13-22.
[13] 1QS 1:1; cf. Brownlee, *The Dead Sea Manual of Discipline,* pp. 6-7.
[14] *Op. cit.,* p. 31, n. 2.

Levi and Aaron" (i.e., priests and Levites), and six "from Israel" (i.e., laymen) (CD 10:4-7). We should like to know more about these details of organization, but about all that we can say positively is that there was noticeably a division between priesthood and laity, with the weight on the side of the laity, and that these smaller groups appear to have had some esoteric knowledge—as the context in each case shows. This is important in making comparisons with early Christianity, for in the early Church there was no distinction between priesthood and laity, and there was no esoteric knowledge in the hands of a select few. In fact, Paul's letter to the Colossians is directed in part against any such idea.

The term *hā-rabbîm* is used frequently, sometimes to be translated "the many," as in the *Manual of Discipline,* and sometimes to be translated as "the great ones," as in the *Habakkuk Commentary.*[15] Just how the term is to be understood is not entirely clear, and scholars have not yet reached agreement.

WAS QUMRAN PART OF A LARGER MOVEMENT?

You are probably wondering how we can explain some of the apparent differences we have found between the various documents. One suggestion that commends itself is that the Qumran group was only one of a number of similar (but not identical) groups. The *Damascus Document,* for example, refers to a group in "Damascus." Its terms and descriptions are slightly different from those of the *Manual of Discipline,* which (we suppose) belonged to the Qumran Community. But the close relationship of the two docu-

---

[15]Perhaps this is an oversimplification. "The many" in 1QS includes priests, elders, and the rest of the people (1QS 6:8-9), whereas the expression in 1QpHab. refers to kings and rulers (1QpHab. 4:2, referring to Hab. 1:10).

ments suggests that the same group made use of them. If the unifying factor were the larger group, this would explain the differences satisfactorily. But a satisfactory hypothesis is not necessarily a true one. Is there other evidence that will support this theory?

We have already noted the reference to a minimum of ten males (1QS 6:3). The *Damascus Document* refers to "the meeting of the cities of Israel" (CD 12:19) and "the meeting of the camps" (CD 12:23, with some restoration of the text), with the words "groups of ten men as the minimum" (CD 13:1) closely connected in the text to these other references. "The camp supervisor" is mentioned in CD 13: 7, and "the supervisor of all the camps" has his duties outlined in CD 14:8-9. Rabin thinks that "the Many" of the *Manual of Discipline* is the same as "all the camps" in the *Damascus Document* (although, he points out, "the Many" in the *Damascus Document* is to be equated with the dwellers of only a single camp).[16] A careful study of the description of a "session of the Many" in the *Manual of Discipline* and that of the order of "the meeting of all camps" in the *Damascus Document*, has, however, left me unconvinced that they are identical.[17] Nevertheless, I believe that the *Damascus Document* clearly indicates the existence of a number of similar communities, and I have no doubt that Qumran was somehow part of a larger movement.

TERMS OF ADMISSION

The process by which a "volunteer from Israel" (1QS 6:13) could become a member of the Community is set forth in the sixth column of the *Manual of Discipline*.

---

[16]Cf. Rabin, *The Zadokite Documents,* p. 69, n. 9, 1. Cf. 1QS 6:12 with CD 14:9.
[17]Cf. 1QS 6:8-23 with CD 14:2-12.

He first presented himself to the "official" (1QS 6:14, identified with the "Supervisor" by most writers) to be examined concerning his understanding and his deeds. If he proved to be an apt candidate, the officer was to "bring him into the covenant" and to "cause him to understand all the laws of the Community" (1QS 6:15). This closely parallels provisions in CD 13:11 and 15:10.

After this, he was to stand before the Many, and they were carefully to consider him, then vote to admit or to turn away (1QS 6:16). If he was admitted, he "must not touch the 'Purity' of the Many until he had been thoroughly investigated by them as to his spirit and his deeds (1QS 6:17). This took a full year, during which time he could not share in the property of the Many (1QS 6:17).

At the end of this time, the "novice" was again examined by the Many, who asked concerning his relation to Torah. If the vote was again favorable, his wealth and property were conveyed to the "custodian of the property of the Many" (1QS 6:20), with the stipulation that these were to be entered to his credit but not to be spent for the Many. He could not "touch the drink of the Many" until the end of the second year (1QS 6:20-21).

At the completion of the second year, he was once more examined, and if it was decided to admit him, he was enrolled in the rank of his assigned position "for Torah and for judgment and for purity," and his property, counsel, and judgment belonged to the Community (1QS 6:22-23). The details concerning his property were obviously to safeguard the Commnuity against claims that might arise if a novice were rejected on the final vote. Once again, it is important to note the details of admission, for in a comparison of Qumran and Christianity these matters are of primary significance.

We may therefore summarize the results of our study thus far. The Qumran Community was a closed group, consisting of men, women, and children, into which one could gain admission only after a long and careful process of examination. It was divided into Priests, Levites, and the rest of the people, and there were ranks or orders of membership. There were various levels of hierarchy, with chief priests and courses, and also various administrative and/or judicial levels, with councils composed of both priests and laity. The group was quite likely part of a larger organization of similar groups, but these local units were not identical in all respects. The members were Jews and made use of the Scriptures and terminology of Judaism, but they had repudiated Jerusalem Judaism and the official hierarchy.

Further study will add more details to this picture of the Qumran Community.

CHAPTER SIX

Practices of the Qumran Community

WE HAVE MENTIONED, in passing, a number of the practices of the Community, but there is value in putting them down in order.

WATER PURIFICATION

One of the significant practices was water purification, which was probably a kind of baptism. The technical term is "water of impurity" (1QS 3:4, etc.), a Biblical term found in Numbers 19:9 ff., translated "waters of separation" (K.J.V.) or "water for impurity" (A.S.V., R.S.V.). In the *Manual of Discipline*, the following words are found: "so that he may purify himself with water of impurity and sanctify himself with rippling water" (1QS 3:9). The passage is difficult, for the words translated "rippling water" mean "rushing, dashing waves." Moreover there is a parallel in the fourth and fifth lines of the same column: "nor cleanse himself with waters of impurity, nor sanctify himself with seas or rivers" (1QS 3:4-5). It is not immediately obvious just how a group calling itself "the penitents of the desert" (4QpPs. 37 2:1) could have developed a ritual using terminology having to do with the sea, waves, rivers, etc. Even more difficult is the problem whether two stages of washing, or perhaps even two separate ritual acts, are in-

tended: one a "purifying"[1] and the other a "sanctifying,"
or whether the two terms are merely parallel. From 1QS
3:4-5, quoted above, the latter seems more likely.

Persons not in the Covenant—which evidently means those
who had not been admitted to the Community—were not
permitted to "enter into the water to touch the purity (or
cleanness) of men of holiness" (1QS 5:13).[2] This statement, taken together with the rules for admission to the
Community described in the previous chapter, indicates that
baptism, or water cleansing, was not an initiatory rite, but
rather was reserved for those already in the Covenant. The
importance of this point will become apparent, but we note
in passing that there is a basic difference between Christian baptism, which is initiatory in that it is administered to
the person coming into the covenant, and Qumran water
purification which is not initiatory.

The term "enter into the water" seems to indicate that a
large quantity of water was necessary. The *Damascus
Document* confirms this: "Let no man bathe in water that
is dirty or less than the quantity that covers up a man"
(CD 10:11).[3]

We should note that baptism was not in itself effectual.
A man "while in iniquity" could not cleanse himself with
water for impurity (1QS 3:4). Rather, it was through God's
spirit[4] of true counsel that his iniquities could be atoned,

---

[1]Following the emendation in Brownlee, *The Dead Sea Manual of
Discipline*, p. 13, n. 16.

[2]We shall discuss the term "purity" later.

[3]Christians should be slow to press this point as an argument in
favor of immersion, since that which is symbolized by ritual washing
in Qumran cultus is not equivalent to that which is symbolized in
Christian baptism.

[4]It is difficult, if not impossible, to know whether to use a capital S
when translating the word for "spirit," for sometimes the spirit in
QL seems to be divine and sometimes merely a human spirit devoted
to God.

and through a holy spirit disposed toward unity in his truth that he could be cleansed. It was through an upright and humble spirit that his sin could be atoned, and through the submission of his soul to all God's ordinances that his flesh could be cleansed "so that he may purify himself with water for impurity" (1QS 3:6-9; cf. 1QS 5:13-14). In other words, it was only after the cleansing was accomplished that the water could be entered. The water did not cleanse the sinner.

In this respect there is a similarity to Christian baptism, for, except in sacramentarian theology, baptism is not considered to have power to cleanse. On the other hand, we must not forget that Christian baptism is initiatory and not repeated; in Qumran the ritual cleansing was repeated, perhaps annually, and was not initiatory.

The Renewing of the Covenant

The *Manual of Discipline* mentions an annual examination of each member in the presence of his fellows, with reference to his spirit and his deeds (1QS 5:24-25). As a result of this examination there could be promotion "according to his understanding," or he could be retarded "according to his perversions." Each of the members was permitted to "reprove his fellow in truth and humility and loving devotion." Brownlee suggests that the annual re-enactment of the Covenant was the most probable time for the admission of new members, the annual examination and promotion of old members, and the renewal of the Covenant vows by all members.[5] When you read the *Manual of Discipline*, you

---

[5]Brownlee, *The Dead Sea Manual of Discipline*, p. 53. Cf. 1QS 2:19 ff. for the annual vows and 1QS 1:16 for the admission of new members.

are impressed with the emphasis upon rank in the Qumran Community. It would seem that the "promoting" or "retarding" of members in the annual examination was somehow connected with the rank each one held.

An annual meeting is described in the *Damascus Document*, with the heading: "The Order of the Meeting of All Camps" (CD 14:3-12). Four classes were mustered: priests, Levites, the children of Israel, and the proselytes. The order states, "They shall be asked about everything" (CD 14:6). The inclusion of the proselyte with the other three classes lends support to Brownlee's suggestion that the admission of new members took place at the annual meeting. In passing, we note that whereas the minimum unit in the Covenant was ten men (CD 13:1), the annual meeting was numbered "by thousands, and hundreds, and fifties, and tens" (1QS 2:21-22). It was this group that was under the "Supervisor of all the camps" (CD 14:9).

THE STUDY OF TORAH

The Community is described as "a Community in the Torah" (1QS 5:2). If we are to understand several statements in the literature of Qumran literally, one of the major emphases in the life of the Community was the study of Torah. For example, consider the following passage from the *Manual of Discipline:* "In whatever place the ten are, there shall not cease to be a man who expounds the Torah night and day" (1QS 6:7). It is stipulated that this expounding was to be done orally, each to the other. Further, the Many were to "keep awake in Community a third of all the nights" to read aloud from the book and to expound the laws (1QS 6:7-8). The exact meaning of this is not clear, but it seems likely that the Community was divided

into three "watches," each of which was to spend a third
of the night reading the law.[6]

In the list of fines in the *Manual of Discipline* there is a
fine of thirty days for sleeping "during a session of the
Many," and a fine of ten days for leaving "without permission and without good reason as many as three times at a
single session" (1QS 7:10). Since this follows the passage
regulating the reading, it seems quite likely that the fines
were imposed for failure to pay due attention and respect
to the reading of the Scriptures. A similar provision may be
implied in the *Damascus Document,* where we read, "In a
locality of ten, let there never be absent a man, a priest,
instructed in the book of the Hagu" (CD 13:2).[7] Just what
"the book of the Hagu" was, we do not yet know. Some have
thought it was the *Manual of Discipline;* others, an esoteric
work now lost; still others, the Scriptures themselves. On
such matters, an open mind is the best present attitude.

COMMUNAL LIFE

Life in the Community was of a communal nature, including the common meal. The following passage from
the *Manual of Discipline* is noteworthy: "When they ar-
range the table to eat, or the wine to drink, the priest shall
first stretch out his hand to invoke a blessing" (1QS 6:4-6).
There is a similar passage in 1QSa 2:11 ff. The latter is
usually taken to be a communion, or sacramental meal; and

---

[6] I have a vivid memory of visiting about ten synagogues in *Me'ah
She'arim*, in Jerusalem, on Pentecost, several years ago. The male
members, from boys up, were reading the Scriptures. My guide,
Rabbi Jacob Sonderling, of Los Angeles, whom I chanced to meet in
the hotel, told me that such continuous reading of the Scriptures can
be found in those synagogues any night of the year. It is an attempt
to fulfill literally such scriptures as Joshua 1:8. Cf. Sir. 51:23.
[7] The evidence from 1QSa 1:7 indicates that this should be
emended in CD to read Hagî.

some writers read the former passage also as a sacramental meal. As a matter of fact, some have argued that this is the precursor of the Lord's Supper of the New Testament. We shall have more to say later; for the present, let us admit that there are parallels. It is well for us to remember that parallels can be found between Christianity and almost every known religion or philosophy. The Lord Jesus did not resent it when men found in Him something reminiscent of John or Elijah or Jeremiah or one of the prophets (Matt. 16:14). Christians often make the mistake of drawing their lines of defense where they are most difficult to maintain. What if there are similarities between the Qumran communion and the Lord's Supper? Nowhere in Qumran Literature is there any indication that a saviour died for his people, and nowhere is there any claim similar to the words, "This is my body which is [broken] for you."

Yet, when we read the *Manual of Discipline* more carefully, we notice that the words in 1QS 6:4-6 seem to apply to any meal. Just a few verses before that we find the rule: "and together they shall eat, and together they shall bless, and together they shall take counsel" (1QS 6:2-3). It would require a strained exegesis indeed to make this apply to just the sacramental meal, especially when read in context.

The communal life included also "their mind, their strength, and their property" (1QS 1:11-12). This suggests that the means of producing wealth, as well as the wealth itself, was to be held in common. There is emphatic repetition on this point.[8] We have already noted the custody of the property of a novice.[9] The reference to the "custodian of the property of the Many" in this connection (1QS 6:20) suggests that there was a common fund. It is reasonable to

[8] Cf. also 1QS 2:24f.; 5:1ff.; 6:2ff.; 7:6ff., and other references.
[9] Cf. p. 76.

suppose that such a common fund was in the background of the regulation in the *Damascus Document,* where the wages of two days every month were to be put in the hands of the supervisor and the judges to be used for orphans, the poor and needy, the old man, the prisoner, the maiden without a relative, the virgin with no one to give her in marriage, and all the work of the corporation (CD 14:13-16).

Note, however, that this is not pure communism.[10] There was provision for wages (CD 14:13). There was also a system of graded fines for designated offenses (1QS 6:25– 7:25). Just how this system of fines worked is not entirely clear. If a member lied "in the matter of wealth," he was fined "one-fourth of his food allowance" (1QS 6:25). Then follows a series of fines expressed in terms of time periods ranging from a few days to one year. Brownlee suggests that we are to understand "one-fourth of his food allowance" as the amount of the fine in each case.[11] However, one regulation states "should he have committed an inadvertence against the property of the Community so as to destroy it, he shall repay it in full; but should he be unable to pay it, he shall be fined for sixty days" (1QS 7:6-8). This certainly seems to imply that there was financial responsibility, or at least a system of work rewards. I am inclined to read the fines in 1QS 6:25–7:25 as stated in periods of time, therefore in terms of earning capacity, rather than food allowance.[12]

---

[10]On this point (and several others) I must dissent from A. Dupont-Sommer, *The Jewish Sect of Qumrân and the Essenes* (London: Vallentine Mitchell, 1954), p. 65.

[11]Brownlee, *The Dead Sea Manual of Discipline,* p. 27, n. 58.

[12]The word translated "fined" can also be translated "punished," which complicates this discussion still further. Burrows, *The Dead Sea Scrolls,* pp. 379-381, translates it the latter. But what does "he shall be punished one-fourth of his food allowance" mean? It is patently a punishment in the form of a fine.

The Community was to have no traffic with nonmembers: "All who are not reckoned in his covenant are to be separated, both they and all they have" (1QS 5:18). Further on we read, "Their property shall not be intermingled with the property of the men of deceit who have not cleansed their ways by separating themselves from perversity and by walking in perfection of way" (1QS 9:8-9).[13] The *Damascus Document,* however, has a slightly different regulation: "Let no man of all the members of the Covenant of God trade with the Children of the Pit, except for cash" (CD 13:14-15).[14] This last clause (literally, hand to hand), if properly interpreted, is another indication of private wealth. However, the argument cannot be pressed on such shaky ground.

That there was a communality of mind, strength, and wealth, in the Qumran Community is beyond question. Whether this was so complete as to exclude private wealth or any kind of work rewards is, in my opinion, less clear. Again I have the feeling that some scholars, in their zeal to make a good case for the identification of the Qumran group as Essenes, have read more into the text than it really justifies. Perhaps even the various Essene communities had different characteristics.

It is risky to suggest a parallel from a different period, I know. But I am tempted to refer to the difference between the *Moshav* and the *Qibbutz* in modern Israel. Life in the *Qibbutz* is communal, even to the extent that

---

[13]The careful reader may note that my quotations often follow Brownlee or Burrows, or (in the case of CD) Rabin. In each instance I have carefully worked over the Hebrew text; but if one of these scholars has given the translation a nice turn, why should I sacrifice that just to be original? This is a blanket acknowledgment of my debt to them.

[14]Following Rabin. However, I have been unable to find support for his interpretation of *kaf le-kaf,* "for cash."

there is no private wealth. Each contributes all he has (if anything) when entering, and thereafter gives according to his ability and receives according to his need. If he leaves the *Qibbutz*, he takes nothing with him, for the wealth belongs to the *Qibbutz*. In the *Moshav*, on the other hand, the communal life is modified. Each contributes his goods to the *Moshav*, but retains title. He receives earnings (usually in kind) according to his production. If at any time he wishes to withdraw from the community, he may take what is his.[15]

It would seem that the provisions of the *Manual of Discipline* tend to indicate a community something like the *Qibbutz*, whereas the *Damascus Document* rather suggests a community something like the *Moshav*. And, just as the modern Israeli looks with favor and even approval upon both kinds of communal life today, it may have been that the members of the Covenant of which Qumran was a part (and I would not be adverse to the inclusion of Essenes in the larger picture) were willing to tolerate and approve different expressions of communal life. The effort to analyze, categorize, and uniformize, is a Western trait which I have not found strongly developed in the Middle East.

THE PURITY

A technical term, *tohŏrâ*, "cleanness, purity," is found in QL (particularly 1QS and CD), which apparently indicated something well known and highly sacred in the Community,

---

[15]While this very sketchy description is from my own observations, the reader can read a similar description of the *Moshav* and the *Qibbutz* in E. Reiger, *Everyday Hebrew* (Jerusalem, Israel: Goldberg's Press, 1954), pp. 160-248, with an English translation of much of the text. The hero and heroine of the story reconcile their own different preferences in the *Collective Moshav*, which has features of *Qibbutz* and *Moshav*.

but which is not defined for us. Our present task is to study
the passages in which the term occurs, to learn what we can
about it.

The rule concerning "everyone entering into the Congregation of the Community" (which seems to be a technical
term for the novitiate) states that he "may not enter into
the water to touch the Purity of the holy men" (1QS 5:13).
After he has been examined by the Supervisor of the Many,
he is put on probation for a full year, during which time
"he must not touch the Purity of the Many" (1QS 6:16-17).
At the end of the second year, if successful, he is admitted
into the Community, enrolled in his proper rank among the
brethren "for Torah, for judgment, for Purity, and for the
transfer of his wealth" (1QS 6:22).

If a member lied about the matter of his wealth, they
were to "exclude him from the Purity of the Many for one
year, and he shall be fined one-quarter of his bread" (1QS
6:25). If he spoke against any of the priests in wrath, he
was to be fined for one year and "set apart by himself
from the Purity of the Many" (1QS 7:3). For slandering
his fellow, he was to be "excluded for one year from the
Purity of the Many," and fined; but if he slandered the
Many, he was to be "banished from them to return no more"
(1QS 7:16). A man who departed from the spirit of the
Community to walk in the stubbornness of his heart, and
then repented and returned, was to be fined for two years;
"in the first he shall not touch the Purity of the Many, and
in the second he shall not touch the Drink of the Many"
(1QS 7:10-20). On the other hand, if a man departed from
the council of the Community after having been in it for
ten years, he could never return, and "any man of the men
of the Community who shares with him in his Purity or in

his property" was to be the same as the one who had been banished (1QS 7:24-25).[16]

A member of the Community who willfully removed a word from all that Moses commanded could not "touch the Purity of the holy men; nor shall he have any knowledge of any of their counsel until his deeds are purified from every kind of perversity" (1QS 8:17-18). If he transgressed a word of the Torah inadvertently, however, he was to be "excluded from the Purity and from the council" for two years (1QS 8:24-25). In a capital offense, two witnesses were required, and when their witness was in hand, "Let the man be set apart from the Purity only" (CD 9:21).[17] But in a matter of property, one witness was sufficient "for setting apart from the Purity" (CD 9:23).

A careful examination of these rules indicates the following:

> It is necessary to enter into water to touch the Purity;
> Torah, judgment, the Purity, and community of property are separate categories;
> The Purity is distinct from the bread (or food allowance);
> The Purity is distinct from the Drink of the Many;
> The Purity is distinct from the knowledge of the council;
> Separation from the Purity was a grave punishment, only less severe than separation from the council and/or separation from the Community.

The word *ṭohŏrâ* ("purity") is cognate with the verb *ṭāhar*, "to purify," which is used in the following passage:

> He cannot *purify* himself by atonement,
> Nor cleanse himself with water-for-impurity,

---

[16] The text is somewhat fragmentary at this point, but there is little question about the restoration.
[17] This is not entirely clear to me.

> Nor sanctify himself with seas or rivers,
> Nor *purify* himself with any water for washing (1QS
> 3:4-5).

In the light of the poetic structure it is obvious that this purification is related to ritual washing. This fact suits the conditions for each of the specifications which we have just set forth concerning the Purity. An easy conclusion would be to identify the Purity with the tank found in the Qumran ruins and which the archaeologists concluded had been used for ritual washing or baptism.

However, easy conclusions are often incorrect. And the word *ṭohŏrâ*, as Saul Liebermann has pointed out,[18] is used in rabbinic literature for ritually clean articles, including vessels, utensils, garments, and particularly food. Joseph Baumgarten concludes that the Purity cannot be water, since nonmembers are not to "enter into water to touch" it.[19] Brownlee says that the Purity may consist of such items as food, vessels, rites, or even the bodies of the holy men.[20] Burrows always translates the term, "the sacred food."[21] Since the Purity is distinct from the food allowance (1QS 6:25), it is impossible to look upon the Purity as food, unless it be food of a sacramental meal.[21a] The juxtaposition of the Purity of the Many with the Drink of the Many in 1QS 7:20 would, in that case, suggest a sacra-

---

[18]"The Discipline in the So-Called 'Dead Sea Manual of Discipline,'" *JBL*, 71 (1952): 203.
[19]"Sacrifice and Worship among the Jewish Sectarians of the Dead Sea (Qumran) Scrolls," *HTR*, 46 (1953): 148 n. 22. Cf. 1QS 5:13-14.
[20]*The Dead Sea Manual of Discipline*, p. 21, n. 37.
[21]*The Dead Sea Scrolls*, p. 377 ff.
[21a]C. Rabin, *Qumran Studies* (New York: Oxford University Press, 1957), p. 8, says "The Purity is ritually pure food," "common meals, from which the applicant and the first-year novice are excluded."

mental meal in which there were the two elements: food (or bread) and drink.

It is probably premature to try to identify the Purity more definitely than this.

We can now summarize certain characteristics of the religious life of the Qumran Community. It was a group stressing ritual washing or baptism in connection with ritual purity. This baptism, however, was not an entrance rite, but a rite repeated perhaps annually. It did not effect ritual cleanness, but rather required sanctity as a prerequisite.

An annual meeting was held, for the purpose of examination of the membership, promotions and demotions, probably the admission of new members, and the renewal of the covenant.

The Community was devoted to the study of the Torah, or Law of Moses.

A Communal life was practiced by the Community which included community of mind, strength, and goods. There are indications, however, of private wealth or work rewards.

A certain cult-object or rite, known as the Purity, was highly revered. Banishment from the Community was the only punishment more severe than excommunication from the Purity.

These are only some of the more obvious practices of the Qumran Community. As we study their theology in more detail, we shall be able to add other points. Final conclusions on any point should be withheld until our picture is complete.

CHAPTER SEVEN

The God of Qumran

WITH THE REALIZATION that what we say is subject to correction, we can describe the religious beliefs of the Qumran Community. What we have seen so far has prepared us to recognize that the theology of Qumran is not greatly different from the theology of Judaism proper. Two risks are to be avoided: conclusions drawn from similarities without due regard for differences, and the opposite conclusions drawn from differences without due regard for similarities.

THE KNOWLEDGE OF GOD

We have already noted the large number of Biblical manuscripts represented in the fragments. Obviously, the Community possessed, and probably used, the Old Testament. This is further confirmed by the number of Biblical quotations and allusions found in the sectarian documents. For example, if we examine the footnotes in Brownlee's translation of 1QS[1] or Rabin's edition of CD,[2] we find a very large number of references to the Bible. The presence of commentaries on various scriptural books further supports our conclusion that the Qumran Community pos-

---

[1]*The Dead Sea Manual of Discipline, passim.*
[2]*The Zadokite Documents, passim.*

sessed the Old Testament, and likely drew its theology from
the Old Testament.

On the other hand, we have also noted the presence of
non-Biblical works among the fragments found in the caves.
To what extent were these used? And to what extent would
the doctrines derived from them differ from the doctrines
drawn from the Biblical books? Did the Qumran Community accept other works than the Old Testament Scriptures as canonical?

In the *Damascus Document* the Book of Jubilees is
quoted by name.[3] Moreover, fragments of certain deuterocanonical books in Hebrew have turned up.[4] Now, in determining the canon of the Old Testament as found in the New
Testament, Protestant Christian scholars have generally
taken two lines of evidence: the quotation of an Old Testament book in the New Testament, and the existence of a
Hebrew form of the·writing in question. On this basis of
these principles, the deuterocanonical works have been excluded from the Protestant Bibles. Whether these norms
are valid or not, I do not wish to discuss at this point. If
they are valid, perhaps we can use them with reference to
the Qumran Community. In that case, we would have to
conclude that certain writings other than the Old Testament books were considered canonical to Qumran.

A safer approach to the problem is to study the theology
found in the Qumran writings and then to make a comparison with the theology found in the Old Testament. When
we undertake this study, we notice almost at the outset an
esoteric element in Qumran theology. There is the mysteri-

---

[3]Cf. Burrows, *Dead Sea Scrolls*, p. 247; Rabin, *Zadokite Documents*,
p. 75; cf. CD 16:4.
[4]Cf. p. 46.

ous *Book of the Hagu*,[5] the peculiar nature of the so-called commentaries on several Old Testament books, and above all the stress upon knowledge and the ranking according to knowledge in the Community.[6] These factors suggest a cautious approach.

THE NATURE OF GOD

In the *Order of Warfare*, there is an extended passage (1QM 10:12-18; 11:1—12:5) in which the nature and works of God are set forth. He is the God of the Fathers (1QM 13:7), the Creator of the earth and its laws (1QM 10:12), the Maker of all things (1QS 3:15; 1QH 10:9; cf. CD 2:21). He created the laws of earth's watercourses, the circle of the seas and the reservoir of the rivers (1QM 10:12-13). To Him are attributed the fruits, animals, birds, man and his generation, the confusion of tongues and the division of the peoples, the habitation of the tribes and their fixed times, the course of the years and the times of eternity (1QM 10:13-18; cf. CD 2:9-10).

He determines the times of war, marches with His chosen people into combat, gives courage (1QM 10:4-9), delivers Goliath into the hand of David, and humiliates the Philistines (1QM 12:1-3); in fact, all power is from Him (1QM 18:13), all knowledge (1QS 3:15), all wisdom (1QS 4:2; 1QH 10:2, 8). There is none like Him (1QM 10:8).

He has a controversy with all flesh (CD 1:2). He caused a remnant to remain (CD 1:4). His wrath was kindled against the faithless backsliders (CD 1:21), but in His grace He raised men of understanding from Aaron and men of wisdom from Israel (CD 6:2-3). "Those whom He hated

---

[5]CD 10:6; 1QSa 1:6.
[6]For example, 1QS 2:22.

He caused to stray" (CD 2:13). He made conciliation for the trespass of the members of the Covenant, and pardoned their impiety (CD 3:18). It is through His righteousness that man's transgression shall be blotted out (1QS 11:3); it is from the fountain of His righteousness that man's justi-- fication flows (1QS 11:5); and even if this elect man should totter, God's dependable mercy is his salvation forever (1QS 11:12).

This, of course, sounds very much like the theology commonly held by Jews and Christians, and indicates that the Community of Qumran was indeed closely related in theology to the Judaism of its day. But other points must be considered.

DUALISM

The term *dualism* conveys a number of ideas. To the philosopher it may suggest the division of the universe into matter and spirit. To the student of religion, on the other hand, it may suggest either the ethical concept of good and evil, or the cosmological concept of two eternal beings locked in a struggle for the control of the universe. Various shades of these ideas will be found.

There is an ethical dualism in the Bible, portrayed under various images and figures of speech, but in general setting forth the conflict between good and evil in this present world. In the Book of Proverbs, for example, there is set forth before man the two ways (Prov. 2:13-15). In the Gospel of John the conflict is between light and darkness (John 1:5; 3:19; 8:12). Other examples could readily be given.

Cosmological dualism is best set forth in Zoroastrianism, particularly in the later form where Angra Mainyu, often translated "the evil spirit" (or Ahriman, to use his later name), is the creator of evil and is opposed to Ahura Mazda (or Ormuzd), the creator of good.[7] In later Zoroastrian scriptures, these two beings are essentially coeval, i.e., they have existed from the beginning. However, they are not co-eternal, for Ormuzd shall triumph at last over Ahriman.

Bible students will at once see that the Biblical doctrine of Satan is to be considered as part of the discussion of Biblical dualism. At times, Satan seems to be almost the counterpart of Ahriman. Satan is not coeval with God, for God created him; but Satan is prehuman, for he was created before man. There are some scholars who hold that the idea of Satan was brought into the Old Testament in the Persian period, through Zoroastrian influence. We need not discuss this point here, for we are concerned with the Qumran materials rather than with the Bible. However, I believe our discussion of the question as it relates to Qumran will have implications for Biblical studies as well.

QUMRAN DUALISM

In the *Manual of Discipline* there is a long passage which is dualistic in viewpoint (1QS 3:13—4:26). We should note, however, the basic monism at the very outset, for this must control our conclusions concerning the dualism: "From the God of knowledge exists all that is and will be" (1QS 3:15). That this is not later modified, the following passage clearly teaches: "After they exist, according to their ordinances . . . they fulfill their task; and nothing can be changed. Under His control are the laws of all" (1QS 3:15-16). Then is set forth the dualistic teaching. "He created man for dominion

---

[7] I am fully aware that I have greatly simplified the matter at this point. But, first, this is not the place to go into a detailed and critical study of Zoroastrianism, and, second, we are not helped in our present task by complicating the problem unduly.

over the world and assigned him two spirits by which to walk until the season of His visitation" (1QS 3:17-18).

The two spirits are described as the spirits of truth and perversion (1QS 3:18-19), the prince of lights and the angel of darkness (1QS 3:20-21). The angel of darkness not only has control of sons of perversion (1QS 3:21), but it is also because of him that the sons of righteousness go astray (1QS 3:22), for he has in his command spirits who have been allotted to him who strive to trip the sons of light (1QS 3:24). But the God of Israel and His angel of truth have helped all the sons of light (1QS 3:25). It was God who created the spirits of darkness and established their ways (1QS 3:25-26), but He has loved "for all the duration of the ages" the spirit of light, while as for the other, "He has loathed its counsel, and all its ways He has hated forever" (1QS 3:26–4:1).

There are two ways in the world, as the result of the activities of these two spirits. The way of the spirit of truth is to enlighten the heart of man, and to accomplish in him the works of God (1QS 4:2-6). The results will be healing and abundant peace during a long life, bearing seed (natural children, or spiritual works?), and eternal rejoicing and a crown of glory and clothes of majesty in eternal light (1QS 4:6-8). The way of the spirit of perversion is the way of greed, indolence, wickedness, falsehood, pride, and every sort of evil (1QS 4:8-11). The results will be plagues, eternal ruin, perpetual disgrace, the shame of destruction in the 'fire of the dark regions, mourning, and no remnant or survivor (1QS 4:12-14).

All of mankind is under the influence of these two spirits, and everyone walks in their ways (1QS 4:15). God has set them (i.e., the two spirits, as the feminine pronominal suffix indicates) in equal parts until the last period, with per-

petual enmity between them (1QS 4:16-18). He has appointed a period for the existence of wrongdoing; but
there is an appointed time, a season of visitation, when He
will destroy the spirit of wickedness forever (1QS 4:18-20).
Then He will purge by His truth all the deeds of man,
cleanse him through a holy spirit (or perhaps, Holy Spirit)
from all wicked practices, sprinkle him with a spirit of truth,
and give the upright insight into the knowledge of the
Most High (1QS 4:20-23). For the present, however, these
spirits strive within man's heart, and "according as man's
inheritance [is] in truth and righteousness, so he hates evil;
but insofar as his heritage is in the portion of perversity and
wickedness in him, so he abominates truth" (1QS 4:23-26).

The basic monism of the passage should be noted, i.e.,
that there is only one Supreme Being, for this is stressed
from beginning to end. But even more important, we should
note that it is never quite clear whether man as an individual is the arena of this struggle. It is the tendency of
those who hold to a cosmological dualism (including, unfortunately, many Christians who have an exaggerated
doctrine of Satan), to assume the "balcony attitude." The
struggle between good and evil in the world is something
that they observe, but in which they never really participate. But in the Qumran teaching, as set forth in the passage just considered, man is involved in the struggle. Moreover, what does the passage in 1QS 4:23-26 mean? Does
it mean that man (i.e., mankind) is divided into two groups:
those who hate evil, and those who abominate truth? Or
does it mean that man (i.e., the individual) has a struggle
within his own heart, with the result that he is divided in
his own loyalties; to the extent that his inheritance is in
truth and righteousness, he hates evil; but to the extent
that he is a child of perversity and wickedness, he abomi-

nates truth? We shall have to return to this problem when we discuss the subject of the doctrine of Man in Qumran Theology.

Is This Zoroastrian Dualism?

A number of writers have stressed the Zoroastrian character of Qumran dualism. Dupont-Sommer, for example, says: "Until now no ancient document of Jewish origin had ever been produced which bore so clearly as this book of instruction the mark of Iran."[8] Likewise, K. G. Kuhn says:

> This Gnostic structure of the new text can scarcely have sprung up from Jewish tradition—there the presuppositions for it would be lacking; while they would be genuinely present in this sect. But it agrees surprisingly with the original preaching of Zoroaster, and thereby is set forth anew the old question of the Parsee influence on Judaism.[9]

The problem is complicated by several factors. The date of Zoroaster's birth, for one thing, is placed anywhere from 6000 B.C. to 569 B.C. Obviously, the more recent his birth, the less opportunity for his ideas to spread westward. In my opinion, the evidence presented by Herzfeld settles the date at 569 B.C.[10] In the second place, Zoroastrianism itself underwent a process of development. In the matter of dualism, it passed from an ethical dualism in the Gathas (or older poems, generally attributed to Zoroaster) to a cosmological dualism in the later writings. Herzfeld says that the teaching that Ahriman is the creator of evil is not

---

[8]*The Jewish Sect of Qumrân and the Essenes*, p. 128.

[9]"Die in Palästina gefundenen hebräischen Texte und das Neue Testament," *ZTK*, 47 (1950): 211.

[10]Ernst Herzfeld, *Zoroaster and His World* (Princeton: Princeton University Press, 1947), I: 19, 29. This is the traditional date of 258 years before Alexander.

found until 1,500 years after Zoroaster[11]—which, of course, is much too late for direct influence upon either Qumran or the Old Testament.

If the objection is made that the forces bringing about such a development in Zoroastrian dualism were operative prior to the actual change, this will be readily admitted. We shall then raise the question: Were those forces from within Zoroastrianism, or were they external? If they were external, then the case for Zoroastrian influence on Qumran and on the Old Testament is lost: for it was in that case a non-Zoroastrian influence. In my opinion, the matter is not yet solved. It is, however, a subject to be handled by those more expert in Zoroastrianism than I would claim to be. I would simply put forth this suggestion: the dualism of Qumran is more similar to the dualism of earlier Zoroastrianism than to that of later developments, but the eschatology of Qumran is more similar (as we shall see) to that of later Zoroastrianism than to that of the earlier form. A satisfactory solution of the problem must account for both these facts.

SUPERHUMAN SPIRITS

When we were discussing the concept of dualism, we had occasion to note the teaching of two spirits, but we were not sure whether these two spirits were opposing forces in an individual, or forces or beings outside of the human race. Kuhn, in the light of one of the most crucial passages in the *Manual of Discipline* (1QS 4:23), remarks that both spirits are in man and maintain their struggle within him, while the upright man longs for the eschatological salvation when God will take from him the spirit of evil.[12] Braun,

---

[11]*Ibid.*, I: 316.
[12]K. G. Kuhn, "Die Sektenschrift und die iranische Religion," *ZTK*, 49 (1952): 301, n. 4.

likewise, says "One sometimes gets the impression that it is a matter of two spiritual currents rather than two definite entities.[13]

On the other hand, there are passages in the Qumran writings that seem to support the idea of spiritual beings. The rule over all the sons of righteousness is "in the hand of the prince of lights," whereas the rule over all the sons of perversion is "in the hand of the angel of darkness" (1QS 3:20-22). The term "prince of lights" is found set over against Belial in the *Damascus Document:* "For in ancient times Moses and Aaron arose by the hand of the prince of lights,[14] and Belial raised Jannes and his brother by his evil device" (CD 5:18).[15] A passage in the *Order of Warfare* supports the view that spiritual beings are meant. In this work a liturgy blesses God and curses Belial and all the spirits of his lot (1QM 13:1-5). God is blessed for His works and judgments, and also because He made Belial, the angel of hostility, to hinder, and then made him to fall into darkness (1QM 13:7-11).[16] Belial "desires to do evil and to make guilty, and all the spirits of his lot are angels who wish to hinder" (1QM 13:11-12). In the easy transition from God to Belial throughout this passage, and in

---

[13]F.-M. Braun, "L'arrière-fond judaïque du quatrième évangile et la Communauté de l'Alliance," *RB*, 62 (1955): 13.

[14]Rabin says that this cannot refer to God Himself, for the phrase, "by the hand of," is only used of second causes in CD. Cf. *The Zadokite Documents,* p. 20. For the use of Beliar (a variant of Belial) in the New Testament, cf. II Cor. 6:15. F. Hvidberg, *Menigheden af den Nye Pagt i Damascus* (Copenhagen, 1928), pp. 103, 245, reminds us that the expression "Father of Lights" is found in James 1:17.

[15]Cf. "Jannes and Jambres" in II Tim. 3:8. This was pointed out by S. Schechter, *Documents of Jewish Sectaries* (Cambridge: University Press, 1910), I: xxxvii.

[16]I have followed van der Ploeg's translation here (and elsewhere in 1QM), although I think it is questionable at this point.

the attribution of will to Belial and his angels, there are evidences that the people of Qumran looked upon Belial and his angels as true beings.

The title *Mastema* is used in the *Damascus Document*, where it appears to be a proper noun, "the angel of the Persecutor" (or perhaps, "the persecuting Angel"; CD 16:5 —cf. "the angel Satan" in II Cor. 12:7, and the form "the Satan," regularly used). In the *Manual of Discipline*, however, the word occurs as a common noun, "in the dominion of his persecution" (1QS 3:23). The name *Prince Mastema* occurs several times in the Book of Jubilees (Jub. 11:5; 17:16; 18:9, etc.) Mastema is usually taken to be another name for Belial, which can be supported by a study of the use of the two words in the *Damascus Document* (CD 4:13; 5:18; 8:2; 16:5). However, there is a difficult passage in the *Order of Warfare* (1QM 13:10-11), which van der Ploeg translates: "And Thou hast made Belial for hindering, the angel of hostility. . . ."[17] The Hebrew, however, seems to say quite clearly, "And Thou hast made Belial to destroy the angel Mastema."[18] If we are not to take Belial and Mastema as separate beings, either one or both of the names in this passage must be understood as common nouns. Unfortunately, the text is damaged immediately following this clause, so that context does not help us.

In the *Order of Warfare*, four angels are named, and their order is given:

> And on the bucklers of the towers shall be written: on the first Mi[chael the prince, on the second Gabriel, on the third] Sariel, on the fourth Raphael.[19]

---

[17]*Et Tu as fait Bélial pour nuire, l'ange de l'hostilité* . . . "La Règle de la Guerre," VT, 5 (1955): 387.

[18]*w'th 'śith bli'l lśht ml'k mstmh.*

[19]The restoration is assured by the mention of Michael and Gabriel in the sentence immediately following. Cf. 1QM 9:15-16.

Michael is named in Daniel (10:13, 21) and Jude (v. 9); Gabriel is named in Daniel (8:16; 9:21) and Luke (1:19, 26) and Sariel is mentioned in a Greek fragment of Enoch (20:6). According to a passage in Enoch, the four principal angels are Michael, Raphael, Gabriel, and Phanuel (En. 40:9-10). Other lists are given in the literature of Judaism; and R. H. Charles observes that "it would be a mere waste of time to attempt to reconcile the angelology of these various passages."[20]

A striking passage is found in the *Order of Warfare*, which I believe merits printing in full (restorations in brackets):

> And you, be strong and do not fear them for they [are nothing], their desire is for Tohu and for Bohu,[21] and their work is as [power]less. And [they shall not conquer] Israel. Every one who is and who shall be and [(*lacking*)] with all who shall be eternal. Today (is) his appointed time to subdue and to humble the prince of the dominion of iniquity. And he shall send (or, has sent) an eternal help for the lot of his [witn]ess in the strength of the angel who was mighty to serve, Michael in eternal light to illumine with joy the e[lect of I]srael (with) peace and blessing for the Lot of God, to exalt among the gods (or angels) the ministry of Michael and the dominion of Israel among all flesh. Justice shall rejoice [in] the heights, and all the sons of His truth shall shout in eternal knowledge.[22] (1QM 17:4-8).

The agency of Michael in the defeat of the prince of the dominion of iniquity, and the exaltation of Michael among the spirit-beings at the time of Israel's exaltation among the

---

[20]*The Book of Enoch*, translated by R. H. Charles (Oxford: Clarendon Press, 1893), p. 118.

[21]These Hebrew words are found in Gen. 1:2, translated usually, "without form and void."

[22]Restorations follow van der Ploeg in most cases. The translation, however, is my own.

human beings, are points which seem to be unique in Qumran angelology.[23]

In the light of this study, it seems safe to conclude that the theology of Qumran, to the extent that we have investigated it, is the theology of Judaism. It is the same God who is worshiped. The so-called dualism of Qumran is ethical, rather than cosmological. The spirit beings are those of the Old Testament. If we were to add any qualifying statements, we would be inclined to say that the Qumran Community stood closer to the apocryphal and apocalyptic writings of Judaism in the development of theology. It seems unnecessary to look outside of Judaism for direct influences, although we readily admit that there were several influences at work in the area during the period in survey, and it would be remarkable indeed if evidence of them was not to be found in Qumran. Further study of the theology of Qumran will help to bring out this point.

[23]It might be valuable to study this passage in the light of Assumption of Moses 10:1-2.

CHAPTER EIGHT

Man and His Salvation in Qumran

CLOSELY RELATED to the idea of God in any religion is the idea of man and his relationship to the deity he worships. In fact, it is almost impossible to make a clear-cut subdivision of the field of theology (for example, the classical divisions of Theology, Anthropology, and Soteriology) simply because each so largely involves the other. Can God be truly God (i.e., an absolute Being) and man still be man (i.e., a free being)? If man is a free being, then is not God limited? And if God is not limited, then is not man caught within a deterministic system? Or again, is God good or just? If He is good, how can He be just? If He is just, He must punish, and if He punishes and destroys, then He is not good. Is He all-powerful? Then why does He not destroy evil? So men reason, round and round in circles: arguments that strike each generation as new—but which in reality can be found as far back as religious literature is found.

THE PROBLEM

The basic idea in the Old Testament seems to be morality based upon the free will of man. Man had, of course, been laid under moral obligation by the revealed will of God. In the story of Eden, for example, man was free to eat of the tree or not to eat. He was not compelled by his nature to eat of that tree, for his basic appetites could be satisfied by the other trees, all of which were freely given to him. Nor was he compelled by outside forces. The serpent did not command him to eat; and even the command of God not to eat of that particular tree allowed for the free expression of man's will by pronouncing a judgment in the event of disobedience. Man, however, was not in ignorance concerning the matter, for God had revealed His will to man. This concept underlies the rest of the Old Testament.

If man sinned (i.e., disobeyed the revealed will of God), the effects of that sin could affect his children's welfare, even for generations (Exod. 20:5). But this can hardly be looked upon as rigid determinism. Jeremiah sets forth unequivocally the principle of personal responsibility, over against a popularized form of determinism, in the passage Jeremiah 31:29, 30.

With the introduction of the idea of two mutually hostile spirits striving for the dominion over man (or even controlling men as their agents), the platform was erected for a deterministic system. Some writers hold that the introduction of this idea into the Old Testament was a result of Persian influence. For example, it is sometimes pointed out that whereas pre-exilic II Samuel says that the Lord incited David to number Israel and Judah (II Sam. 24:1), post-exilic I Chronicles attributes this action to Satan (I Chron. 21:1).[1] We have already discussed the problem of Persian influence in connection with dualism.[2] We would only add here that there are careful scholars, with

---

[1] It should be noted, however, that in I Chronicles, the word occurs without its customary article, and may possibly mean "an adversary" rather than "the Satan."

[2] Cf. pp. 98-103.

no theological ax to grind, who think the idea of Satan is
thoroughly Jewish. Two examples are quoted:

> The belief in Satan, as we find it in the Old Testament,
> is thoroughly Jewish, yet it would hardly have assumed
> its actual form without the indirect influence of the belief
> in Ahriman against which it became a protest.[3]

> It would be absurd to think of Satan and his angels as
> borrowed from Angra Mainyu and the daevas.[4]

When we stop to think about it, we can see how a dualistic system can develop at the popular level from the
doctrine of a creature who is more than human and less
than divine (such as Satan is portrayed in the Bible).
There are many "Bible believers," who, in spite of the
monism of the Bible, have managed to construct about
Satan a dualistic system, including in his power such elements as disease, misfortune, and even death. Even the
doctrine of the "permissive will" of God is on the threshold
of dualism. And the evangelist who zealously calls upon
his hearer to "get on God's side and help defeat the Devil,"
is perilously close to dualism and a finite God. Yet who
would try to trace these things to Zoroastrianism!

After all, there is an observable difference between the
conduct of "good" people and "bad" people; and when this
is explained as the result of the influence of two spirits, as
it seems to be in Qumran theology, a quasi-dualism is already established. Along with this, there is an increase in
the idea of determinism and a decrease in the idea of free
will. Grossouw's statement is, in my opinion, an oversimplification, but nevertheless worthy of consideration:

---

[3] K. F. Geldner and T. K. Cheyne, "Zoroastrianism," *Encyclopaedia
Biblica* (New York: Macmillan Co., 1899-1903), IV: 5428.
[4] J. H. Moulton, "Zoroastrianism," [*Hastings'*] *Dictionary of the
Bible* (New York: Charles Scribner's Sons, 1919), IV: 988.

"Their mastery over man's moral actions seems to be absolute, the consequences of which would be that these actions are determined and no longer free."[5]

FREE WILL

In several passages in QL the free will of man is stressed. The emphasis on good works which is found throughout the *Manual of Discipline* would serve to underscore this viewpoint, as would the emphasis on repentance. The men outside the Community are described in terms which certainly stress responsibility:

> For these are not reckoned in His covenant, for they have not sought or inquired after Him in His ordinances to know the unconscious sins into which they have strayed, incurring guilt; while the conscious sins they have done willfully (1QS 5:11-12).

Likewise in the *Damascus Document* we find passages stressing responsibility and choice:

> . . . all flesh that were on the dry land when they died, and they became as though they had not been, through doing their own will and not keeping the commandment of the Maker (CD 2:20-21).

> Through it the first members of the covenant became culpable, and they were given over to the sword, when they forsook the covenant of God and chose their own desire and went about after the stubbornness of their hearts by doing each man his own desire (CD 3:10-12).

A careful reading of these passages is sufficient to lead to the conclusion that free will and human responsibility is a basic part of Qumran theology.

---

[5]W. K. M. Grossouw, "The Dead Sea Scrolls and the New Testament," *Studia Catholica*, 26 (1951): 293.

DETERMINISM

On the other hand, there are many passages in QL that stress a kind of determinism.

If we follow Grossouw's explanation (p. 107) and trace the deterministic elements to the doctrine of the two spirits, then we can offer in evidence the long passage in the *Manual of Discipline*, which we have already discussed.[6] The prince of light is to rule over the sons of righteousness, and the angel of darkness over the sons of perversion (1QS 3:20-22). Man's heart is enlightened by the spirit of truth (1QS 4:2). Greed, indolence, wickedness, falsehood, pride and haughtiness of heart, lying, deceit, cruelty, gross impiety, quick temper, blasphemous tongue, blindness of eyes and dullness of ears, stiffness of neck and hardening of the heart to walk in the ways of darkness, are all the work of the spirit of perversion (1QS 4:8-11).

From the passage, "and Belial raised Jannes and his brother by his evil device" (CD 5:18-19), it would seem that the Evil Spirit is even directly responsible for putting his agents in the world.[7]

The determinism of the Qumran literature may also be traced to their doctrine of creation. In this respect, there would be a similarity to the view sometimes expressed against the Biblical doctrine of creation: If God made man with a sin-potential, then God is ultimately responsible for man's sin. In the *Manual of Discipline*, for example, we find the following:

> From the God of knowledge exists all that is and will be.
> Before they existed, He established all the design of them.

---

[6] 1QS 3:13—4:26; cf. pp. 95-98.
[7] Cf., in this connection, Matt. 13:38-39, "The tares are the children of the wicked one; the enemy that sowed them is the devil."

And after they exist, according to their ordinances, they fulfil their task; and nothing can be changed (1QS 3:15-17).

Similar ideas can be found in the *Thanksgiving Hymns:*

A man's way is not established except by the spirit which God created for him (1QH 4:31).

For what is man? . . . What can I plan unless Thou hast desired it, and what can I think apart from Thy will? What can I accomplish unless Thou hast established me, and how can I be wise unless Thou openest my mouth? (1QH 10:5-7).

Thou hast cast for man an eternal lot with spirits of knowledge to praise Thy name (1QH 3:22).

We must keep in mind, however, that these last quotations are from devotional literature. The observation that man "prays like a Calvinist and preaches like an Arminian" is but a somewhat simplified expression of the fact that man is more aware of his finitude in the presence of Deity. Similar passages could be found in the Biblical Psalms and in other devotional passages in the Bible. Only a Pharisee (and I think an unusal one at that!) would pray, "I thank Thee that I am not like other men." Other men, increasingly so as their piety deepens, would stand before the mystery of godliness and confess in reverence that any values to be found in their works must have had their origins in the divine will.

A third possible source of the doctrine of determinism is the doctrine of election. It might be profitable to attempt to determine priority with reference to these two doctrines: was it because man felt that all things were foreordained that he came to believe that he was among the elect; or was it because he believed himself to be elect that he arrived at the corollary of predestination?[8] We shall be content here simply to set forth the relevant material.

> To those whom God chose He has given them as an eternal possession; and He has given to them an inheritance in the lot of the holy ones; and with the sons of Heaven He has associated their assembly for a Community council; their assembly will be in the Holy Abode as an eternal planting (1QS 11:7-8).

> Then the priests shall bless all the men of God's lot, who walk perfectly in all His ways . . . and one shall not fall from the status of his office, nor rise from his allotted place (1QS 2:2, 23).

> And all the spirits allotted to him [strive] to trip the sons of light; but the God of Israel and His angel of truth have helped all the sons of light (1QS 3:24-25).

The following passage is revelatory in what it implies as well as in what it expresses:

> These are the ordinances in which the wise man is to walk with every living being . . . to do God's will . . . and to hold firmly to those chosen . . . ; to treat every man according to his spirit; and to bring him near according to the cleanness of his hands . . . but to conceal the counsel of the Torah in the midst of men of perversity; . . . but to admonish with true knowledge and righteous law those who choose the way. . . . Let there be eternal hatred toward the men of the Pit in the spirit of secrecy (1QS 9:12-24).

Perhaps we should remember that we are not dealing with professional theologians or philosophers in the Qumran writers. Several scholars have noted that the Qumran Community was not given to deep abstract thinking.[9] Raymond

---

[8]Cf. Eph. 1:4-5, where election precedes ordering, and Rom. 8:29, 30, where predestination precedes calling.

[9]Cf. J. Coppens, "Les documents du désert de Juda et les origines chrétiennes," *Cahiers du Libre Examen*, 1953, p. 85.

Brown says, "This seems particularly true in the problem of predestination and free will—a problem at the root of the domination of man by the spirits of light and darkness."[10] They were grappling with a deep problem at approximately a popular level, it seems to me, and we should no more expect to find a neat solution to the problem in QL than we would find in the average minister's sermons. For that matter, the Bible itself seems to maintain a paradox with reference to determinism and free will.

ELECTION

We have already seen that refusal to do God's will indicates that a person belongs to the "sons of darkness" (p. 107, above). It is not clear, however, that the opposite is true: namely, that to do the will of God makes one a son of light. We look in vain for any teaching concerning sons of light outside the Community. It seems reasonable to conclude that the first stage of "salvation" is equated with membership in the Community. Names of the Community such as "the men of God's lot" (1QS 2:2) and "the elect of mankind" (1QS 11:16) confirm this conclusion. Brown says, "Apparently the sectarians felt that no one could do what God wanted unless he was acquainted with the Torah as explained in the Qumrân Community."[11]

There appears to be no propaganda whereby members can be secured for the Community from the nonmembership. In this we can only point to the parallel in Judaism proper[12] where there was a sizable body of proselytes with no organized missionary program; we suggest that it was

---

[10]R. E. Brown, "The Qumran Scrolls and the Johannine Gospel and Epistles," *CBQ,* 17 (1955): 412.

[11]R. E. Brown, *art. cit., CBQ,* 17:415. Cf. 1QS 5:15-16.

[12]E. Schürer, *Geschichte des jüdischen Volkes* (3d and 4th ed.; Leipzig: J. C. Hinrichs, 1901), III: 150-188.

the uncertainty of the times and dissatisfaction with exist-
ing religious systems that led men to try new or different
movements. The Qumran Community received its share of
these malcontents.

Admission to the Community required confession of sin:
"We have perverted ourselves . . . we have done wickedly,
we [and our fathers] before us" (1QS 1:25). This sin called
forth the righteous judgment of God, but in addition there
was also gracious compassion (1QS 2:1). God is long-
suffering, and a multitude of forgiveness is with Him (CD
2:4). God shall make conciliation for them (CD 4:10).

Brownlee uses the expression "the chosen of grace" to
translate *beḥîrê rāṣôn* in an important passage in the *Manual
of Discipline* (1QS 8:6). In his notes to the translation he
compares this with the "election" of grace in Romans 11:
5, and the similar idea in Galatians 1:15 and II Timothy
1:9.[13] Raymond Brown takes exception to this translation
as seeming "a little too Christian, influenced by Rom. 11, 5
. . ."[14] It would be helpful to know what Hebrew word
Paul had in mind (if any) when he used the word *charis.*

According to the *Concordance to the Septuagint,* the
word *charis* is used to translate six different Hebrew words:
ḥēn (38 times), *ḥésed* (twice, both in Esther), *ṭôb* (once),
ráḥam (once), *gedûlā* (once), and *rāṣôn* (three times, all in
Proverbs).

Thirteen different Greek words are used in the Septuagint
to translate *ḥésed,* the most common being *eleos* (172
times), and the next in frequency *eleēmosunē* (only 8
times). It would hardly seem that this word lay behind
Paul's use of *charis.*

Fourteen different Greek words are used to translate

---

[13]Brownlee, *The Dead Sea Manual of Discipline,* p. 33.
[14]R. E. Brown, *art. cit., CBQ,* 17: 413, n. 42.

rāṣôn in LXX, the most common being *dektos* (21 times), and after that *thelēma* (13 times) and *eudokia* (eight times). This seems no more likely to be the word behind Paul's *charis*.

Five different words are used to translate *ḥēn*, the most common being *charis* (61 times) and after that *eleos* (16 times).

The other three words are used only once each.[15]

It therefore seems safe to conclude that *ḥēn* would be closest to Paul's idea of grace. Brownlee's translation of *rāṣôn*, in my opinion, is highly unlikely.

The idea of election, or God's sovereign choice and good pleasure, seems to be stressed somewhat more strongly in the Qumran literature, to judge from this word, than in the New Testament concept of grace.

PERSEVERANCE

The sanctity of the members of the Community, as F.-M. Braun points out, is always precarious.[16] The members can never forget that they belong to a sinful humanity, for the annual ritual reminds them of it (1QS 3:6-12). Their devotional literature likewise reflects this view:

> I know that righteousness does not belong to a man, nor to a son of man blamelessness of conduct. . . . For I remember my guilty deeds, together with the faithlessness of my fathers, when the wicked rose against Thy covenant, and hapless against Thy word. Then I said, "For my transgression I am left outside of Thy covenant" (1QH 4:30-35).

---

[15]Counts were made from Edwin Hatch and Henry A. Redpath, *A Concordance to the Septuagint* (Oxford: Clarendon Press, 1897; reprinted photomechanically, Graz, Austria: Akademische Druck- und Verlagsanstalt, 1954), 2 Vols., *in locis*.
[16]F.-M. Braun, *art. cit.*, *RB*, 62:21.

The prince of darkness and his evil spirits not only have control over the sons of darkness, but they even tempt the sons of light: "It is because of the angel of darkness that all the sons of righteousness go astray. . . . And all the spirits allotted him [strive] to trip the sons of light" (1QS 4:22-26). Backsliding is possible, and punishment can extend even to exclusion for serious cases (1QS 6:24–7:25; note the excommunication in 1QS 7:22-25).

Yet there is a sense of security: "And I, if I totter, God's dependable mercy is my salvation forever" (1QS 11:12). "All the sons of Thy truth Thou wilt bring in pardon before Thee, cleansing them from their transgressions in the abundance of Thy goodness and the greatness of Thy mercy, to make them stand before Thee to the ages of eternity" (1QH 7:29-31).

CHAPTER NINE

The Law

A SUBJECT OF GREAT IMPORTANCE in understanding the Christian message is the Law, and the Qumran literature will contribute to this understanding.

According to the New Testament, man is saved by the grace of God through faith apart from works of law (cf. Rom. 3:28). There are only three conceivable systems of salvation: you save yourself, God saves you, or you work with God for your salvation. The Christian Church—and by that I mean every part of it, Protestant and Catholic, Western and Eastern—has always and unequivocally branded as false and heretical any system teaching that man can save himself. This point cannot be too strongly stressed, for it is only in modern times that churches claiming to be Christian have been permitted to set forth as Christian the Humanistic teaching that man is his own saviour.

The way that man earns his own salvation in a religious system is by keeping a prescribed set of teachings. It is not difficult to find religions in the pagan world that make salvation contingent upon the keeping of religious law. However, the religion of the Old Testament and the religion of Judaism is *not* among these systems. Both the Old Testament and Judaism depend upon God for salvation.

This is not generally recognized by Christians who stress

115

the difference between Law and grace in the Bible. The popular view, as I have found it expressed many times, holds that man in the Old Testament was saved by keeping the Law of Moses. It is argued that this is what Paul is decrying in his Epistles to Romans and Galatians. But this is a distortion of what Paul is saying, which, in my opinion, has led to one of the most serious misinterpretations of the Bible to be found in evangelical Protestant theology in the present day. As a matter of fact, Paul himself protests against such distortion, for *he argues for the Gospel of grace from the Old Testament!*

There were those who were teaching, erroneously, that salvation was by the works of law. Paul points out to them that God's promise was by faith, and the giving of the Law 430 years later could not and did not annul that promise. (Read Galatians 3, particularly verses 10, 11, 15-18).

Now Paul was a Jew. He had been trained in Judaism. If his training under Gamaliel means what it seems to mean, he was trained as a rabbi. He certainly understood the Jewish concept of the Law. After his conversion, he recognized the distortion that had taken place in the Jewish view of the Law. But was this distortion to be found throughout Judaism? Or was it merely the Pharisaic interpretation? At this point the Qumran materials take on significance.

The Law in Qumran

There is great stress on the Law in QL. Those who constitute the Community dedicated themselves "to become a community in Torah [Law] and in property" (1QS 5:2). The convert to the Covenant took a "binding oath to return to the Torah of Moses according to all that he commanded, with wholeness of heart and wholeness of soul"

(1QS 5:8). Wherever ten members were gathered, "there shall not cease to be a man who expounds the Torah day and night continually, orally, each to his fellow" (1QS 6:6-7). The severest punishment—total and permanent excommunication—was reserved for the one who "transgresses a word of the Torah of Moses highhandedly or in fraud" (1QS 8:22-23).[1]

Did the Qumran group look upon the Torah as a series of restraints, things to be done or avoided, in order to merit the favor of God? There was such a view of the Law in Judaism, as we know not only from Paul's reaction against it, but also from the internal strife in Judaism concerning interpretations, with more rigid and less rigid applications. The schools of Hillel and Shammai could hardly have sprung up without this view of the Law.

On the other hand, the Torah was also viewed as a doctrine or instruction, a source of joy and gladness. George Foot Moore says: "The principle is one frequently affirmed and illustrated by rabbis: The Laws were given that men should live by them, not that men should die by them."[2] It is obvious that the Law, when viewed as regulation, can only condemn; it is only when it is viewed as instruction that it can lead to fullness of life.[3]

---

[1] I have rejected here the translation by Brownlee (following H. L. Ginsberg) as "openly or clandestinely," cf. *The Dead Sea Manual of Discipline*, p. 35, n. 39. The expression "with a high hand" is Biblical (cf. Num. 15:30), and its meaning is clear. The highhanded or presumptuous sin, in contrast to the inadvertent sin, was without forgiveness. The following word, "in fraud," is also a Biblical word.

[2] G. F. Moore, *Judaism* (Cambridge, Mass.: Harvard University Press, 1927), II: 19. His chapter on "The Perpetuity of the Law," I: 263-280, should be read in this connection.

[3] Motor vehicle laws are a case in point. As regulations, they can only serve to condemn offenders. As instruction, they help to develop safe drivers. Even here, men divide into two classes: those who try to do no more than the law requires; and those who try to live according to the spirit of the law.

The word *tôrā*, usually translated "law" is probably derived from the root *°wry* or *°wrw* (cf. Ethiopic *warawa*, "he threw"), from which is also derived the Hebrew verb *yārā*, "he threw, shot."[4] The noun derivative *môrê* can mean both "teacher" and "archer," and, to judge from the long-*ô* following a preformative *m-*, is a *Hif'il* participle meaning "one who causes to shoot."[5] The picture of sending ideas like arrows into the mind would not be, in my opinion, too far removed from the root meaning of the word. Torah, or "instruction," then, would be the idea that enters the mind or life. This is certainly the concept that lies behind the scriptural passages that refer to the *study* (not the "keeping"!) of the Torah, as well as the many rabbinic teachings along the same line.[6]

THE WALL AND THE WELL

It may be that the two attitudes toward the Law which we have just discussed underlie the figures of "the wall" and "the well," used in the *Damascus Document*.

God gave His commandments to "the first members of the covenant"; but they "digged a well" (CD 3:10, 16). They also "built a wall" (CD 4:12). The well is specifically identified as the Law: "the well is the Torah" (CD 6:4; cf. *Sifre Deut.*, 48). The man who despises it shall not live (CD 3:17). Those who entered the new covenant in the land of Damascus had forsaken the well of living water (CD 19:35). On the other hand, the "builders of the wall"

---

[4] For a discussion of the legal vocabulary in the Qumran documents, cf. M. Delcor, "Contribution à l'étude de la législation des Sectaires de Damas et de Qumrân," *RB*, 61 (1954): 539-544.
[5] *Wilhelm Gesenius' hebräisches und aramäisches Handwörterbuch über das alte Testament*, ed. Frants Buhl (17th ed.; Berlin: Springer-Verlag, 1917, reprinted 1949), *in loc.*
[6] Cf. Moore, *op. cit.*, II: 239-247.

who have "walked after Ṣaw—the Ṣaw is a preacher—" (CD 4:19), have gotten caught in whoredom. Then follows a long passage in which the whoredom is discussed, followed by a discussion of the day of the Lord's visitation. Then: "All this they did not consider, who built the wall . . . and preaching to men with lies preached to them . . ." (CD 8:13 = CD 19:25). A few lines later, we read the climax: "God hates and abhors the builders of the wall, and His wrath is kindled against them and against all those that walk after them" (CD 8:18).[7]

The Pedagogical Aspect

The instructive character of the Law is brought out in such ideas as "to seek God in His ordinances" (1QS 1:2), "to purify[8] their mind by the truth of God's ordinances" (1QS 1:12), the "knowledge of righteous laws" (1QS 3:1), "zeal for righteous laws" (1QS 4:4), and "studying the Torah" (1QS 8:15). One who wished to enter the Community took an oath "to return to the Torah of Moses" (1QS 5:8)—suggesting that the keeping of the Law as practiced by the Jews outside of Qumran was not the true Torah. Negatively, the instructional character of Torah is implied in the regulation prohibiting a member of the Community from so much as answering the questions of a perverse man concerning Law and judgment (1QS 5:15-16). This would suggest that the truth imparted by the Torah belongs only to the sons of truth.

The instructional character of Torah may also be seen in

---

[7]There may be an intentional reference to this wall of the false builders in 1QS 8:7, where the council of the Community is described, "that is the tried wall."

[8]The word is *le-bārēr.* In Ps. 2:12 the word *bar,* translated "son" in K.J.V., is translated in the Vulgate as *disciplinam,* a cognate of the verb used here. We might translate the passage, "to discipline their mind . . . ."

an eschatological figure mentioned in the *Damascus Document,* called "the one who inquires into (or interprets) the Torah" (CD 6:7).[9] This person is also identified with "the Commander"[10] whose time of activity is "during the whole epoch of wickedness" (CD 6:7). Of him we read: "The nobles of the people are they that have come to dig the well with the commands which the Commander has commanded" (or "with the staffs, which the Staff has instituted"—Rabin). Another person to arise "in the end of days" is "the one who teaches righteousness" (CD 6:11; cf. Hos. 10:12). In these various figures and descriptions, the emphasis upon the instructional nature of the Law is obvious.

THE PROSCRIPTIVE ASPECT

The restrictive and legislative nature of the Law, however, is also present in the Qumran writings. It is seen by implication in the objective of those who dedicate themselves "not to transgress a single one of God's provisions," and this is further spelled out, "not to advance their times, not to lag behind any of their seasons; nor to swerve from His true ordinances, to go either right or left" (1QS 1:14-15).

It is the *Damascus Document,* however, that sets forth in detail the proscriptive character of the Law. There sins are set forth which include robbing the poor, despoiling widows, and murdering orphans (CD 6:16-17), incest and whoredom (CD 7:1-2), false witness (CD 9:3-5), idols in

---

[9]For a study of this personage, cf. N. Wieder, "The 'Law Interpreter' of the Sect of the Dead Sea Scrolls: The Second Moses," *JJS,* 4 (1953): 158-175.

[10]Better, "Lawgiver," or "Staff"; but I want to bring out the play on words in the passage.

the heart (CD 20:8-10), murder of Gentiles (CD 12:6-7), and selling grain, wine, slaves, or especially clean beasts and birds to the Gentiles which they in turn might use for profane sacrifices (CD 12:9-11).

Ceremonial items expressly mentioned include keeping the Sabbath day "according to its exact rules" (CD 6:18), observing other appointed times (CD 3:14; 6:19), which most likely included the "seasons," "moons," "holy days," "beginnings of years," "weeks of years," and "season of release," mentioned in the *Manual of Discipline* (1QS 10: 5-8; also CD, *passim*). A "fast-day according to the finding of the members of the new covenant in the land of Damascus" (CD 6:19), probably a holy day peculiar to the sect, was also specified.

Laws of consanguinity are probably referred to in CD 7:7-9, and specific degrees of consanguinity expressly forbidden are mentioned, similar to those in the Mosaic Law, with the stipulation that "the rules of incest are written with reference to males and apply equally to women" (CD 5:8-11). "Marrying two women in their [masculine] lifetime" is named as harlotry (CD 4:21). The exact intent of this law is not clear, due to the presence of the masculine plural suffix. Ginzberg held that it was aimed at polygamy rather than divorce.[11] Schechter held that the Law forbade divorce,[12] which is in my opinion difficult to maintain, since provision for divorce is clearly found in the *Damascus*

---

[11]L. Ginzberg, "Eine unbekannte jüdische Sekte," *Monatsschrift für Geschichte und Wissenschaft des Judentums*, 56 (1912): 294.

[12]S. Schechter, *Documents of Jewish Sectaries*, I: xxxvi, n. 3. Schechter's reasoning is spelled out in his "Reply to Dr. Büchler's Review of Schechter's 'Jewish Sectaries,'" *JQR*, 4 (1913-14): 455, as follows: the Mosaic Law allowed divorce, therefore the author of CD could not deny it; but by forbidding a man to take a second wife while the first was living, he made divorce practically impossible.

Document: "And likewise with regard to him that divorces, and he [. . . (*broken away*)]" (CD 13:17).[13]

Dietary laws are behind the following passage from the *Damascus Document:*

> Let no man defile his soul with any living being or creeping thing by eating of them, from the larvae of the bees to all the living things that creep in water. And as for fish, let them not eat them unless they have been split while alive and their blood has been poured away. And as for all locusts in their various kinds, they shall be put into fire or water while they are alive, for this is what their nature requires (CD 12:12-15).

Other laws included the distinction between clean and unclean, holy and profane (CD 6:17), defilement resulting from the unclean (CD 12:16-18; cf. 1QM 14:3 for ritual washing of garments after battle), and the nature and sanctity of the oath (CD 15:1–16:13).

We have already discussed the technical term *ṭohŏrâ,* "Purity," on pages 86-90.

SACRIFICES

An important matter in Qumran theology is the subject of sacrifices. When Schechter published the *Zadokite Fragments* (CD) in 1910, there was a prompt and extended discussion of the relationship of that sect to other sects of Judaism.[14] Charles, on the evidence of laws relating to animal sacrifices and the Temple, concluded that "the Zadokites were not Essenes, since they inculcated the duty of ani-

---

[13] I read *mgrš* as *mᵉgârēš.* To read it as *migraš,* "open field," with Schechter, *Documents of Jewish Sectaries,* I: liii, n. 22, makes absolutely no sense in context.

[14] An excellent survey of the discussion will be found in Hvidberg, *Menigheden af den Nye Pagt i Damascus,* pp. 9 ff.

mal sacrifice."[15] Baumgarten has restudied this problem in
the light of the Qumran materials,[16] and his work is the basis
for the following discussion.

In the *Habakkuk Commentary* there is severe criticism of
the priests, particularly a "wicked priest" (1QpHab. 8:8-13).
When he violated the principles of holiness, the group
which had accepted him rebelled. "Later priests of Jerusalem" (1QpHab. 9:5) were regarded in the same light.
The "wicked priest" persecuted the Teacher of Righteousness (1QpHab. 11:5), and used the "resting of the Day
of Atonement" as the occasion to cause the people to stumble on that day (1QpHab. 11:7).[17] The defiling of the
sanctuary at Jerusalem is also mentioned in the *Damascus
Document* as one of the "three nets of Belial" (CD 4:15-
18; Jerusalem is not specifically named, however). It was,
in fact, this defiling that led the sectaries to avoid the
Temple rather than participate in the desecration (CD
6:11-14). The sect is called a "house of division (or Peleg)
who went out from the holy city and put their trust in God
in the epoch when Israel sinned and made the sanctuary
unclean" (CD 20:22-23). Baumgarten points out that it was
not objection to animal sacrifices as such, but objection to
profaning the Temple by the priests, that led to the schism:[18]
a very important point.

In the *Damascus Document* there is mention of a ram

[15]Charles, *The Apocrypha and Pseudepigrapha,* II: 790.
[16]J. Baumgarten, "Sacrifice and Worship Among the Jewish Sectarians of the Dead Sea (Qumran) Scrolls," *HTR,* 46 (1953): 141-
159.
[17]S. Talmon, "Yom Hakkippurim in the Habakkuk Scroll," *Biblica,*
32 (1951): 556, thinks the sect had instituted a calendar reform, and
the sole purpose of the "wicked priest" was to intercept this unauthorized holy day. We shall discuss the calendar later.
[18]Baumgarten, *art. cit., HTR,* 46: 145.

for a sin-offering (CD 9:14). Further on there is a pro-
hibition against offering at the altar what had been unlaw-
fully acquired (CD 16:13). In another passage, a man is
forbidden to send to the altar a burnt offering, a cereal
offering, or frankincense, by the hand of any man affected
with any type of uncleanness (CD 11:19-20). Schechter
and Büchler, among others, held that the Zadokites continued to offer sacrifices outside the Jerusalem sanctuary,
Büchler even locating the place of sacrifice in Damascus.[19]
Ginzberg, however, rejected any such possibility, as does
Baumgarten.[20]

Turning to the *Manual of Discipline*, Baumgarten first
notes that it differs fundamentally from the *Damascus
Document* in that the latter contains both general Halakah
based on Biblical law and specific rules of the sect, whereas the *Manual* contains only sectarian regulations. This
would explain the fact that there is no law concerning animal sacrifice in the *Manual*. The Community is called "an
institution of holy spirit of eternal truth to atone for the
guilt of transgression" (1QS 9:3). The Community (or its
practices) has expiatory value "more than flesh of burnt-
offerings and than fats of sacrifice" (1QS 9:4), and prayers
are for judgment "as a fragrant offering of righteousness"
(1QS 9:5). Perfection of way is like giving an acceptable
oblation (1QS 9:5).

Gustav Hölscher had previously attempted to interpret
the sacrificial laws in CD figuratively.[21] This view has

---

[19]S. Schechter, *Documents of Jewish Sectaries*, I: xv; A. Büchler,
"Schechter's 'Jewish Sectaries,'" *JQR*, 3 (1912-13): 457-461; cf.
M. Delcor, "Le sacerdoce, les lieux du culte, les rites et les fêtes dans
les documents de Khirbet Qumran," *RHR*, 144 (1953): 5-41.
[20]L. Ginzberg, *art. cit., MGJW*, 56: 446; Baumgarten, *art. cit., HTR*,
46: 146.
[21]"Zur Frage nach Alter und Herkunft der sogennanten Damaskusschrift," *ZNW*, 28 (1929): 21-46.

gained no noticeable following. However, it is clear that
the Qumran sect made very little mention of sacrifices in its
literature. No altar has been discovered at Qumran, and
there is no historical evidence of any cult with a place of
sacrifice outside Jerusalem, except the Temple of Onias
in Egypt—and that was not recognized by the religious
authorities.[22] There is on record in QL strong antipathy
against the Jerusalem priesthood, and several statements
prohibit any relationship with them.[23] It therefore remains
to be proved, in my opinion, that the Qumran Community practiced ritual sacrifice of animals. The sect seems
to have followed the more spiritual teachings of the prophets[24] rather than the sacrificial Levitical code. Even circumcision is mentioned in a spiritualized aspect (1QS 5:5).

Since this view of the Law concerning sacrifices could
exist in Judaism, and did exist in Qumran, it makes the
attitude of the "Hellenists" in the Book of Acts more under-
standable, and prepares the way for teachings such as those
found in the Epistle to the Hebrews. The attitude toward
the Law against which Paul reacted was that of the
Judaizers, a group which stemmed from Jerusalem, and
had probably been under the influence of the teachings of
the Jerusalem priesthood. Yet Hellenist Jews, Jews who had
returned from the Diaspora where ritual sacrifice was not
observed, lived almost in the shadow of the Temple and
felt no need of the sacrificial system. Legalism was largely

[22]Cf. Schürer, *Geschichte des jüdischen Volkes*, III: 146-147.
[23]The statement by L. Arnaldich, "Los sectarios del Mar Muerto y
su doctrina sobre la 'Alianza,'" *EstBib*, 11 (1952): 363, is to the
point: "En ningún texto de los manuscritos de Mar Muerto se hable
de la subida a Jerusalén con ocasión de ciertas festividades, ni se
hace mención de los sacrificios en el Templo. Es muy posible que los
sectarios no acudieran al Templo para no contaminarse al contacto
con los hijos de la iniquidad."
[24]Cf. the expansion of Micah 6:8 in 1QS 5:4-5.

the development of the Pharisees; and it was due to the Pharisees that, after the destruction of the Temple, all the minute details of the Temple and its cultus were treasured up in the Talmud against the day when the Temple would be rebuilt. Had the Pharisaic attitude toward the Law been the universal view of Judaism, it seems highly unlikely that Christianity could have developed within Judaism its Gospel of salvation by faith apart from works of law. The reaction against it was so violent on the part of the Judaizers that only Paul stood firm. Even the other apostles were moved from their foundations (cf. Gal. 2:11 ff.). But Paul could successfully argue his point, partly, at least, because the spiritual concept of the Law was already recognized in Judaism.

These facts should have been clear to us entirely apart from the Qumran discoveries. Yet, as in so many other cases, we failed to see the full significance of the available data until one fresh bit of evidence came to light. It would be foolish and unnecessary to claim that Christianity was the *first* revolt against Legalism; it would be enough to say that it was the *first successful* such revolt!

The Sabbath

In one respect the Qumran Community seems to have followed a legalistic approach that was unmitigated: in the matter of the Sabbath. Here we find only the proscriptive Law.[25]

---

[25]Perhaps it was because of the prevalence of this view of the Sabbath in Judaism that Jesus deliberately undertook to violate the Sabbath laws. For a very stimulating discussion of the Sabbath controversy and its central place in the ministry of Jesus, see A. G. Hebert, *The Throne of David* (London: Faber and Faber, 1941), pp. 143-163.

There is an entire section on the Sabbath in the *Damascus Document* (CD 10:14–11:18), which calls for cessation of work on the Sixth Day "from the time when the orb of the sun is distant from the gate by its own fulness" (CD 10:15-16). Specific prohibitions on the Sabbath include: speaking a lewd or empty word,[26] lending, bloodshed, speaking of labor to be done the next day, walking in the field to be near the place where one must work the next day, traveling more than 1,000 cubits, eating food prepared on the Sabbath, eating that which was lost in the field, drinking water unless it is in the camp, bathing or drinking when on the road or when required to draw water, sending a proselyte to work as one's substitute on the Sabbath, putting on dirty clothing on the Sabbath, starving oneself voluntarily on the Sabbath, and traveling more than 2,000 cubits for a beast pastured outside the town.

The law goes on to forbid on the Sabbath: using the fist as a hammer, carrying anything into or out of a house (or even a *sukkā*, "tabernacle"), opening a sealed vessel, carrying medicaments upon oneself, picking up a stone or dust in the house, the carrying of a child by a pedagogue, urging on a slave or hired laborer, or assisting a beast in birth on the Sabbath day. This latter law is noteworthy in its statement, "even if she drops [the new-born] into a cistern or pit, let him not keep it alive on the Sabbath" (CD 11:13-14), for it is in contrast to the popular practice reflected in Matthew 12:11.

The *Document* continues by proscribing spending the Sabbath in a place near Gentiles, profaning the Sabbath for the sake of property or gain (although it was permitted to save human life that had fallen into water or into a place

---

[26]The word used here lies behind *raka* in Matt. 5:22.

from which it could not get out), or placing an offering on an altar on the Sabbath, "except the burnt-offering of the Sabbath" (CD 11:18).

CHAPTER TEN

The Qumran Calendar

INTEGRAL WITH THE LAW, both in the Old Testament and in Qumran literature, is the observance of holy days. We have discussed the Sabbath at some length. Moons, holy days, years, and exact epochs are mentioned in QL. The Day of Atonement has an important place in the history of the sect (1QpHab. 11:7). There is no good reason to suppose that the Qumranians did not observe the other holy days of the Jewish religious year.

But soon after the publication of the Qumran documents scholars perceived that there was a sectarian attitude toward the calendar. Talmon, for example, took a cue from Dupont-Sommer (with whom he disagreed in other matters), and found significance in the words "caused them to stumble on the fast day, the day of their resting" (1QpHab. 11:8). He presented evidence to show that "the Bne Zadok employed a calendar calculation which differed from the one adopted by the official authorities, namely by the 'Wicked Priest' and his followers."[1]

Dupont-Sommer undertook, by extensive critical revision of the passage, to show the sacred character of the Qumran calendar. Some of this material was expanded into a long section on "The Holy Seasons" in his work on *The*

---

[1] S. Talmon, *art. cit., Biblica,* 32: 551.

Jewish Sect of Qumran (pp. 104-117), in the course of which he put forth the Pythagorean theory and the mystical significance of the number 50. Brownlee noticed interesting connections between QL and the Book of Jubilees,[2] and others have written more extensively on the subject. But it was Mlle Jaubert who made the first careful study of the Qumran calendar.[3] Her article led Julian Morgenstern, who is probably the outstanding authority on calendration in the ancient Middle East, to publish an article setting forth several refinements on Mlle Jaubert's conclusions, while substantiating her basic thesis.[4]

THE PENTECONTAD CALENDAR

According to Morgenstern, the old calendar of Palestine was a pentecontad calendar, i.e., it consisted of periods of 50 days, with the necessary intercalation to bring what was essentially an agricultural year into harmony with the solar year. In ancient times, about the only important reason for having a calendar was to integrate other activities (religious and civil) with the seasons of planting, cultivation, and harvest. We know, for example, from Assyrian records, that the military campaigns were planned to fit into the agricultural calendar, and were interrupted so the men could go home for plowing and planting.[5]

---

[2] W. H. Brownlee, "Light on the Manual of Discipline (DSD) from the Book of Jubilees," *BASOR*, 123 (October 1951): 30-32.

[3] A. Jaubert, "Le calendrier des Jubilés et de la secte de Qumrân, les origines bibliques," *VT*, 3 (1953): 250-264.

[4] J. Morgenstern, "The Calendar of the Book of Jubilees, Its Origin and Its Character," *VT*, 5 (1955): 34-76. Cf. his articles in *Hebrew Union College Annual*, 1 (1924): 13-78; 3 (1926): 77-107; 10 (1935): 1-148; 20 (1947): 1-136; and 21 (1948): 365-496.

[5] It may well be that this was a major reason why smaller kingdoms were able to continue to exist. In Sennacherib's Annals, for example, we find frequent examples of kings or kingdoms who were conquered on a certain campaign, and who had to be conquered again on a subsequent campaign, or even on several campaigns. An uninterrupted military campaign would certainly have wiped them out.

According to Morgenstern's reconstruction, the New Year's Day was the day of the cutting of the first sheaf. Then followed a "fifty" which was the grain harvest. The last day of the "fifty" was the festival of first-fruits. Each of the "fifties" ended with a festival day, although the names or nature of some of these are not known. After the fourth "fifty" was an intercalated "seven" the festival of ingathering, and after the seventh "fifty" was the festival of unleavened bread. This will be clearer in tabular form.

Day of cutting the first sheaf.	1
First "fifty," grain harvest.	49
"End," festival of first-fruits.	1
Second "fifty"	49
"End," undetermined festival.	1
Third "fifty"	49
"End," undetermined festival.	1
Fourth "fifty"	49
"End"	1
Festival of ingathering ("seven")	7
Fifth "fifty"	49
"End"	1
Sixth "fifty"	49
"End"	1
Seventh "fifty"	49
"End"	1
Festival of unleavened bread ("seven")	7

Total 365

A similar calendar continued among the fellahin of Palestine even down to modern times, called "the seven fifties,"[6] and named as follows:

Easter

Pentecost

---

[6] Arabic, *es-sabi' hamsinât.* This was recorded by T. Canaan in 1913, and is quoted by Morgenstern, *art. cit., VT,* 5:45.

> Grape Watching
> Grape Pressing
> Festival of Lydda
> Christmas
> Fasting

It is obvious that two of these remain in the Christian church year, the first (Easter to Pentecost, which preserves the name "fifty"[7]) and the last (the Lenten season). Agricultural vestiges are also apparent.

Such a calendar, of course, plays havoc with the weekly Sabbath, for seven times each year an eight-day week is introduced. And, just as those who are zealous for the regular observance of a seven-day week are today opposed to the calendar reform periodically discussed, so they were in Judaic Palestine. According to Morgenstern, the sweeping reforms in Judaism at the end of the fifth century B.C. included the outlawing of this pentecontad calendar. "Normative Judaism" was in the process of formation. "Peripheral Judaism"[8] resisted the reforms, and when this resistance led to the repudiation of normative Judaism, "sectarian Judaism" was brought into being. In the main, this seems to be a reasonable analysis.

Calendar Reforms

To maintain the regularity of the seven-day cycle throughout the year, the "end days" of the "fifties" were removed, and made into an additional week. Each of the "fifties" thus became a 49 (the name was never used), or seven seven-day weeks, which, added to the two festival "sevens," plus the newly made week, resulted in a calendar of 52

---

[7]The word *Pentecost* comes from the Greek word for "fifty."
[8]Morgenstern takes over the term "normative Judaism" from Moore, *Judaism,* I:3, and coins the term "peripheral Judaism."

weeks. The year was then divided up into four quarters, each of three months or 13 weeks, which became the calendar of the Book of Jubilees.[9] Because of the close relationship between the Qumran Community and the Book of Jubilees, it is probable that this calendar was also used by the Qumranians.

The calendar of "normative" Judaism, however, was a lunar calendar. In other words, it was determined entirely by the moon, with months of 29 and 30 days. There is no connection between such a year and the solar year, as the Mohammedan calendar will prove (for example, the fast-month of Ramadân moves throughout the solar year in planetary fashion, coming approximately eleven days earlier each year). For a nomadic people, this is not important, but for an agricultural people, the year must be somehow harmonized with the seasons, which are in turn related to the sun or solar year. Judaism accomplished the harmonization by intercalating an entire month three times in eight years, as necessary for Passover to follow the vernal equinox. This is reflected in the Christian Easter, which is dated by the moon's relation to the solar year.

One effect of this calendar reform was to change the nature of the "fifty" or seven-week period. Before the reform, a "fifty" began with the first day (for convenience, and without any implication, let us call it the "Sabbath"), and ended with the intercalary festival day. The next "fifty" began again with the "Sabbath," and so on. But after the "end days" were removed, it became necessary either to use the succeeding Sabbath to round out the "fifty," or to turn the "fifty" into a 49. To clarify this, let us suppose that the "week" began and ended with Sunday—how could the fol-

---

[9]Jaubert, *art. cit., VT*, 3:253. Cf. also Jub. 6. In Jub. 6:23, such a year is traced to Noah.

lowing week also begin and end with Sunday, for one Sunday could not both end one week and begin another.

The Book of Jubilees solved the problem by turning the "fifties" into 49's. The concept of the "week" (or better the heptad) had been carried over to the yearly cycle. Seven years was known as a "week" or heptad (cf. Dan. 9:24-27). And seven such heptads of years made a "Jubilee." Here again, the results of calendar reform are visible, for the Jubilee in normative Judaism was 50 years (Lev. 25:8-10),[10] whereas the Jubilee in the Book of Jubilees was forty-nine years (Jub. 4:29-30).[11]

THE QUMRAN CALENDAR

The reason for this circuitous discussion will become apparent as we consider certain passages in QL. The Community was comprised of men who had dedicated themselves, among other things, "not to advance their times and not to lag behind any of their appointed seasons" (1QS 1:14). If the annual renewal of the covenant in 1QS 1:18–2:18 is to be equated with the celebration in the Book of Jubilees described as "the feast of weeks . . . to renew the covenant every year" (Jub. 6:17), then there would seem to be symbolic significance in the renewing of the covenant—for according to the Book of Jubilees (and only there[12]), the feast of weeks commemorates the establishment of the covenant with Noah (Jub. 6:15-17).

---

[10]The technical word for this 50-year period, as we know from the studies of Julius and Hildegard Lewi, "The Origin of the Week and the Oldest West Asiatic Calendar," *HUCA*, 17 (1942-43): 1-52, was in Assyrian *dârum*. This is unquestionably reflected in the Hebrew word *dôr*, "cycle, generation, age."

[11]In Jub. 10:16, 950 years is 19 jubilees, 2 weeks, and 5 years, or $19 \times 49 \ (= 931), + 2 \times 7 \ (= 14), + 5$.

[12]Cf. R. H. Charles, ed., *The Book of Jubilees* (London: Society for Promoting Christian Knowledge, 1917), p. 63, n. 1.

In the *Manual of Discipline* there is an extended passage (1QS 9:12–11:15) in which there is a cryptic discussion of the *'áleph,* the *mêm,* and the *nûn* (1QS 10:1).[13] The *nûn* is to unlock God's eternal mercies "at the beginnings of seasons in every period that will be." Following this, a number of terms are used, including "moons," "holy days in their establishment" (is this a slap at the new calendar which was not "established"?), "seasons," "the beginnings of years in the establishment of their appointed times," "the season of reaping" and the "season of summer-fruit," "the season of sowing" and "the season of green herbage," and "the beginning of their sevens to the appointed time of manumission" (i.e., the release associated with the year of Jubilee in the Old Testament).

The last four terms quoted have been compared with the Gezer Calendar.[14] There is some similarity in the terms, although the significance of the Gezer Calendar is not clear. Without going into the details here (I have done it elsewhere),[15] let me suggest that the comparison is not to be found in the Gezer Calendar, but in the covenant with Noah. We have just seen that the annual renewal of the covenant in the *Manual of Discipline* may be connected with a similar idea in the Book of Jubilees (1QS 1:18–2:18; Jub. 6:15-17). In the Book of Jubilees the time for the ritual is the feast of weeks, commemorating the establishment of the covenant with Noah.

In the Biblical account of the covenant with Noah, the

---

[13]These are three letters of the Hebrew alphabet, pronounced *ah'lef, maim,* and *noon.* We shall discuss them later.

[14]Cf. Brownlee, *The Dead Sea Manual of Discipline,* p. 41, n. 24.

[15]W. S. LaSor, "A Preliminary Reconstruction of Judaism in the Time of the Second Temple in the Light of the Published Qumrân Materials," an unpublished Th.D. dissertation, School of Religion, University of Southern California, 1956, pp. 237-238.

terms *seedtime, harvest, summer,* and *winter,* are used (Gen. 8:22). Let us set these down alongside the terms in the *Manual of Discipline.*

Manual of Discipline	Genesis 8:22
qāṣîr, "reaping"	*qāṣîr,* "harvest"
qáyiṣ, "summer-fruit"	*qáyiṣ,* "summer"
zéra', "sowing"	*zéra',* "seedtime"
déše', "green herbage"	*ḥóref,* "winter"

The parallel is obvious in all but the last pair. But the season of greenness in Palestine is winter, the rainy season (approximately December to February), just as it is in Southern California. This makes the parallel complete.

It is, of course, possible that the expressions in Genesis are simply to be taken as merism.[16] On the other hand, there may be the basis here for symbolism, such as the Qumran Community loved to develop. The passage in the *Manual of Discipline* reads,

> this to this,
> the appointed season of harvest to summer-fruit,
> and the appointed season of seed to the appointed season of greenness.

If we diagram the passage in Genesis, in the following manner, and connect the elements in accordance with the *Manual of Discipline,* the result is as follows:

An interpretation of this, in the light of the context, would

---

[16]Merism: a form of synechdoche in which a totality is expressed by the use of two contrasting parts.

then be somewhat as follows: "when the limit of their measures fulfills its allotted day" (1QS 10:6-7), God will bring together the seasons of the year to form a seasonless, perfect age.

Whether this interpretation be right, the reference to the year of Jubilee immediately following, "the appointed time of manumission,"[17] is unmistakable. The use of the year of Jubilee to symbolize the ultimate redemption of man is not unknown, and perhaps lies behind the words of Isaiah 61:1-3, part of which was quoted by Jesus in the synagogue at Nazareth (Luke 4:18-19).

In the *Damascus Document* there are numerous statements or terms indicating affinity with the Book of Jubilees, the most convincing of which is the quotation of the title of the book, "The Book of the Division of Times into their Jubilees and Weeks" (CD 16:4). The entire document shows marks of this division of time into "epochs" (*qēṣ, qiṣṣim*). God foreknew the "number and explanation of their epochs" (CD 2:9). Epochs ending with Noah, Abraham, and Moses, are implied (CD 3:1-10), each closing by forsaking the covenant, and another epoch ended with the sons of Zadok (CD 3:14; 4:1). The sons of Zadok are called the elect of Israel, about whom are revealed "exact statements" of names, genealogies, "the epoch of their existence," the length of their exile, and their works (CD 4: 4-6). An "epoch of the desolation of the land," (CD 5:20), and the "whole epoch of wickedness" (CD 6:10) are mentioned, but it is not clear whether these are the same. They appear to refer to the time of the exile of the sect, the sojourning "in the land of Damascus" (CD 6:5). If so, then,

---

[17]The same word is used in Lev. 25:10, in connection with the year of Jubilee, and also in Isa. 61:1.

this was "the last epoch" (cf. I John 2:18). There is, however, no mathematical indication of these epochs such as is found in the Book of Jubilees.

One cannot help but wonder whether the influence of these movements, found in Qumran literature and in the Book of Jubilees, had not penetrated much farther afield, and whether this influence (I do not say the same group of persons or the same sect) was not in sight when Paul, for example, referred to the feasts and festivals in Colossians 2:16 ff., or the genealogies in I Timothy 1:4.

There is one possibly significant matter in this discussion for the student of the New Testament. As is well known, the date of the Last Supper in the Synoptics (Matthew, Mark, Luke) does not agree with that in the Gospel of John. In the one, it is the Passover; in the other, it is the day before the Passover. Now if John is marking Passover according to the calendar used by the Qumranians, while the other Gospels are following the "orthodox" calendar, the problem can be resolved. Mlle. Jaubert puts the Last Supper on *Tuesday* evening. This is in keeping with an early Christian tradition, but not many scholars have been willing to make such a clear break with established Christian tradition. One might speculate on the possibility that the crucifixion actually occurred on Thursday, the Passover beginning at sundown that day; evidence, however, does not at present support such speculation.[18]

---

[18]Materials discovered in 4Q clearly support the view that the Qumranians used the calendar of Jubilees and Enoch; cf. J. T. Milik, *Ten Years of Discovery in the Wilderness of Judaea* (London: SCM Press, 1959), pp. 107-113. On the date of the Last Supper, see A. Jaubert, *Le Date de la Cène* (Paris, 1957), and E. Vogt, "Dies ultimae coenae Domini," *Biblica* 36 (1955): 403-408. For other references, see W. S. LaSor, *Bibliography of the Dead Sea Scrolls 1948-1957*, §§ 3356-3367.

CHAPTER ELEVEN

What of Qumran Gnosticism?

A NUMBER OF WRITERS have stressed the use of the word
knowledge and similar words and ideas in Qumran
literature, reaching conclusions that are quite varied as to
the relationship of QL to Gnosticism. Since the problem
of the relationship of Christianity to Gnosticism is also the
subject of a considerable amount of discussion, it is fitting
that we make some effort to discuss the subject in the
present work.

WHAT IS GNOSTICISM?

It might be well, in handling a subject as complex as
this, to begin with definitions. Unfortunately, this has often
not been done, and I would venture the observation that
most of the scholars who have written on the subject of
Gnosticism and the Dead Sea Scrolls have no common idea
of what they mean by Gnosticism.

The words *gnosis*,[1] *Gnostic*, and *Gnosticism* are cognate
with our word *knowledge*. But obviously it is not Gnosticism just because the words *know* or *knowledge* are used. I
know that two plus two equals four. No one, to my knowledge, has called that Gnosticism. I know the secrets of my
fraternity. Who would call that Gnosticism? Yet, there are
some who have discussed the Gnostic elements in QL on the
basis of the knowledge of mysteries (or "secrets"—it would
be the same word in the original languages, whether Greek

---

[1]The words are pronounced *nō'sĭs, nŏss'tĭck,* and *nŏss'tĭ-sĭzm.*

or Hebrew) of the sect. When we come to a passage such
as: "No one knows the Father except the Son and anyone
to whom the Son chooses to reveal him" (Matt. 11:27),
most scholars decide this is Gnosticism. But is it?

Robert P. Casey has a good discussion of the various ideas
of Gnosticism, and a sketch of the development of critical
studies of Gnosticism in the past fifty years, in his chapter
on "Gnosis, Gnosticism, and the New Testament" in *The
Background of the New Testament and its Eschatology.*[2]
He points out that "all religions assert a claim to special
knowledge and all religions based on revelation depend on
the acceptance of revealed truth as necessary for salvation" (p. 55). If, then, these points (viz., special knowledge
revealed and the necessity of reception of it for salvation)
are taken as the basic definition of Gnosticism, I would
suggest that all religions are Gnostic. Obviously, this is not
a satisfactory definition. Personally, I am not convinced
that Casey has not gone far afield in his own approach to
the problem—but he has helped to clarify the subject.

One of the difficulties in the study of Gnosticism has been
the almost complete absence of source material. We did not
possess materials by the Gnostics; we only possessed materials about them. Moreover, we possessed conflicting materials about them, which opened the door too wide to sub-
jectivism. We lacked the controls necessary to add a reasonable degree of certainty to subjectivity.[2a] Certainly, this
situation is not being helped by grasping at any Jewish or

[2]The "Dodd Anniversary Volume," edited by W. D. Davies and
D. Daube (Cambridge: at the University Press, 1956), pp. 52-80.
[2a]This situation will rapidly be rectified with the publication of the
Chenoboskion discoveries of 1946—almost as important as the Dead
Sea Scrolls. For description, cf. V. R. Gold, "The Gnostic Library
of Chenoboskion," *BA* 15 (1952): 70-88; H. C. Peuch, *Coptic Studies
in Honour of Walter Ewing Crum* (Boston: The Byzantine Institute,
1950), pp. 91-154.

Christian writing that includes the word *knowledge,* and
adding that to the study of Gnosticism! For a definition to
be definitive, its edges should be made increasingly sharp
and not increasingly fuzzy.

One of the characteristic elements of Gnosticism was
dualism—but dualism of the cosmological (matter-spirit)
type, rather than the ethical type. God (if we may introduce the word for the sake of convenience) is pure spirit.
An ethical concept is usually added, that spirit is good and
matter is evil. Created matter, therefore, being evil, cannot
have come directly from God who is spirit and good. The
attempt to solve the problem of evil is usually part of
Gnosticism, and it is achieved by the removal of creation
from God by interposing a series of "emanations" and a
Demiurge. I oversimplify greatly when, for clarity, I suggest that emanations from God brought the Demiurge
into existence, and it (he?) in turn was responsible for the
creation of matter by other emanations.

A second characteristic of Gnosticism is the claim that by
special knowledge, available only to those who are initiated
into the secrets of this system, man becomes spiritual and
therefore good. This stress on knowledge is basic to Gnosticism (hence the name); but as I understand Gnosticism, the
dualistic concept of the universe is integral with knowledge
in the system. Without either one or the other, I seriously
question that a religious or philosophical system should be
called Gnostic.

The Christian Church in the second century and following
resisted Gnostic invasions because (1) esoteric knowledge
(i.e., for the initiated only) was put in the place of faith,
thus tending to divide the Church into gradations of believers, and also because (2) the labeling of matter as evil
led to a denial of the bodily resurrection and to a denial

of the true human nature of the Lord Jesus Christ (or Docetism).

That there are points of contact between Christianity and Gnosticism should not be denied. God is Spirit. How He could have brought matter into being is indeed a "mystery." The Bible says He "created" (Gen. 1:1)—and does not explain it further. In these days of modern science, when we know· that matter is composed entirely of nonmatter revolving about nonmatter at tremendous speed and held by tremendous forces, it is more of a mystery than ever. But to say that spirit is good and matter is evil entirely misses the point—for all of the wickedness of man proceeds not from his material being, but from his "heart" (i.e., his essential being, under the motivation of his will). Moreover, the resurrection of Jesus Christ is designed to teach us, among other things, that the body of man is forever a part of his being.[3] And again, knowledge is necessary for salvation in Christianity (knowledge of Christ, that is)—for revelation becomes a meaningless term unless that which is revealed by God becomes that which is known by man.

Now, against the background of this discussion,[4] let us look at the concept of knowledge in the Qumran writings.

THE SOURCE OF KNOWLEDGE IN QUMRAN DOCTRINE

The source of knowledge in Qumran teaching is God. He is "the God of knowledge" (1QS 3:15; cf. I Sam. 2:3), "the source of knowledge" (1QS 10:12), and it is "by His knowl-

---

[3]The resurrection body, according to I Cor. 15:44, is a "spiritual body," it is true. But it is still a body—otherwise, what is the point of the entire fifteenth chapter?

[4]It must be kept in mind that I have greatly oversimplified a complex subject.

edge" that everything has been brought into being (1QS 11:11). The Qumran worshiper says of Him that He is the one who "opens the heart of Thy servant unto knowledge" (1QS 11:16); "Thou hast taught all knowledge" (1QS 11: 18). The blessing of the priests included the prayer: "May He . . . illumine thy heart with life-giving wisdom, and favor thee with eternal knowledge" (1QS 2:3). It is the way of the spirit of truth "to enlighten the heart of man" (1QS 4:2), and to "make his heart tremble with . . . mighty wisdom which believes in all God's works . . . and a spirit of knowledge" (1QS 4:2-4).

The psalmist sings: "These things I know from Thy understanding. . . . I am a thing formed of clay, . . . without understanding" (1QH 1:21-23) whereas God is "the God of knowledge" (1QH 1:26). Again, he exults: "Thou hast given me knowledge of Thy wondrous mysteries. . . . Who that is flesh could do aught like this; what thing formed of clay could do such wonders?" (1QH 4:27-28). "God loves discernment; knowledge and wisdom (*dá'at wehokmā*) He has set up before Him" (CD 2:3).

It follows therefore that the men of His covenant "shall bring all their mind" (1QS 1:11) as well as their strength and property, when entering the Community. They are appointed their place in the Community "according to knowledge" (1QS 2:22). In a meeting of the Many, each was to present "on request his knowledge" (1QS 6:9, following Brownlee). The priesthood (literally, Aaron) had "knowledge of all to enact laws and to offer up an agreeable odor" (1QS 8:9). If Rabin's interpretation is correct, the members (or a judicial council among them) are "men of knowledge" (CD 20:4).[5]

---

[5] The Hebrew, however, is *'anšê tammîm.*

This knowledge can be mediated by God's agents. The most important mediator in this respect is the Teacher of Righteousness, who is the one "to whom God has made known all the mysteries of the words of His servants the prophets" (1QpHab. 7:5). God raised for the remnant "a teacher of righteousness to lead them in the way of His heart and to make known to the last generation, the congregation of the faithless" (CD 1:11-12). In these two quotations, the significant word is "to make known" or "to cause to know." It is not clear whether this Teacher of Righteousness is to be identified with "the priest" of the last generation who seems to serve a quite similar function; but at any rate this priest was "given unto the Ch[ildren of Israel for a teach]er to give the meaning of all the words of His servants the prophets" (1QpHab. 2:8-9). The psalmist was made by God "a reproach and derision to the treacherous, but a counsel of truth and understanding to those whose way is straight" (1QH 2:9-10). The camp Supervisor had the responsibility of instructing "the many in the works of God" and causing "them to understand His wonderful mighty works" (CD 13:7). Even though this last sentence does not contain the word *knowledge*, it is probably to be understood in that sense, particularly in the light of the following statement: "For Thou hast given me knowledge of Thy true counsel and hast made me wise by Thy wondrous works."[6]

The false prophets, "interpreters of lies and seers of deceit," are castigated because "they withheld the draught of knowledge from the thirsty" (1QH 4:9, 11). Rather "they did not [heed] Thy [instruction]; they did not listen

---

[6] 1QH 11:3-4, after Burrows. He has, it is true, restored [*hôda'*]*táni*, but the restoration seems plausible.

to Thy word; for they said of the vision of knowledge, 'It is not right,' and of Thy heart, 'It is not that.' "[7]

THE PURPOSE OF KNOWLEDGE

Knowledge is given by God, in the first place, according to the Qumran writings, to influence the walk of men of truth. "They walk in wisdom or folly" (1QS 4:24). Understanding is connected with deeds, much the same as faith is connected with action in Christian doctrine, as the examination of the novice by the Supervisor indicates:

> The man who is supervisor . . . shall examine him as to his understanding and his deeds. And if he grasps instruction, he shall bring him into the covenant to turn to truth and to turn away from all perversity (1QS 6:14-15).

Conversely, knowledge is for the purpose of correcting transgressors:

> According to his sin shall men of knowledge reprove him (CD 20:4).

However, it is made clear in the context, as well as in many other passages, that this knowledge is not given to reprove men outside of the covenant (cf. 1QS 9:17, 22). Careful reading of the section dealing with the two spirits (1QS 3:13—4:26) will confirm this observation.

This is not the purpose of knowledge in Gnosticism. Rather in Gnosticism the purpose of knowledge is liberation from the material fetters of life. Except in extensions of this teaching, it has no moral or ethical significance. The manner of life is not the means of determining knowledge, but knowledge is its own test. The importance of this point should not be overlooked.

---

[7]Burrows' restoration.

Yet there is an esoteric nature of knowledge implied in numerous statements in QL, many of which deal with the "mysteries." It should be noted that this esoteric knowledge is not limited to the future. Certain activities of community life, such as enacting laws (1QS 8:9) and being made aware of the judgments (the word is used chiefly of those in daily life), belong to knowledge. One who wished to turn from his corrupt way must stand before the Supervisor—and until that time "let no man cause him to know judgments" (CD 15:10-11). This applied not only to the entrant, for even the man of the Community who had willfully removed a word from all that God had commanded might not "have any knowledge of their counsel" until he had been thoroughly purified (1QS 8:17-19).

A study of the particular words used in the Qumran writings to denote some "mystery" or "counsel" is very much to be desired. In order to make such a study one would need a concordance to the literature of Qumran—and none has yet appeared. The word *sôd*, "secret" or "counsel," seems to have had an esoteric connotation, for the Supervisor of all the camps was required to be "master in every secret of men" (CD 14:9-10). There are "counsels of covenant" (CD 7:5) and "counsels of spirit" (1QS 4: 6).[8] Whether these "counsels" are the same as those for which the word *rāzîm*, "mysteries," is used, or whether "mysteries" have to do with God and "counsels" have to do with men, is not clear. The evidence at hand is too little to be conclusive. On the one hand, the expression, "His wonderful mysteries" (CD 3:18), suggests the divine counsel; but "the truth of the mysteries of knowledge,"

---

[8]In this expression, as in the preceding, the absence of the definite article (not "the covenant" or "the spirit") is not immediately explicable.

taken in context (1QS 4:6), seems to apply to that common body of instruction intended for the spiritual life of the members of the covenant.

The word *rāz*, which is used quite often in QL (if one may rely on an impression gained from repeated reading of the texts), occurs nine times in the Aramaic portion of Daniel.[9] Mandelkern defines it as "counsel, pertaining to eschatology."[10] It is translated in both Septuagint and Theodotian by *mustérion*. In the *Habakkuk Commentary* the word has eschatological overtones: "The final end delays and is left for all of which the prophets spoke; for the mysteries of God are to be marvelous" (1QpHab. 7:7-8).

Other words that should be studied are: *sātar*, particularly the form *nistārôt*, "hidden things" (cf. CD 3:14); *bîn*, "understand," particularly in the *Hif'îl*, "cause to understand," but also the form *mᵉbônan*, "instructed," with reference to the *Book of the Hagu* (CD 13:2); and *śākal* in the *Hif'îl*, "to understand, be wise," and in the noun form *śékel*, "insight" (1QS 2:3).[11]

SIGNIFICANCE

If we define Gnosticism rather closely, there are clearcut distinctions between it and Christianity, and between it and Qumran theology. On the other hand, if we define Gnosticism rather loosely, there are elements of Gnosticism (so-called) in both Christianity and Qumran theology. This fact is in itself illuminating.

---

[9]Since the word is borrowed from Persian, it is not necessary to look upon it as Aramaic in QL.

[10]*sôd, le-dá'at ha-'ăhărônîm; Veteris Testamenti Concordantiae*, p. 1343.

[11]In this passage, *śékel hayyîm*, "wisdom of life" (i.e., wisdom that gives life) is paralleled by *dá'at 'ôlămîm*, "knowledge of eternity" (i.e., knowledge that gives eternal life). The form *śôkel* occurs in CD 13:11.

For a half-century, scholars have been trying to solve the problem of Gnosticism in the New Testament. Various approaches have been used. The New Testament writings that came into the area of Gnosticism were dated late. This was not a satisfactory solution, as even the critics were finally willing to admit. Gnosticism was dated earlier. But this was not without difficulties, for Gnosticism *per se* is not to be dated prior to the second century A.D. Various developments of the theory of pre-Christian Gnosticism (or perhaps better, pre-Christian *gnosis*) were advanced.

Since Gnosticism (or should we call it Ur-Gnosticism, to try to keep the record straight) was looked upon as a Hellenistic development, the major problem has been to find sources for it in the Hellenistic world of thought. This has not been too satisfactory. Attempts have been made to define "Hellenistic" in such a way as to include other cultural strains; for example, "Hellenistic" is sometimes defined as the synthesis that resulted from the Macedonian conquest. This is, obviously based upon a sound observation, for such a synthesis did occur. To take just one example that is of great importance for the Christian: when as a result of Hellenization, the Old Testament was translated into Greek, not only were the religious concepts of the Old Testament widened by the meanings of Greek terms, but also—a point too often overlooked!—the Greek language itself took on shades of meaning that it previously did not have.[12] In this case, "Hellenization" has meant the

---

[12] It is for this reason that the study of New Testament theological terminology must include the Hebraic background as well as the Hellenistic background of the words. A scholar of classical and Hellenistic Greek, without the knowledge of the Semitic world and particularly the Hebrew Old Testament, can never fully understand the New Testament.

addition of non-Hellenic elements to the Hellenic modes of thought and expression.

But when the term *Hellenistic* is defined so as to include non-Hellenic elements, and when Ur-Gnosticism is called Hellenistic in the sense that a non-Greek element has influenced a non-Greek religion (Christianity in its early form)—*just where does that leave us?* Let us face the facts squarely, without trying to cover them with weasel-worded labels. What this means is simply this: the so-called "Gnostic" elements in Christianity have not come from the Greek thought-world at all. Scholars who have recognized the force of this have talked in terms of a pre-Christian Jewish Gnosticism.

Something like this pre-Christian Jewish Gnosticism is found in the Qumran theology. It is not cosmologically dualistic. It does not quite have the doctrine of knowledge found among the later Gnostics—but it is tending in that direction. It does not have the speculative characteristics of Philonic Judaism. But it does put sufficient stress on esoteric knowledge that a system of ranks had developed within the membership. What was the source of it? The answer is not yet clear. Persian, Hindu, and Mandaean similarities have been pointed out by various scholars; but while the similarities are marked, the arguments are not yet convincing for any one of these sources. It seems quite reasonable to suppose that Greek Gnosticism developed as a result of this same undercurrent coming into contact with Greek, particularly Platonic philosophy. Greek Gnosticism and Qumran "Gnosticism" would then have a common root (or roots) in the as-yet-unknown source of the undercurrent.

The implications of this for the study of the New Testament are important, for it is no longer necessary to try to explain all of the "Gnostic" elements in the New Testament on the basis of Hellenism. We now have fairly clear evidence that the vocabulary and thought found in the so-called Gnostic portions of the New Testament could well have been developed within the Judaic background of the New Testament, and could even have been aimed at trends in Judaism that were moving in the direction of something similar to Gnosticism.

A new set of terms to cover these various strands would be of real service; for to use the label "Gnostic" indiscriminately is to make the clear communication of ideas all but impossible.

CHAPTER TWELVE

The Messianic Idea in Qumran

THE TERM *messiah* (i.e., the common noun *māšîᵃh*, "anointed") is found about 40 times in the Old Testament, but never, with the possible exception of Daniel 9: 26, as the title of a specific eschatological[1] character. In the apocryphal[2] literature the term becomes a title, as for example, the Messiah (to use the Hebrew form; cf. Enoch 48:10), or the Christ (to use the corresponding Greek form) of the Lord (cf. Ps. Sol. 17:36). In the rabbinic literature, the term is a proper name, the Messiah, both in Hebrew (Mishnah *Berakot* i. 5) and in Aramaic (Mishnah *Sota* ix. 15), and the compound name, Messiah King, is found frequently in the Targums (Jer. *Berakot* 5a on Hos. 3:5, etc.). The New Testament period, as well as the Qumran, is to be placed at about the same time as the apocryphal writings, and a few centuries earlier than the rabbinic writings.

This brief sketch of the historical development of the use

---

[1]Eschatology (pronounced *ess-kǎ-tol'o-jee*) is the doctrine of the end of the world (or age) and the persons and events associated with that period.

[2]The Apocrypha (*uh-pŏk'rĭ-fuh*), "hidden," are the books which were not admitted to the Old Testament canon. They are therefore not accepted as authoritative for doctrinal purposes. The word, as commonly used, meaning "spurious," is a popularization; many things in the apocryphal writings are not spurious.

of the term helps us to see one problem in clearer light: both in Qumran writings and in the New Testament we are dealing with a term which for the particular group using it may or may not have yet developed the significance of a proper name. It is important that we try to discover whether the Qumranians thought in terms of the Messiah, a specific, individual character associated with the end-time, or in terms of an anointed one who was just one of a number of anointed ones.

ONE, TWO, OR THREE MESSIAHS?

It is generally accepted that the word *Messiah* occurs as a title in QL. Burrows, for example, says: "The word 'anointed' or 'Messiah' is clearly used for one who is to come at the end of the present age."[3] Rabin and other scholars capitalize the word when it occurs, thus indicating that they understand it as a proper noun.

Strangely enough, the scholars have spent little time debating the question whether there was *a* Messiah in Qumran eschatology; rather they have debated whether there were *two* Messiahs. This fact needs to be explained for the sake of those who are not familiar with the background.

When the *Damascus Document* was first published, the expression "the Messiah of Aaron and Israel" was noted in three places (CD 19:11; 20:1; 13:21). Some scholars interpreted this in the obvious sense of one Messiah over Aaron and Israel. But other scholars, chiefly rabbinic scholars who were familiar with the rabbinic doctrine that there were two Messiahs: one priestly (descended from Aaron) and one Davidic, saw in this passage the two-Messiah doctrine. This required a simple emendation in the text,

---

[3] M. Burrows, *The Dead Sea Scrolls*, p. 264.

the addition of the smallest letter, to read "the Messiahs of Aaron and Israel."

The doctrine of two Messiahs is found according to common interpretation in the *Testaments of the Twelve Patriarchs*,[4] fragments of which have been found now in the Qumran caves. The Levitical or priestly Messiah, according to the rabbis, was to be a second Moses, in accordance with Deuteronomy 18:18 ("a prophet like you I will raise up"). According to Wieder,[5] this interpretation was held by Jews in the early Christian period. He supports this contention by two illustrations, one rabbinic, the other Christian. For example, Rabbi Jochanan ben Zakkai quotes God's promise to Moses: "When I bring Elijah the prophet unto them, the two of you shall come together" (Deut. Rab., iii, end). Or when John the Baptist was being interrogated, after he denied being Elijah, he was asked, "Art thou that prophet?" (John 1:21). Wieder says this refers to the prophet in Deuteronomy 18:18, and that "he is here unequivocally distinguished from both the Messiah and Elijah."[6] Dupont-Sommer also points out a reference to "the prophet" in I Maccabees 4:45, 46.[7]

After the discovery of the Dead Sea Scrolls, this discussion was renewed with new vigor when, in the *Manual of Discipline,* the expression "the Messiahs [plural!] of Aaron and Israel" was found (1QS 9:11). Not only did this reading fit the facts which the scholars favoring two Messiahs

---

[4]Test. Reuben 6:7-12; Test. Levi 8:14; Test. Judah 24:1-3; Test. Dan. 5:10-11; and Test. Joseph 19:5-9. Cf. Charles, *The Apocrypha and Pseudepigrapha,* II: 294.

[5]*Art. cit., JJS* 4: 170.

[6]*Ibid.,* p. 169.

[7]*The Jewish Sect of Qumran,* p. 136, n. 15. He also refers to I Macc. 16:41 (in both French and English editions), but the chapter ends at verse 24, and I have been unable to trace the passage he intended.

had adduced, but the critical canon of the "more difficult reading" supported the reading in 1QS. On the other hand, the reading in CD could readily be explained as a "dogmatic emendation" by a mediaeval scribe,[8] since the doctrine of two Messiahs had by that time been forgotten.[9] This argument collapsed, however, with the discovery of 4QD[b] where the singular form is found.

However, I question whether it is grammatically possible to use the expression "the Messiahs of Aaron and Israel," when you mean to say "the Messiah of Aaron and the Messiah of Israel." This is contrary to Hebrew idiom, as I have tried to demonstrate more fully elsewhere.[10] The only time such an expression can be used, according to the evidence I have examined, is when the two parts of the second half of the expression are viewed as a unity or a universalism. For example, "men of blood and deceit" (Ps. 5:7), obviously does not mean to designate one man of blood and another man of deceit. Blood and deceit as a single idea characterizes these men. "The Messiahs of Aaron and Israel," in like manner, refers to "Aaron and Israel" as a unitary idea, priest and laity, or the whole Community, and to the Messiahs (I would prefer to say simply, "the anointed ones") of that Community. Rowley arrived at a similar conclusion by another method of reasoning:

The sect itself therefore represents Israel and Aaron, and

---

[8]The *Damascus Document* discovered by Schechter, see page 50, above, is admitted by all scholars to be a copy from the tenth-twelfth centuries. A "dogmatic emendation" is an alteration which a scribe makes to a manuscript deliberately (rather than accidentally) to bring the passage into harmony with the dogma of his group.

[9]Wieder says it had been suppressed by anti-Christian rabbis, *loc. cit.*, p. 170.

[10]W. S. LaSor, "The Messiahs of Aaron and Israel," *VT* 6 (1956): 425-429. Burrows has challenged the validity of my argument; cf. *More Light on the Dead Sea Scrolls*, p. 299. However, in the light of Gen. 3:5, "knowers of good and evil," I am not convinced that he has made his point.

the title of the Messiah has reference to the character of the sect, and not his personal descent. The Messiah who shall arise from Aaron and Israel is thus the Messiah who shall arise from the sect.[11]

Some scholars see three Messianic figures: one of the Davidic line (a messianic King), one of the Aaronic line (a messianic Priest), and one like Moses (a messianic Prophet).[12] It seems that such theories destroy themselves by their own weight.

Suppose we were to establish a doctrine of the Messiah each time the word *messiah* (i.e., the Hebrew noun) occurs in the Old Testament. We would have a messianic priest (Lev. 4:3), several messianic kings (Saul, I Sam. 24:6; David, II Sam. 19:21; Zedekiah, Lam. 4:20), the patriarchs (Ps. 105:15), and the Persian King Cyrus (Isa. 45:1). Yet the one person we would not have would be the eschatological Messiah.[13]

The rabbinic view, as presented by Wieder, and the Christian view as found in the first chapter of John, in my opinion, do not concern the Messiah. Let us grant that Rabbi Jochanan ben Zakkai put Moses alongside Elijah—what does this prove about the Messiah? In the Johannine account, as Wieder correctly observes, neither Elijah nor "that prophet" is the Messiah—what does this prove about two Messiahs? These passages do not teach two *Messiahs;* they teach two *forerunners* of the Messiah. Moreover, if the doctrine of two Messiahs had been part of normative Judaism in the early Christian period, what happened to re-

---

[11]H. H. Rowley, *The Zadokite Fragments and the Dead Sea Scrolls* (Oxford: Basil Blackwell, 1952), p. 41.

[12]Cf. Milik, *Ten Years of Discovery in the Wilderness of Judaea,* pp. 124-126.

[13]Except possibly in Dan. 9:26, where the indefinite form "an anointed one" is not at all conclusive.

move it? To say this is anti-Christian polemic is nonsense, for where do we find two Messiahs in Christianity?

The question of two Messiahs in sectarian Judaism is beyond my field of specialization; scholars seem to be in general agreement that two Messiahs are found in the literature in view. But whether two Messiahs are found in Qumran Literature is, in my opinion, an entirely different matter. The most lucid discussion I know is given by Millar Burrows,[13a] who favors the thesis of two Messiahs. I find myself still not convinced.

"Messiah" or "Anointed"

We should then turn to the question: Is there a Messiah at all in the true sense, eschatologically speaking, in the Qumran writings? Or is the word *messiah*, whenever it occurs, simply a common noun meaning "anointed one"?

To answer this question, we should have access to a concordance to the Qumran writings; and, as we have said, one is not yet available. I have attempted to run down every use of the word in QL, but I do not suggest that I have been successful in the effort. I have found the word *māšîᵃh* or some modification of it, in the *Damascus Document* (CD), the *Manual of Discipline* (1QS), the *War Scroll* (1QM), and several fragments.[14] I have made a detailed study of these passages elsewhere[15] which I do not feel it necessary to reproduce here. The main points of my study I shall summarize.

The "anointed one/ones" in CD 2:12; 6:1; and 1QS 9:11 may refer to the prophets or other persons of the present or

---

[13a]*More Light on the Dead Sea Scrolls*, pp. 297-311. Note that the Messiah of Aaron is hypothecated in p. 300, and only one Messiah is mentioned where two are suggested, p. 304, among other weak points in the total argument.

[14]The full list of references is: CD 2:12; 6:1; 7:21; (=19:10); 20:1; 13:21; 12:23-24; 14:19; 1QS 9:11; 1Q28a 2:12, 14, 20; 1Q30 1:2; 1QM 9:8; 11:7; 4QPatrBless.

[15]In my unpublished Th.D. dissertation, previously cited.

past, and therefore need not necessarily refer to a future (whether imminent or remote) eschatological figure. I have carefully said "need not necessarily refer," without implying that the eschatological reference is impossible.

On the other hand, the references in CD 19:10; 20:1 and 12:23, 24, seem quite definitely to be related to an eschatological figure. The reference in CD 14:19 is a restoration in a badly broken context, and cannot be unduly pressed. It seems to be eschatological. The reference in 1QS 9:11 we have discussed a few pages previously, with reference to the two-Messiah theory. Our conclusion was that this does not need to be viewed as eschatological. The remaining passages are so important that we must take them up in detail.

THE EVIDENCE OF 1Q28a

Since the passages may not be readily accessible, I shall set down the full text in a baldly literal translation, in lines that follow the obvious syntax. Many restorations are necessary. Instead of using the customary square brackets, which would make the text hard to read, I shall use *italics* to indicate restoration. The amount of a word not in *italics* indicates the amount legible (e.g., if three letters of the English word are in Roman type, it signifies that three Hebrew letters are legible). If the tense can be determined, I have printed the auxiliaries (did, will, etc.) in Roman type.

*This is the sessi*on of the men of the name,
the called ones of the Assembly
to the Council of the Community:
If *God* shall cause him to bear *the* messiah with them
     (?)[16]
they shall enter,
the chief *priest,*

---

[16]This is a very difficult text. Some such emendation as Barthélemy suggests, "shall cause the Messiah to walk with them," seems necessary; *Discoveries in the Judean Desert,* I: 117.

all of the Council of Israel,
and all of the *fathers of the Sons* of Aaron,
the priests,
the called ones of the Assembly,
the men of the name,
and they shall sit b*efore him,*
each according to his importance [literally, glory],
and after(wards) shall *sit the mess*iah of Israel,
and shall sit before him
the heads of the *thousands of Israel,*
each according to his importance
as *his standing* in their camps
and as their journeyings,
and all the chiefs of the *fathers of the congregati*on
with the wise me*n of the Congregation of holiness*
shall sit before them,
each according to his importance;
and *if to the table of* a Community[17] they shall assemble,
*or to drink the n*ew wine,
and the arrangement of the common table
and the pouring of the new wine,[18]
let not a man *stretch forth* his hand
in taking possession of the bread and the *new wine*
before the priest,
for *he shall b*less the first of the bread and the new win*e,*
he shall stretch forth his hand on the bread for the pres-
    ence (?),[19]

---

[17]Or "to a common table."

[18]Barthélemy's restoration on the basis of Prov. 9:2.

[19]Barthélemy reads "on the bread first." But *lpnym* (*l⁰pānîm*) which occurs 21 times in the Old Testament, means "formerly, in former times"; it is never used to mean "first." On the other hand, my suggestion is equally difficult to sustain, and I offer it with no conviction.

and after(ward*s*) *shall stretch for*th the messiah of Israel
his hand on the bread,
*and afterwards they sh*a*ll bless* (i.e.)
all the Congregation of the Community,
each according to his importance;
and this statute
they shall do for every ar*rangement*
when they shall assemble
up to ten me*n*.

A number of things could be said about this important
passage. One of the first observations should be the considerable amount of restoration necessary in the text. Those
not skilled in textual criticism may be tempted to dismiss
all such restorations as the product of imagination. However, those of us who have the privilege of teaching younger
scholars to work in unedited texts know that it does not
take long for a student with imagination to develop the
ability of restoring the portions that have been broken
away. Sometimes the restorations are made on the basis of
parallel passages in the same texts; sometimes they are made
on the basis of parallel passages in other texts; sometimes
they are made on the basis of the requirements of the context; and sometimes (let us admit it) they are made on the
basis of imagination. All four types of restoration are found
in the passage under consideration. I have not bothered to
add notes to all of them. Most of the emendations commend
themselves.

Even though we must not dismiss the work of the critics
lightly, at the same time we must not accept blindly the
critical emendations. Some of the most crucial portions of
this passage, as far as the messianic doctrine is concerned,
are based on restorations of the text.

The passage deals with a meal. As restored, it is a meal of bread and new wine. This suggests a "Communion" service, and there have been scholars who have seen here the precursor of the Christian Lord's Supper. Two figures are prominent in the meal, as restored: the "messiah of Israel" and "the priest." Barthélemy makes much of the fact that (as he restores the text, let it be remembered) the "messiah" is second to the priest. This would seem to indicate most clearly that there were two eschatological figures (at least): the messianic priest (or "messiah of Aaron") and the messianic king.

Let me pause here long enough to say that I fail to see why a Christian should be concerned with any particular solution to this present problem. Whether there is one messiah or two in Qumran theology, whether there was a Communion service with bread and wine—what difference does it make? That Jesus took many ideas of His people and gave them a new significance we must admit. He would have had little opportunity to minister to His own had it been otherwise. That He also added new ideas and new methods we must also admit. He was the first of the scribes of the kingdom to bring out of the treasure-bag things new and old. When we approach the Qumran materials, let it be with no ax to grind, no pet theory to defend. We simply want to know all that we can about the group that was so closely connected in time and space with the formative period of the Christian faith.

The passage under examination in 1QSa has to do with "the end of the days" (1QSa 1:1). But this term is part of the description of the Community, which seems to be called "the whole Congregation of Israel in the latter days" (much as the Mormons call themselves "The Church of Jesus Christ of the Latter Day Saints"). The passage that follows, therefore, is not necessarily eschatological other than to the extent that the Community thought of itself as a Community of the end-period.

In the lines that follow (1QSa 1:6, 7), the purpose is spelled out: "And this is the rule for all the hosts of the Congregation for every native in Israel, and from his yo[uth they shall instr]uct him in the Book of *hhgy.* . . ." This does not appear to concern any particular individual figure, eschatological or otherwise; but rather it has to do with the entire Congregation. Indeed, if we can press the statement in 1QSa 1:4 ("from tots to women"), it is concerned with those born in the Community. The young member is to receive instruction for ten years. Then, at the age of twenty, he passes from the authority of his family to the Community. And so his progress is described.

Next comes a description of a convocation of the entire assembly, whether it be a matter of judgment, a common deliberation, or a military mobilization (1QSa 1:25, 26). Rules of purity necessary for participation are discussed.

Then comes the passage with reference to the "messiah." But at this point the manuscript is damaged, with a large piece missing from the right side of the column, and another large piece missing from the center.[20]

The part that would most clearly support Barthélemy's position is doubly difficult: the word *God* is a restoration with no context to require it; and the main verb in the passage must be emended to give a satisfactory reading. It is a sort of unwritten law in critical studies never to criticize a scholar's emendation unless you have a better suggestion to make. I have no better suggestion. Yet in the interest of objectivity, I must insist that we recognize the fact that a

---

[20]This is clearly shown in the photograph, *Discoveries in the Judean Desert*, I, Plate XXIV.

crux interpretum is in this case resting on two legs, both of which are hypothetical. This is shaky foundation, indeed! Again, Barthélemy has translated the word *'aḥar* in lines 14 and 20, *ensuite* ("afterwards"). In each case, a restoration is necessary in the following word. Now, when *'aḥar* is followed by a finite verb in Hebrew, it means "afterwards"; but when it is followed by an *infinitive construct*, it means "after." It would be equally possible to restore this latter form in each instance, which would result in the following readings:

> And after the anointed one of Israel is seated, then shall sit before him the heads of the thousands of Israel . . . .

> And after the anointed one of Israel has stretched forth his hands on the bread [. . .] then the whole Congregation of the Community shall bless . . . .

If such readings were to be established, then the "anointed one" (Barthélemy's "Messiah"), instead of being subservient to the priest, would be identical with him.

But most damaging to Barthélemy's theory, in my mind, is the fact that the context here is strongly like the context in the *Manual of Discipline* (1QS 6:2-8) where the communal meal is described. The meeting in each case is called a "session" (*môšāḇ*). The "stretching forth of the hand" to bless, the bread, the wine, the arranging of the table, the presence of a priest, the quorum of ten, and the study of the Torah (if the Book of *hhgy* is the same as the Torah)— all are mentioned in each case.

The fragment on which Barthélemy has based so much, then, *could* be simply a description of a common meal. In fact, it would seem from the context to be the meal of the entire assembly on any occasion of importance (cf. 1QSa 1: 25, 26).

OTHER PASSAGES

In a fragment formerly identified as 4QpGen49, now 4QPBless *(Patriarchal Blessings)*, we read of the "coming of the Messiah of righteousness, the sprout (or scion) of David." The expression "sprout of David" is found again in 4QFlor *(Florilegium,* see above, p. 47), and is clearly a Messianic title. Other Messianic titles are found: "branch" and "rod" in 1Q28b 5, where Messianic passages from Isa. 11:1; Gen. 49:9; and Num. 24:17 are cited (4QTest, we have pointed out, is a collection of such Messianic passages); and "prince" in 1Q28b 5:20; 1QM 5:1, 2; CD 5:1; 7:20. These passages, plus the use of the name "Zadok"— which can readily be linked to David—indicate that the Community had a Messianic hope. But the detailed nature of that hope is not given.

CONCLUSIONS

That the Qumran community believed in a Messiah of some kind is now established. That this Messiah was Davidic is, I believe, also clear. That there was another Messiah—not a "second" but the principal Messiah of Aaron, to whom the Davidic Messiah was second—is not yet, in my opinion, established. One of the most important facts to note is the absence from the Qumran Literature of the apocalyptic "Son of Man" concept.[21] In this respect, Qumran seems to stand closer to normative Judaism than to the apocalyptic Jewish sects. In my opinion it is becoming increasingly clearer that the teachings and claims of Jesus can in no way be traced to Qumran (or, as it is often called, "Essene") origin.

---

[21]Further observations, together with the evidence, will be found in my study of "The Messianic Idea in Qumran," in *Studies in Honor of Abraham A. Neuman,* edited by M. Ben-Horim, B. D. Weinryb, and S. Zeitlin (Leiden: E. J. Brill, 1962), pp. 343-364.

CHAPTER THIRTEEN

Other Points in Qumran Eschatology

THE TEACHER OF RIGHTEOUSNESS

A N IMPORTANT FIGURE in the Qumran writings is the "Teacher of Righteousness," whom God raised up for the remnant "to lead them in the way of His heart and to make known to the last generation, what He would do to the Congregation of the faithless" (CD 1:11, 12). It was to him that "God has made known all the mysteries of the words of His servants the prophets" (1QpHab. 7:5). This language identifies the figure as eschatological, hence we must attempt to discover his relationship to, or identity with, the "messiah."

The name (môrê haṣṣédeq), incidentally, is variously translated, and you will see it as "the Master of Justice," "the Doctor of Justice," and other names. Teicher even uses the name "the True Teacher," and goes on to say that the identification of the True Teacher with Jesus is "proved beyond doubt."[1] It is my opinion that Teicher's main tenet—viz., that the Qumran literature was produced by the Jewish Christian sect of the Ebionites—has been once and for all set aside by the archaeological and other evidence which requires an earlier date. Moreover, the expression môrê haṣṣédeq can hardly be translated "the True Teacher." Even if ṣédeq could be shown to mean "true" (which is highly

---

[1] J. L. Teicher, "The Habakkuk Scroll," *JJS,* 5 (1954): 53.

improbable), the grammatical structure requires the second word to be a noun and not an adjective.[2]

An extensive work on the Teacher of Righteousness, by A. Michel, appeared in 1954.[3] He commences his study with the *Habakkuk Commentary* in which the Teacher of Righteousness is named seven times (1QpHab. 1:13; 2:2; 5:10; 7:4; 8:3; 9:10; 11:5). From this he proceeds to a survey of the historical cadre of the *Commentary*, making full use of the apocryphal literature. This is followed by a study of the *Damascus Document*, Daniel, Maccabees, the Kittim, the Man of the Lie, the House of Absalom, and the Impious Priest. It is obvious that he is attempting a historical identification of the Master of Justice—and in his final chapter he gathers the various strands together.

Regardless of his conclusions, it must be admitted that Michel has gathered together into one fully documented volume a vast amount of material. Omitting details not pertinent to our present study, we may summarize his findings as follows: the Teacher of Righteousness might be identified as a priest in the *Habakkuk Commentary*, but he is clearly distinguished from the priests in the *Damascus Document;* he is not one of the judges; he has the characteristics of a prophet, but that name is not applied to him; he was persecuted; in the *Damascus Document* he is portrayed as dead, but it is not stated that his death was violent; and the death of the Teacher was the occasion, if not the cause, of the

---

[2]I admit that the *st. cstr.* could be a genitive of quality, and hence "teacher of (the quality of) righteousness" could mean "righteous teacher." In this instance, however, the context suggests that the expression, each time it occurs, is an objective genitive.

[3]*Le Maître de Justice d'après les documents de la Mer Morte, la littérature apocryphe et rabbinique* (Avignon: Aubanel Père, 1954) xxxiii + 335 pp. To this must be added an important work by H. H. Rowley, "The Teacher of Righteousness and the Dead Sea Scrolls," in the *Bulletin of the John Rylands Library* 40 (1957): 114-146.

exile of the sect to Damascus (*op. cit.*, pp. 265-320).

Of course, not all scholars are in agreement with all of these points. At the same time, some insist on many more points than Michel does.

THE TEACHER OF RIGHTEOUSNESS AND JESUS

One of the most frequently quoted scholars, in this respect, is Dupont-Sommer, who in one place writes: "The Galilean Master, as He is presented to us in the writings of the New Testament, appears in many respects as an astonishing reincarnation of the Master of Justice."[4] In Dupont-Sommer's opinion, the Teacher was a priest (cf. 1QpHab. 2:8), who was persecuted by the Man of the Lie while the House of Absalom remained neutral (cf. 1QpHab. 5:10, 11). He was judged, beaten, and tortured (cf. 1QpHab. 8:13– 9:2), swallowed up, stripped, and murdered (cf. 1QpHab. 11:2-8). Dupont-Sommer admits that the words *death* and *put to death* do not occur in QL, but he reads the idea in from the context together with a comparison of Isaiah 57: 1, 2. Then he concludes his study with the words: "Yes, the Master of Justice was really put to death."[5]

Dupont-Sommer further identifies the Teacher of Righteousness with the "New Priest" in the Testament of Levi (Test. Levi 18:2), and says: "After his earthly career and his ignominious death, he is now to be translated to an eschatological plane, invested with full Messianic glory, and enthroned as chief of the universe."[6] He is convinced that the "Messiah of Aaron and Israel" of the *Damascus Document* is the Teacher of Righteousness, and it is by this Teacher, the "Elect," that God would effect His final judg-

---

[4]*The Dead Sea Scrolls*, p. 99.
[5]"Le Maître de justice fut-il mis à mort?" *VT*, 1 (1951): 215.
[6]*The Jewish Sect of Qumran and the Essenes*, pp. 51, 52.

ment, when he would come again. "He has been taken away, but he lives still, and his glorious return is awaited."[7]

It has been suggested that Dupont-Sommer holds that the Teacher of Righteousness was raised from the dead. I have not found any express statement to this effect in his writings. He does use the word *apotheosis* (incidentally in a passage which he takes to refer to the Teacher, but which seems quite clearly to refer to the Wicked Priest [1QpHab. 11:7-8]). He does speak of the Teacher as still living, and as expected by the Community to return. But he omits to say anything about the resurrection. Possibly the misunderstanding has come about from Dupont-Sommer's use of the term *raised up* (*enlevé*) to translate the *Niph'al* of the verb *'āsap* —but his explanation of the term makes it clear that he means "snatched away" by death, or "gathered" to the fathers.[8]

Even so, there is enough said in Dupont-Sommer's publications, some of which have been taken up and expanded by other writers, to have caused much consternation to many sincere Christians. Was nearly every significant event in the life of Jesus Christ anticipated in the writings about the Teacher of Righteousness in the Qumran sect? Then what becomes of the uniqueness of Christ? Were the stories that we read in the Gospel about the teachings, sufferings, death, resurrection, and second coming of Christ only a variation of similar stories that were commonly current about other teachers?

It is well to remind ourselves at this point of two important facts.

First, the much-discussed "uniqueness" of Jesus Christ

---

[7] *The Dead Sea Scrolls*, p. 44. Cf. *Observations sur le Commentaire d'Habacuc découvert près de la Mer Morte* (Paris: Adrien Maisonneuve, 1950), p. 21.
[8] Cf. *art. cit.*, VT, 1: 200.

should not be tied to His teachings, nor even to His sufferings and death. There have been other teachers, and there have been other martyrs. The Bible does not put the burden of uniqueness at these points: rather it singles out as the one significant point the Incarnation. And it is not merely that *Christ said* that He was God in the flesh, or that *men said* that He was the Incarnate; rather, the uniqueness is placed in this fact: *that Jesus Christ is God in the flesh.* Father Divines can make their claims, and the disciples of Teachers of Righteousness can have their beliefs about their masters—but only Jesus Christ is the Incarnate Son of God. We do not believe that this fact is true simply because the New Testament says so; we believe that the New Testament says so because the fact is true. This is confirmed by the Holy Spirit (I John 4:2; 5:9). It was because the Incarnation was a fact, and because the Holy Spirit testified to the fact, that the apostles wrote it into the New Testament Scriptures.

In the second place, we need to remember that the views of Dupont-Sommer and others who go along with him in much of his writing are not the only views. Many scholars equally learned and equally familiar with the Qumran materials, do not at all agree that Jesus is anticipated in the Dead Sea Scrolls. Nor can it be charged (as Edmund Wilson has done by innuendo)[9] that the scholarly conclusions are influenced by theological presuppositions. The simple fact is that scholars of all shades of theological presuppositions, or of none at all (if that be possible), have differed with Dupont-Sommer's conclusions.

---

[9]Cf. "A Reporter at Large: the Scrolls from the Dead Sea," *The New Yorker*, May 14, 1955, p. 95. The same is found in his expansion of this article, *The Scrolls from the Dead Sea* (New York: Oxford University Press, 1955).

WAS THE TEACHER OF RIGHTEOUSNESS AN INDIVIDUAL?

Vermès, for example, holds that "Doctor of Justice" is more a descriptive title than an eschatological figure. In his chapter on the Doctor of Justice,[10] Vermès points out that while the work of the individual was closely related to the ultimate victory of the people of God, yet salvation was placed not in the Teacher, but in his message. "His saving role is none other than that of a doctor who teaches justice." This Teacher was a new Moses, but he was not to be confused with the Messiah.[11] In fact, Vermès is of the opinion that "the texts published to date teach us very little about the messianic beliefs of the sect," and adds: "the Messiah also was to be a teacher of righteousness" (*loc. cit.*).

Brownlee has approached the problem from an entirely different angle by studying the "Servant of the Lord" passages in 1QIs[a].[12] He shows that righteousness was one of the deepest cravings of the Qumran Community, and that the advent of the messiah was anticipated because of the teaching of righteousness that he would bring. The text of Isaiah 51:5 has been emended in 1QIs[a] to read "his" instead of "my," with the following personification of righteousness:

> My righteousness draws near speedily,
>   My salvation has gone forth,
>   And his [MT, my] arms will rule the peoples;
> The coastlands wait for him [MT, me],
>   And for his [MT, my] arm they hope.

---

[10]*Les manuscrits du désert de Juda,* pp. 90-108.

[11]*Ibid.,* p. 118; cf. also J. van der Ploeg's review of The Dead Sea Scrolls of St. Mark's Monastery, *Bibliotheca Orientalis,* 8 (1951), p. 13.

[12]The Servant of the Lord in the Qumran Scrolls," *BASOR* 132 (Dec., 1953): 8-15; 135 (Oct., 1954): 33-38.

This variant and its significance has been included in an article by one of Brownlee's recent doctoral candidates, John V. Chamberlain, in which he discusses the functions of God (judgment, righteousness, deliverance, salvation, and counsel—all of which can be included in the term *Torah*) as messianic titles in the Qumran Isaiah scroll.[13]

However, the problem of the identification of the Teacher of Righteousness with the Servant of the Lord is not quite so simple. Many students of Isaiah have recognized the probability that the Servant of the Lord in Isaiah has corporate significance, as well as individual. (In fact, some scholars, in my opinion mistakenly, have insisted that only the corporate group, Israel, is meant by the Servant in Isaiah.)

This corporate idea is taken over into the Community in the *Manual of Discipline*, according to Brownlee. So, just as there is a blending of the personal and national elements in the Servant of the Lord in Isaiah, even so is there a blending of the ideas of the Teacher of Righteousness and the teaching ministry of the Community in Qumran. There is the tendency in a group that thinks of itself as the eschatological community (i.e., the only ones remaining faithful, and therefore the only ones who will be saved in the final catastrophe to come upon the world) to identify itself with the person who symbolizes par excellence that which the Community symbolizes. We can find this not only in various Adventist sects, but even in New Testament Christianity, where the Church (the "called-out ones") is frequently identified with Christ. It therefore becomes quite difficult, if not impossible at the present time, to draw a clear-cut distinction between the Teacher of Righteousness as an

[13] J. V. Chamberlain, "The Functions of God as Messianic Titles in the Complete Qumran Isaiah Scroll," *VT*, 5 (1955): 366-372.

ideal and the Teacher of Righteousness as a messianic individual.[14]

Thus we see the complexity of this problem. Was the Teacher of Righteousness a historical character in the past, when the Qumran writings were produced (as many have suggested); or was he an eschatological character to come; or was he both at once, a historical figure who was killed and was to return (as Dupont-Sommer holds); or was he just an ideal toward which every teacher, and indeed, the entire Community, was to strive? While scholars of repute maintain different views, it is unwise for us to be dogmatic in our conclusions. There is little doubt, as I understand the texts, that some outstanding figure of the recent past had so impressed the Community that he became known as the Teacher of Righteousness. That he was expected to return is, to me, less clear. But that he represented an ideal so basically right that it had to be part of the messianic age seems to be a minimum interpretation. Beyond this, I would prefer not to go at the present time.

OTHER PERSONALITIES

For want of a better place we may include in this chapter a few remarks about other eschatological personalities in the Qumran writings.

It was the duty of the Teacher of Righteousness to speak, and the responsibility of the Community to listen (CD 20: 27-34). The "Man of the Lie" is the subject of reproach because he did not believe all that the Teacher of Righteousness had spoken from the mouth of God (1QpHab. 2:2-3). The "Preacher of Lies" misled many by instructing them in

---

[14]The suggestion has been made that a possible basis for the idea of the Teacher is to be found in Isa. 30:20, 21. Here, again, we see how the one and the many may blend, for in Isa. 30:20, the word is plural, "teachers."

works of falsehood (1QpHab. 10:9-13). The "Wicked Priest" persecuted the Teacher of Righteousness, and worked abomination in Jerusalem and defiled the sanctuary of God (1QpHab. 11:4–12:10).

Much has been written about these characters, but I think it would add little to our present study to go into details here. In the New Testament "many antichrists" and "the spirit of Antichrist" are expressions used to summarize any force opposing the work of Christ as seen by His early Church. Christian scholars have come to different conclusions concerning the interpretation of these terms. Likewise in the Qumran materials there is the idea (but not by name) of an "anti-Teacher of Righteousness." It is possible that distinct individuals were in the minds of the writers for the different expressions used, but at the present time and in the light of the available materials, we can only hypothecate these identifications.

One character deserves more than a passing reference: "the Searcher of the Law," who appears in the *Damascus Document* (CD 6:7; 7:18). He is identified with "the Staff" in CD 6:7, and with "the Star" in CD 7:18. Wieder, who calls him "The Law Interpreter," has prepared a study of the figure, drawing upon Biblical and rabbinical materials, in which he shows that the Law Interpreter was a second Moses, an eschatological figure but not the Messiah.[15] The exact term, says Wieder, is not found in rabbinic literature (p. 167), but the parallels are unmistakable. He ties this Law Interpreter in with his view of two Messiahs (see p. 153), but goes on to say of the Law Interpreter, "His authority seems, namely, to have been limited to the transition period and was to terminate with the beginning of the Messianic age proper" (p. 172, citing CD 6:10-11).

---

[15]Wieder, *Art. cit.*, *JJS* 4:158-175.

Again we would raise the question whether we are dealing with two "Messiahs" or two "forerunners." Both the
New Testament and rabbinic literature, probably having
a common source in the teaching reflected in Malachi 4:5,
had a doctrine of the forerunner whose task was not to
bring about the final period of judgment, but to prepare
the people for the greater figure who would. To use the
adjective *anointed* (*māšîᵃḥ*) of the forerunner (or forerunners) would not cause any more difficulty than does the
use of the term for Cyrus (Isa. 45:1). But to use the proper
noun, *the Anointed,* or its Hebrew or Aramaic original,
the Messiah, for the forerunner, when it is usually reserved
for the great apocalyptic figure himself, is to introduce unnecessary confusion.

The End of the Age

The end of the age, which was upon them, was to be a
time of suffering (1QS 3:23), but not to the destruction of
the people of God (1QpHab. 5:3-4). God would deliver
them from the house of judgment for the sake of their
labor and their faith in the Teacher of Righteousness
(1QpHab. 8:2-3). In the *Order of Warfare,* this seems to
be set forth as an eschatological battle in which "the dominion of Kittim" will come to an end (1QM 1:6). The people of God would pursue and destroy the enemy to eternal
destruction, specifically "for all the lot of Belial" (1QM
1:5). It is "the vengeance of His [God's] anger against all
the Sons of Darkness" (1QM 3:9), "the anger of God with
fury against all Belial and all the men of his lot without
remnant" (1QM 4:1-2). The house of judgment was to be
brought up for judgment, and God would judge it "with fire
of brimstone" (1QpHab. 10:5). On the day of judgment,
God would "destroy in the sea all the worshippers of 'wood,'

and from off the earth the wicked" (1QpHab. 13:4). It was to be an eternal defeat (1QM 18:1). The following passage from the *Thanksgiving Hymns,* while set in a background of personal remorse and self-judgment, seems to be a picture of the last judgment:

> The foundations of the mountains are given to the flames; the roots of flint become torrents of pitch. It devours to the great abyss; the torrents of Belial burst into Abaddon; the sentient beings of the abyss roar with the noise of the eruptions of mire. The earth cries aloud at the ruin which has been wrought in all the world; all its sentient beings shout; all who are upon it go mad and melt in utter ruin. For God thunders with the noise of His might, and His holy dwelling re-echoes with His glorious truth; the host of heaven utter their voice; the eternal foundations melt and shake; and the war of the mighty ones of heaven rushed about in the world and turned not back until the full end decreed forever; and there is nothing like it.[16]

On the other hand, the people of the Covenant will have "everlasting blessings, eternal rejoicing in the victorious life of eternity, and a crown of glory, together with raiment of majesty in eternal light" (1QS 4:7-8). Vermès refers to this as "union with God."[17] Is this a spiritual eschatology, immortality, or bodily resurrection? Scholars differ in their interpretations.

Van der Ploeg, for example, sets forth his reasons for belief at least in personal immortality.[18] The Community not only exists in this world, but has its counterpart in the after-life. The faithful has been brought from the Sheol of Abaddon to an eternal height (1QH 3:20). He has been formed from the dust for an eternal company (1QH 3:22),

---

[16]1QH 3:31-36, M. Burrows, *The Dead Sea Scrolls,* p. 405.

[17]*Les manuscrits du désert de Juda,* pp. 119-122.

[18]J. van der Ploeg, "L'immortalité de l'homme d'après les textes de la Mer Morte," *VT,* 2 (1952): 171-175.

and "will stand in his place with the army of the holy ones," and "come together with the congregation of the sons of heaven" (1QH 3:23).

Vermès thinks that there is more than immortality: that nothing less than resurrection is implied. He bases his view on a passage in the *Manual of Discipline*, which reads:

> And then God will purge by His truth all the works of man, by tearing away every spirit of iniquity from his garments of flesh and by purifying him by the holy spirit from every impious activity. He will pour out on him a spirit of truth as lustral waters, washing all lying abominations, and He will lead him by the lustral spirit in order to teach the righteous the knowledge of the most High, and to instruct the perfect in the wisdom of the sons of heaven.[19]

Vermès says: "It is incontestably a matter here of men in flesh and bone."[20] However, the *crux interpretum*, "garments of flesh," is not so read by other scholars. Vermès would agree that the resurrection of the body is not openly taught in QL, but he explains this as due to the belief that the Community was living in the end-time, and therefore would not pass through death. "Entrance into eternity was conceived of as a sort of *assumption* in a purified and sanctified body, and not as a resurrection."[21]

My readers at several points, without any need of having it pointed out, will be reminded of similarities to Christian doctrine. Once again, however, we need to observe the differences. Christianity, which has all too often been labeled as "other worldly" and an "interim ethic," unmistakably has its teaching for the undefined future. It is neither

---

[19]1QS 4:20-22 (Vermès). This translation varies at points from the Hebrew text, but not in relevant passages.
[20]*Les manuscrits du désert de Juda*, p. 122.
[21]*Loc. cit.*

correct to speak of New Testament Christianity as expecting to end with that generation nor to deny that expectation. The only right explanation of the New Testament attitude, it seems to me, is that of possible imminence: that is, the Lord could return at any time. Some teachings indeed were in line with such immediacy. But other teachings were also present that prepared the Church for generations of service here on earth. Therefore, the New Testament could continue to be used. It was not necessary to throw it away when Christ failed to return. If this seems to be a paradox to the modern mind, I would suggest that it is only because we fail to grasp the full significance of imminence: it can happen at any time—which may be soon or distant.

In the Qumran literature, on the other hand, there is no provision for generations to come. Only immediacy of the end was taught. Perhaps one of the reasons for the disappearance of the sect was its failure to see beyond its own generation.

CHAPTER FOURTEEN

Were the Qumran Sectarians Essenes?

M ANY ATTEMPTS HAVE BEEN MADE, even from the very first, to identify the Qumran Community. They have been compared with Essenes, Pharisees, Sadducees, Zealots, Ebionites, and several other groups. Talmon's word, in my estimation, is good: "But no solution, offered until now, will answer all queries and silence all objections raised by opposing scholars." After long and careful study of the problem, I have come to the conclusion that a final solution is at present impossible for two reasons. First, we do not know enough about the Qumran Community. True, we have considerable material from their library—but we cannot be sure that everything in the library expressed the viewpoint of the sect. The picture is rather confusing at the present time, and there are numerous contradictions that need to be resolved.

In the second place, we do not have a clear picture of Judaism of that period. Almost all, if not all, of the materials that have come down to us present Judaism through the eyes of the Pharisees. It is possible that these materials were written from a somewhat biased point of view; in fact, it would be remarkable if this were not the case. There is little in the way of objective controls for critical study—or there had been prior to the Qumran discoveries.

Still, all is not hopeless, and much has been learned from the attempts of the various scholars to identify the Qumranians—even when (in my opinion) the conclusions have been erroneous.

If truth could be arrived at by a majority vote, the identification of the Qumranians with the Essenes[1] would be established, for this seems to be the view of most scholars at present. Who were the Essenes, and what do we know about them?

What Do We Know About the Essenes?

Actually, we do not know much about them. The Pharisees and the Sadducees are mentioned in the New Testament; but there is no reference to the Essenes. The Jewish historian Josephus, who lived in the latter half of the first century A.D., determined to know about all three sects, and he tells us that he lived in the desert for a period of time—it is uncertain whether his reference to three years applies to all three, or just to the Essenes—in order to learn about the Essenes. He is our principal source. Yet even his opinion is open to question; in the first place, he finally decided (at the age of 19) to become a Pharisee; and, in the second place, he seems to be dependent on other writers, chiefly Philo, for some of his material on the Essenes. Still, his material in *Antiquities of the Jews* (xiii 5:9; xv 10: 4-5; xviii 1:5) and *Wars of the Jews* (ii 8:2-13) constitutes our principal sources. Philo, Pliny (the Elder) and Dio Chrysostom add other details. The material is presented in full in Schürer's *Geschichte des jüdischen Volkes*, with long quotations in the original languages of the source ma-

---

[1]Pronounced *ess′seen.*

terials.[2] The reader is referred to this work for further study.

Several scholars have discussed the meaning of the name *Essene.* Lightfoot, in an excursus on the Essenes in his commentary on *St. Paul's Epistles to the Colossians and to Philemon,* lists about thirteen suggested etymologies of the word. Most of them are unsound. Among the less improbable are: Aram. *'âsayyâ* "physicians," and Aram. *ḥăsayyâ* "pious ones." An attractive case could be made for a form *'âsayyâ* "doers, workers," if it were not for the fact that the common Hebrew word for "do, make" (*'āśâ*) is not used in the same sense in Aramaic.

The origin of the Essenes is no more certain than the etymology of their name. Josephus introduces them in the time of Jonathan the Maccabee, and mentions Judas by name in the time of Aristobulus (104-103 B.C.). He fails, however, to say whether this was the time of the origin of the sect, and it is not unreasonable to suppose that he was ignorant of that fact.

Reconstructing the Essene sect from the sources, we have the following picture. They lived on the western side of the Dead Sea, not far from Sodom, at some distance from the shore of the sea to get away from its noxious fumes. Engedi was "below" (= to the south of?) them. This is approximately the location of the Qumran caves, and Burrows suggests that the region could scarcely have supported separate groups. He views the geographical argument as "the

---

[2] An English trans. of Schürer is available (in an earlier edition) for those who do not read German readily, under the title, *History of the Jewish People in the Time of Jesus Christ* (2 divs. in 5 vols.; Edinburgh: T. & T. Clark, 1897-1898). The later German ed. is preferable, but the additional material in it is of no great consequence for our purposes.

strongest reason" for identifying the Qumranians with the Essenes.

The Essenes were about 4,000 in number, and lived in many of the towns of Judea (and perhaps Syria). To get away from the immorality of the city-dwellers, they lived chiefly in the villages. Whether these "villages" can be equated with the "camps" of the Qumran sect, it is difficult to say.

According to Philo, no Essene had his own house, but rather all property was held in common. Josephus tells us that they neither bought nor sold with one another, and there was no sign of wealth or poverty. Wages were turned over to a "manager" who bought for the community. There was one purse, common expenses, common clothes, common food, and common meals. Wages received were put into a common fund to care for the sick. In these points the Essenes and the Qumranians are remarkably similar.

The Essene communities were under the rule of "managers" (the word used is not the same as that used for the one who did the buying), and the members did nothing except on the orders of these managers. The title used here (*epimelêtai*) is not greatly different from the title used for the "supervisor" (*mebaqqēr*) of the Qumran Community. Philo and Josephus mention the high regard for the "lawgiver" among the Essenes. This could be the leader of the sect—or it could refer to Moses. It would be interesting to speculate that the "Teacher of Righteousness" of the Qumranians is intended.

ADMISSION TO THE SECT

Membership in the Essene sect was granted only after a probationary period which, according to Josephus, consisted of two stages of one year and two years, respectively.

After that time the novice was permitted to participate in the common meals and to take the "fearful oath" of membership.[3] He bound himself to openness to the brotherhood and secrecy regarding the doctrines to nonmembers. Only adults were admitted to membership, although children were received for training. There are slight differences of detail between the Qumran group and the Essenes, as you can discover by going back over what we have already said about Qumran membership. But once again, the similarity is rather striking.

The Essenes condemned marriage. Josephus knew of a group of "marrying Essenes," but the implication is that this was unusual. Scholars who resist the identification of Qumran with the Essenes point out a basic difference just here.[4] On the other hand, we must admit that Josephus seems to have known only one Essene community from personal experience; and this is insufficient evidence for generalized statements.

Josephus tells us that the Essenes were divided into four classes, according to the time of their entrance. Schürer understands this to refer to children, the two stages of novices, and the members proper. Dupont-Sommer makes the same interpretation. However, a careful study of Josephus at this point (*Wars of the Jews,* ii 8:10) seems to me not to mean this at all; rather he is referring to ranking that was done after the probationary stages were completed.[5] If I am correct, this reminds us of the statement: "If it is decided under God to admit him into the Community, he [the Overseer] shall enroll him in the order of

---

[3]Dupont-Sommer, *The Jewish Sect of Qumran and the Essenes,* pp. 94-95, recalls 1QS 1:16—2:18 in this connection.

[4]Cf. 1QSa 1:4, to which should be added the evidence of the cemetery.

[5]*Diéirêntai de kata chronon tês askêseôs eis moiras tessaras.*

his assigned position among the brethren" (1QS 6:22).[6]

When the postulant, or novice of the first step, was admitted to candidacy, or probation, in the Essene sect, he was given three badges: an apron, a white garment, and a pickax. No parallel to these is known in the Qumran Community.

THE RELIGIOUS LIFE OF THE ESSENES

The Essenes began the day with prayer, after which they went to their work. They reassembled for purificatory washing and the common meal, and returned to their work. This was followed by the common evening meal. Ritual washing and common meals were part of the life of the Qumran Community.

The Essenes are described as men of outstanding qualities and virtue. They condemned sensual desire, ate only to satisfy their needs, and dressed only to cover their nakedness. They did not collect silver or gold. Until the decipherment of the copper scrolls (see p. 34), these points could be compared with the practices of the Qumranians. However, we are now faced with the possibility that the Qumran group did collect silver and gold. Moreover, there is no indication that the Qumranians ever condemned sensual desires except as these led to immoral behavior.

The Essenes repudiated slavery; the Qumranians did not

---

[6]It would be attractive if the following words could be identified with the four classes: "for Torah, for judgment, for purity, and for transferring of property" (1QS 6:22). In such case we should understand the Qumran group to be divided into students and expounders of Torah ("prophets"), judges, priests, and stewards of material things. Josephus' word, *moíras,* is equivalent to the word *góral,* commonly used in QL ('lot'); however, it is difficult to tell whether the same connotations are intended. At any rate, this must be recognized as speculation only.

(cf. CD 12:11). The Essenes forbade the use of oaths; the Qumranians did not (cf. 1QS 6:24–7:25; on the contrary, cf. 1QS 6:27).[7] The Essenes forbade anointing with oil; this is not specifically mentioned in QL, but the several references to "the anointed" could, if taken literally, indicate that anointing was practiced. The Essenes bathed before every meal in cold water; QL does not contain this specific regulation, although ritual bathing was certainly practiced. The Essenes wore white raiment at all times; no such requirement is mentioned in QL. The Essenes were scrupulous to dig a hole (with the pickax given to them when admitted to candidacy) and bury their excrement; the excavations at Khirbet Qumran suggest that a common toilet and septic tank was used. The Essenes were careful to cover themselves (with the apron given them at the time of admission) when bathing; QL is silent on this point.

The Essenes condemned marriage; the Qumranians did not. The Essenes sent gifts of incense to the Temple, but they did not send animal sacrifices and hence were not admitted to the Temple; the Qumranians held antipathy toward the Temple priesthood, but there was no objection to animal sacrifice. In the *Damascus Document* on the contrary, there are provisions for sending offerings to the Temple under certain conditions (CD 9:14; 11:19-20; 16:13). The Essenes were noted for their pacific nature, being even referred to at times as pacifists. Burrows thinks this is "perhaps the most conspicuous apparent divergence between the Essenes and the covenanters."[8] Yet it is a mistake to press this point too far, for Josephus knew at least one

---

[7]There is a section on oaths in CD 7:7-8; cf. also CD 9:9-23, which clearly provides for the use of oaths.
[8]*The Dead Sea Scrolls*, pp. 291-292.

Essene who had been a valiant soldier. At the same time, the Qumran Community should no more be looked upon as less peace loving simply because of statements in the *Order of Warfare* than should Christians be accused of warlike tendencies, as someone has suggested, simply because they sing, "Onward, Christian Soldiers!"

ESSENE DOCTRINE

Josephus attributes to the Essenes belief in an unalterable fate including the abolition of human freedom. The Sadducees, he tells us, held that nothing was dependent on fate, while the Pharisees took a middle ground. Schürer thinks that Josephus is here referring to belief in Providence. We must be cautious whenever we attempt to discuss the theological and philosophical subtleties of any systems with which we do not have a sympathetic and thorough knowledge. With due caution, we suggest that there is a marked similarity between Essene "fate" (as seen through the eyes of Josephus, let us not forget) and Qumran "lot."

The Essenes had high regard for the Law and the Lawgiver, and included the reading of the Scriptures and the explanation of them in their services. Philo tells us that they took a special delight in allegorical interpretation. Though excluded from the Temple, they sent gifts of incense and maintained the Aaronic priesthood. Here the parallels with Qumran are strongly marked. The "allegorical interpretation" of the Essenes could very well describe the hermeneutics found in such Qumran writings as the *Habakkuk Commentary.*

The Essenes interpreted Exodus 16:29, the first mention of the Sabbath, with extreme literalness. The *Damascus Document* calls for the keeping of "the Sabbath day according to its exact rules" (CD 6:18). However, this may be only a common punctilious regard for the Sabbath laws, with no implication of interdependence.

Josephus tells us that the Essenes rose daily before sunrise and addressed prayers to the sun. Schurer resists this as too contrary to Judaic religious thought. There is a school of thought that holds that Solomon's Temple was oriented in such manner that the equinoxial sunrise would fall through the doors upon the holy place inside, thus suggesting an element of sun-worship.[9] The present study is not the place to get into this highly complex problem. However, we may recall that Solomon introduced elements of pagan religions into Israel, and throughout the time of the prophets there were those who worshiped in ways contrary to the revealed truth. It is not beyond reason that some such elements may have come down into Judaic times in the sects of Judaism.[10] One might speculate that some such heretical element would be sufficient reason to explain the lack of mention of the Essenes in the New Testament. At any rate, there is slight resemblance to the Qumranians at this point.[11]

The Essenes had certain "ordinances" which included esoteric books that were not to be revealed to nonmembers, sacred names of angels which were not to be divulged, and the study of the future together with the ability to make accurate predictions. References to these points are found, however, only in passing in the *Wars of the Jews,* and it may be unwise to do more than mention that they resemble such elements in Qumran theology as "the *Book of the Hagû,*" the developed angelology in the *Order of Warfare,*

---

[9]Cf. S. H. Hooke, ed., *Myth and Ritual* (London: Oxford University Press, 1933), pp. 87-110, and other scholars.

[10]In fact, cf. Mishnah *Sukkah* 5:2-4 for evidence that such deviations were known.

[11]Brownlee, on the other hand, sees a parallel in 1QS 10:1.

and the eschatological interpretations of the *Habakkuk Commentary*.

On one point of Essene doctrine Josephus is unusually explicit, namely, on the doctrine of the soul and immortality. The Essenes, he tells us, taught that the bodies are perishable, whereas the souls are immortal, with an ethereal pre-existence and future existence. As presented by Josephus, the view is somewhat Gnostic, and is quite definitely different from the Qumran view. Hippolytus, however, gives us a somewhat different picture of the Essene doctrine, which is more in line with the Qumran teaching. This problem is at present, in my opinion, beyond solution, since we have no way of testing the conflict between Josephus and Hippolytus.

PYTHAGOREAN ELEMENTS

Josephus saw certain Pythagorean elements in Essenism, and similar Pythagorean elements have been pointed out in the Qumran materials by Dupont-Sommer.[12] It may be worth our while to spend some time on this point. As every schoolboy knows after his introduction to geometry, the simplest right triangle has sides of 3, 4, and 5 units (the longest side being known as the hypothenuse), and "the square of the hypothenuse equals the sum of the squares of the other two sides." The Pythagoreans, according to Philo, loved to point out that the simple units of the right triangle could yield only the number 12 ($3 + 4 + 5 = 12$), whereas the squares of the numbers yielded 50 ($3^2 + 4^2 + 5^2$ [or $9 + 16 + 25$] $= 50$). Twelve was the number of the Zodiac cycle, but the pentecontad cycle (i.e., the one based on 50) was better than the Zodiac cycle as the second power is better than the first.

---

[12]*The Jewish Sect of Qumrân and the Essenes*, Ch. VI.

The letters of the Hebrew alphabet, like the Greek, are assigned numerical values. The fourteenth letter (*nûn*) has the value 50. In the *Manual of Discipline* there is a cryptic reference to the sign *nûn* (1QS 10:4), and immediately following are the words, "for the key of eternal mercies." The letter *nûn* as usually written has the shape of a key, hence several scholars have seen here another indication that a play on words is intended. Moreover, the section immediately preceding the reference to the *nûn* contains references to the *'áleph* and the *mêm*. The letters *'áleph*, *mêm*, and *nûn* form the Hebrew word *'āmēn*, or Amen, which is even today a liturgical word. The numerical value of the letters in this word is $1 + 40 + 50 = 91$, or the number of days in three months of the special calendar used by the Pythagoreans. Immediately following the reference to these three letters in the *Manual of Discipline* is a discussion of times, seasons, etc. (1QS 10:5-8).

This somewhat fanciful discussion becomes even more fanciful when we realize that the word *nûn* is cognate with the word for "fish" in Aramaic and Akkadian, it is the sign of the universal soul among the Arabs, and the same letter of the alphabet is given a name meaning "serpent" in Ethiopic. Scholars have not failed to connect these points in various ways with the discussion at hand.[13]

These points, particularly as elaborated by Dupont-Sommer are certainly noteworthy. But the very extravagance of the various theories, and the widespread use of a symbolic meaning for *nûn*—fish—fifty—eternity—should caution us against too quick identification. A common origin, which stems back to the Sumerian period at least (since Sumerian

---

[13] I have failed to find, however, any mention of the fact that the temple of Nin-girsu at Lagash was named *Ê.NINNU* ("House of Ninnu," the sign for *NINNU* being the cuneiform sign for 50).

word signs are used in Hammurapi's Code), and which spreads over much of the Ancient Middle East, would be sufficient to account for the similarities which Dupont-Sommer has brought forth.

Conclusions

That the Qumranians, like the Essenes, were a religious monastic (or semimonastic) sect, all will admit. That there are many points of similarity between the two groups cannot be denied. But certain differences must be noted. The Essenes apparently believed that water could cleanse; the Qumranians believed that water was useless until the heart was clean. The two groups differed in their attitudes toward women, warfare, and sacrifices. The Essenes were a "twice-born" group with a single initiation; the Qumranians apparently held to an annual rebirth. Maximum punishment among the Essenes was death; this was contrary to the spirit of the Qumran group. The Essenes had no private possessions; Qumran had a limited right of property. Gottstein concludes:

> There are such grave religious divergences between the Essenes and the Dead Sea Community as to render this theory highly improbable, *unless we are prepared to allot to the name "Essenes" a meaningless indefiniteness.*[14]

Burrows comes to a more moderate, but basically similar conclusion:

> If several related sects are included under the term Essene, the covenanters may be called Essenes; if by Essene we mean a particular sect, which we assume to be accurately described by the ancient writers, then the covenanters were not Essenes. For the present it seems

---

[14]M. H. Gottstein, "Anti-Essene Traits in the Dead Sea Scrolls," *VT*, 4 (1954): 142. (*Italics* his.)

to me best not to speak of the Qumran sect as Essenes, but rather to say that the Essenes and the covenanters, with other groups of which we know little or nothing, represented the same general type. *It is more important to define the extent of agreement and difference than it is to accept or reject a particular name.*[15]

ADDITIONAL NOTE TO SECOND EDITION

In view of the fact that almost all scholars have now accepted the Essene identification, plus the fact that several reviewers of this work have taken me to task for my cautious conclusion, I fully planned to rewrite this chapter. I have reviewed all evidence carefully, paying particular attention to points raised in the reviews. Two things impress me: there is nothing that I have found to cause me to alter my conclusions as expressed above; more disturbing is the tendency to an almost cultic attitude toward this question on the part of scholars who are otherwise markedly cautious. Once again I am constrained to quote Professor Burrows:

> One must still, however, protest against the current tendency to use together what Josephus and Philo say of the Essenes and what the Dead Sea Scrolls reveal concerning the sect of Qumran, on the assumption that both bodies of data apply to one and the same group. To some it may seem pedantic to maintain this distinction, but for the purpose of accurate historical knowledge it is essential.[16]

---

[15]M. Burrows, *The Dead Sea Scrolls*, p. 294. (*Italics* mine.)
[16]*More Light on the Dead Sea Scrolls*, p. 274.

CHAPTER FIFTEEN

Other Possible Identifications

W E HAVE DEVOTED much space to the Essenes simply because most points of similarity are to be found in that
area. But we must also consider the other Jewish sects of
the period, remembering that there were most certainly
other groups than the Pharisees, Sadducees, and Essenes.

THE PHARISEES

Source materials for a study of the Pharisees are found in
Josephus, the Mishnah (printed in full in Schürer), and to a
lesser extent in the New Testament. The name is obviously
from the Aramaic *perišayyâ* (cognate with Heb. *perûšîm*),
"the separated ones." But from what were they separated?
Suggestions that have been made are: from uncleanness;
and from the Hellenistic party of Judaism. In the latter case
they are supposed to have been the successors of the
Asideans (Heb. *ḥăsîdîm*, "pious ones"), who in turn can
be traced back to the time of the Maccabean conflicts. The
Asideans were originally distinct from the Maccabean party,
but joined them in the revolt against Hellenism, and continued in that fight as long as the objective was the establishment of the Law. When, however, the Hasmoneans (or
Maccabees) took over the political powers, the Asideans
drew more and more away from them. In the time of John
Hyrcanus (135-104 B.C.), they appear as "Pharisees," and
were opposed to the Hasmoneans. John Hyrcanus, indeed,
was a Pharisee at the beginning of his reign, but he with-

drew, probably to join the Sadducees. The Sadducees thereafter and until the Second Revolt became the party with some degree of control over the political life, whereas the Pharisees controlled the religious life of the Jews more or less absolutely. This picture, for all practical purposes, is acceptable, although at many points scholars find details that need further study.

The Pharisees, according to Josephus, numbered about 6,000—a very small percentage of the nation.[1] It is remarkable that although Josephus describes the admission rites for the Essenes, he tells us nothing of the requirements for admission to the Pharisees (even though he himself joined them!). It is also remarkable that, while we know from the New Testament (Matt. 23:15) and from other sources of the great zeal of the Pharisees to make converts to their sect, we nowhere have any account of the means that were used to make converts; and while we know of their exceeding zeal for the Law, we have no knowledge of how this zeal was to be demonstrated to the satisfaction of the group.

A learned group of the Pharisees was known as "the scribes." Previously, their duties had included the safeguarding and transmission of the Scriptures. By New Testament times they seem to have developed rather into students of the Law, and as such "lawyers" or "teachers" they more and more replaced the priesthood. It is possible that the responsibility for judgment (*mišpāṭ*) devolved upon the elders and the responsibility for the Law *(tôrā)* upon the scribes; the priestly duties, of course, being the prerogative

---

[1]T. W. Manson, *The Servant Messiah*, p. 11, puts the population of Jerusalem at 30,-35,000, and Palestinian Jewry at 500,-600,000. On mathematical grounds alone, scholars should have realized that we cannot account for all Jewish sects: 6,000 Pharisees, 4,000 Essenes, and Sadducees fewer in number than the Pharisees, at most adds up to 16,000, or only 3 per cent of the nation.

of the chief priests. On the other hand, the motto of the men of the Great Synagogue: "Be deliberate in giving judgment, and raise up many disciples, and make a barrier about the Law" (*Pirqê Abôt* 1:1), seems to place *mišpāṭ* within the province of the scribes.

The Pharisees are reported to have been divided into seven categories, and while this may indeed be "a round number," it seems to me that it cannot possibly be compressed into the two schools of Hillel and Shammai. We should rather be prepared to find several groups comprising the previously mentioned 6,000 membership.

According to the New Testament, the Pharisees were not only zealous for the Law (the term including there the Legalism of Judaism, or "traditions of the fathers"), but by contrast with the Sadducees, they believed in the resurrection of the body, in angels, and in the later additions to the Canon.

We can see parallels with the Qumran group at several points. There was in each case high regard for the Law. However, this similarity becomes less convincing, as we begin to understand what each group means by the term "the Law." Delcor, for example, sees the Qumranians as "a second stage of Pharisaism" (and the Essenes as a third and hyper-Pharisaic stage). He points out the following parallels. The Qumran belief in the resurrection of the body is more nearly that of the Pharisees than of any other known sect. The attitude toward Temple sacrifices in Qumran is not that of the Essenes. Details such as sympathy for the oppressed poor, the democratic character of the Qumran sect, and the like, are not Essene. In my opinion, Delcor is leaning over backward in his attempt to disprove identification of the Qumran sect with the Essenes. Still, the points he makes must be considered carefully.

De Vaux at first saw a clear Pharisee origin for the Qumran group; later he withdrew his "Pharisee label." But he reminds us of Josephus' record of the crucifixion of 800 Pharisees in the days of Alexander, with the others fleeing for their lives. From such a group may have sprung a sect, Pharisee in origin, but differing in the development of certain points. Something like this seems to be necessary to account for the facts that are known to us, but beyond this we can only speculate.

Saul Lieberman has pointed out interesting parallels between the Qumranians and the *hăbûrā,* or society of the *hăbērîm,* of whom certain facts are recorded in rabbinic sources. The terms used for admission, for example, are similar. There was in each case insistence upon strict ritual cleanliness. There were similar steps in the process of admission. The word for "the many" in Qumran is synonymous with the word *hăbērîm.* The word for "purity" is used in a technical sense by each group. The hatred of the *hăbērîm* toward the *'am hā'áres* ("people or the land," the country folk who were unable to fulfill the legalistic minutiae of the Law), was expressed in the statement of Rabbi Simeon ben Yohai: "An *'am hā'áres,* even if he is pious, even if he is a saint, even if he is honest, cursed be he to the Lord, the God of Israel." This reminds us of the hatred of Qumran toward all who were not "children of the light."[2]

The parallels between Qumran and the Pharisees cannot be denied. On the other hand, we must ask ourselves whether these parallels are of such distinctive character that they require some interdependence between the groups. In my opinion, they can be sufficiently accounted for by a common zeal for the Law, and by the fact that the two

[2]S. Lieberman, "The Discipline in the So-Called 'Manual of Discipline,'" *JBL,* 71 (1952): 204-206.

groups, in the first century B.C., were separated from a common origin by only a brief span of time.

On the other hand, there are elements in QL that sound almost anti-Pharisaic. The "tried wall" of the Community (1QS 8:7) may be an implied rebuke against the "building of the wall" (or fence) of Jerusalem Pharisaism. The doctrine of determinism in Qumran seems to be stronger than the idea of "fate" presented in Josephus' view of the Pharisees. And Dupont-Sommer's questions raise other points: "Where is the matter of the community of goods, of an oath of initiation, of the novitiate, of the sacred meal presided over by a priest, etc., among the Pharisees?" The Qumran sect had, moreover, repudiated the Temple sacrifice and substituted no altar sacrifice in its place. And again, as Lagrange points out, "The sect acknowledges full value to the apocryphal books such as the Book of Jubilees and the Testament of the Twelve Patriarchs, not to speak of an unknown book, the Hagu." Even if Lagrange has overstated his point, as seems likely to me, there is validity in his argument. On the other hand, Marcus' view that the Essenes were a subgroup of Pharisees, differing chiefly in their enthusiasm for apocalyptic speculation, dualism, and pessimistic determinism, seems to ignore important differences while reducing Judaism to Pharisees and Sadducees.

Again we say, the picture is far more complex than has hitherto been recognized. The easy confidence of Zeitlin and others in the rabbinic picture of Judaism (which was recorded by Pharisees who no longer had any opposition party to correct their statements) must give way to a more critical approach to Judaism. The Qumran sect is not Pharisee, in the sense that we have known Pharisaism. Neither is it non-Pharisee. It is part of a complex, in which it stands sometimes closer to, sometimes further from, Pharisaism.[2a]

THE SADDUCEES

The information concerning the Sadducees in Josephus is found in the same passages as the information concerning the Pharisees. Source materials are printed in full in Schürer, as is source material from the Mishnah. The latter is of little value, because of its apparent tendentious character.

The origin of the name of the sect is even more obscure than the names of the Pharisees and the Essenes. The root of the word obviously means "to be just, righteous," and the name has sometimes been taken to be an adjective, "the righteous ones." This form, however, should be *ṣaddîq*, whereas the tradition of the name without exception preserves a form of the word *ṣaddûq*. But there is no lexical support for a form *ṣaddûq*, hence Schürer concluded that a form *ṣādôq* was intended. (In Hebrew, *ṣaddûq* and *ṣādôq* would look exactly alike before the advent of vowel-points.) With the discovery of the Qumran materials, including the *Damascus Document*, the name of the *b⁰nê ṣādôq*, "the sons of Zadok," came into prominence. Hebrew scholars recognized that a form such as *b⁰nê ṣādôq* is interchangeable with the gentilic form *ṣ⁰dôqî*, "Zadokite," just as the form *b⁰nê yiśrā'êl*, "sons of Israel," is interchangeable with the form *yiśrā'êlî*, "Israelite." The plural of *ṣ⁰dôqî* would be *ṣ⁰dôqîyîm*—which would be exactly the form needed to explain the name "Sadducees." This reasoning is without fault—but it does not prove that the "sons of Zadok" of Qumran are the same as the "Sadducees" of other writ-

---

[2a]For a recent study connecting Qumran with the Pharisees, cf. C. Rabin, *Qumran Studies* (Scripta Judaica, II; London: Oxford University Press, 1957). I do not agree with several points, but the work deserves careful study.

ings. Only the interchange of the two names in the same literary material would produce that result.

Why would a group be called by a certain man's name? Three possibilities are obvious: (1) they are the direct descendants of the man (such as the "sons of Israel" in the first generations); (2) they are a group that was founded by the man whose name they bear (such as "Campbellites," "Buchmanites," etc.); or (3) they are a group that either chose or were given the name of a person whom they regarded as an ideal (the "Jacobites," "Augustinians," etc.)

Can Zadok (or Sadôq) be identified? Four possible identifications have been suggested: (1) The first is Zadok of II Samuel 8:17, who served, together with Ahimelech, as a priest in David's court. He is identified as a son of Aaron through the line of Eleazar (I Chron. 24:3), and was instrumental in the return of the Ark (II Sam. 15:24-29). Ezekiel builds up the sons of Zadok (Ezek. 40:46) in his visions of the restored Temple, stating that when the children went astray, the sons of Zadok remained loyal (Ezek. 44:15), and therefore they would be the ministers in the new sanctuary.[3] Bonsirven accepts this identification, and Schürer reluctantly backs into it.

(2) A second Zadok is named in an apocryphal legend in the *Abot de-Rabbi Nathan,* which traces the origin of the Sadducees to a disciple of Antigonus of Socho by the name of Zadok. Many have accepted this view. But Wellhausen shows, I believe correctly, that the story is late; it contains erroneous details, and is obviously not tradition but an effort to explain away a Sadducean heresy.

(3) A third "Zadok" is a hypothecation of scholars who have decided that neither of the preceding two can be ac-

---

[3]Some scholars have objected that Ezekiel has confused a Zadok of a later period with the Zadok of David's day. Even if for the sake of argument this be admitted, it would make no difference, for popular movements can thrive on idealized characters even if factual details have become confused.

cepted, therefore there must have been another. (North calls him "an *ad hoc* eponym.")

(4) The fourth explanation, like the third, is no Zadok in reality, but simply an ideal. The "sons of Zadok" are "the sons of the righteous."

North discusses all of these explanations, and rejects them all. He concludes that the Sadducee sect *"grew out of* and *derived its name from* the Ṣadoqite priesthood."[4] But this is the same as (1) above, without pressing for historical accuracy or true genealogy. In the mind of the people, the priesthood had to be derived from Aaron. No person could decide to *become* a priest; he had to *be born* into the priesthood. And since the time of Ezekiel, at the latest, the Zadokite line of the Aaronic priesthood was the preferred line. At least, such was the ideal.

Josephus lays stress on the aristocratic nature of the Sadducees. They were not the party of the people, but the party of the wealthy. The Sadducees were priests, but not all priests were Sadducees (a point sometimes apparently overlooked). Several priests who were Rabbis were named in Josephus, as well as in rabbinic literature, and Josephus himself was, according to his *Life* (i 2) both priest and Pharisee. Similarly, the record in Acts 6:7 points to priests who were not likely Sadducees.

Originally, the priesthood and the government of the nation had been separate. With the Maccabean revolt, and particularly with the recognition of Simon as high priest and autonomous ruler of the Jews (c. 143 B.C.; I Macc. 13:41-42), the priesthood and the throne were united in a single person. This becomes a pivotal point in the history of the Jewish people, and several movements can be traced to various

---

[4] R. North, "The Qumran 'Sadducees,'" *CBQ*, 17 (1955): 173; (*italics* his). This article is worth careful study.

forms of reaction against this centralization of power. The first reference in Josephus shows the Pharisees and Sadducees to be in a state of hostility, and the Pharisees had the multitude of the people on their side; the Sadducees could persuade none but the rich.

However, the difference between the two groups was not merely a political or social matter. The Sadducees were a religious sect, and they had their own teachings. Josephus singles out one point, namely, the attitude toward tradition: the Sadducees rejected everything that was not found in the written Word. In the light of its context, this has been taken to mean that the Sadducees accepted only the Pentateuch. However, it seems to me that Josephus means the written Scriptures, as opposed to oral tradition, when he uses the word *Law* in this context.

Of course, this becomes a crucial point when we attempt to compare the Qumran sect with the Sadducees. If the Sadducees accepted only the Pentateuch, then the Qumran sect can hardly be Sadducee, as Burrows and Dupont-Sommer have pointed out. On the other hand, if the Sadducees only objected to oral tradition, then the identification becomes less difficult.

According to Josephus, the Pharisees believed in the immortality of the soul and a future life which, in spite of ambiguity in the wording, is probably to be understood as life in a resurrection body. The Sadducees, on the other hand, denied the continuance of the soul and any rewards or punishments in an after-life. The same difference, essentially, is brought out in the New Testament. By implication, as Schürer has pointed out, this would rule out any Messianism except in the most figurative sense. Here there is marked divergence between the Sadducees and Qumran.

The same could be said with reference to the Sadducean nonbelief in angels.

Josephus also points out a difference between the Pharisees and the Sadducees in the matter of divine providence and human freedom. The Pharisees stressed the idea of "fate," but allowed considerable room for human free will and responsibility. The Sadducees, on the contrary, ruled out fate and any suggestion that God was implicated in evil in even the remotest way, and stressed the sovereignty of human choice. Once again, there is a noticeable difference between the Sadducees (at least, as presented by Josephus in this regard) and the Qumran sect.

The Qumranians, it must be obvious, were not Sadducees, in the sense that the Sadducees have been preserved for us in the literary sources. But to say that the *benê ṣādôq* of Qumran were not *ṣedûqiyîm* is a differentiation that the names will hardly allow. We simply *must* account for the names in each case. It is therefore necessary, in my opinion, to conclude that the name *Sadducee* must now be looked upon as a complex, and that the "Sadducees" were a complex sect of which we have previously had only a very restricted and unilateral view.

If North is correct in his conclusion that the Sadducee sect grew out of the Zadokite (Ṣadoqite) priesthood, it would appear to be reasonable to conclude also that the *benê ṣādôq* of Qumran likewise grew out of the Zadokite priesthood. There are many indications of a continuing struggle against the Sadducees in the years following the reign of John Hyrcanus. The struggle erupted in revolt in the days of Alexander Jannaeus. Cavaignac is of the opinion that the Qumran writings reflect this struggle as well as an attempt to restore a true Zadokite priesthood. Vermès also believes that the Qumran priesthood is pressing the claim that it is the legitimate priesthood. The theory is not incredible.

However, the doctrinal differences between Qumran and the Sadducees must be taken into consideration. A suggestion would be that doctrinal degeneration, particularly in eschatological matters, was part of the development of the "Sadducees." Having put their stress on political expediency and having traded the support of the common people for the security and prestige of a wealthy and aristocratic clientèle, they banished "pie in the sky" concepts. To admit the need of Messianic deliverance, or to stress life in the world to come after defeat in this life, would be to deny the humanistic principles basic to their position. Emphasis on free will would fit into this picture. So would hostility to the appeal to tradition by which their principal opponents, the Pharisees, supported their own position. The progressive character of Pharisaism, in contrast to the reactionary character of Sadduceeism, is consistent with this picture.

One thing, however, must be kept in mind: We have no primary source material for the Sadducees. The Pharisees, on the other hand, have preserved much of their viewpoint in the writings of their successors the Rabbis. The Talmudic picture of the Sadducees is, as Schürer notes, "quite foggy." The Qumran writings may reflect elements of Sadduceeism previously unknown to us, and over which we have at present no control.

OTHER JEWISH SECTS

Epiphanius, c. A.D. 375, listed seven Jewish sects, and Pfeiffer adds four Samaritan sects to this list. Allowing for some duplication, while also noting that the Ebionites, the Sampseans, and the Qumranians are omitted, we still have a rather complex picture. To say that the Qumranians are not Pharisees, and they are not Sadducees, therefore they must be Essenes, is uncritical and almost naïve. Certain scholars have apparently felt the force of this logic, and have attempted to compare Qumran with some of the lesser-known sects. Significant details have been brought out by their studies, and these should be brought together in future studies of Judaism. I have attempted to do this briefly elsewhere,[4a] but the work should be done thoroughly and by scholars equipped for the task. I shall mention here only a few points that seem to be particularly significant.

The *Zealots* are mentioned in the New Testament and Josephus. Some have attempted to identify the Zadok of Qumran with the Zadok who was a cofounder, with Judas the Galilean, of the Zealots. It seems to me that there is a basic difference between the Zealots who were ready to fight for their nation and the Qumranians who had written off the nation and retired to their monastery. Moreover, the matter of chronology enters the picture. Certainly the Qumran group was founded a century or more before the Zealots came into existence.

Marcus, recalling Ginzberg's demonstration of the existence of a conservative and a liberal wing in Pharisaism, comes to the conclusion that the Essenes formed a third division, a "left-wing Pharisaism." Burrows goes a step farther and puts the Sadducees at the extreme right and the Zealots at the extreme left, with the three groups of Pharisees in between. If the Qumran group can be identified with the Essenes, he reasons, this alignment seems "quite plausible." I would be inclined to put the Qumran sect on the other side, next to the Sadducees. Actually, there is little difference between an aristocracy that occupies a Temple and a monasticism that dwells in the desert. Both are out of contact with the world. The chief difference would

---

[4a]See pp. 222-244, below.

be that, whereas the Sadducees believed "You can't take it with you," and so they wanted it here and now, the Qumran group gave up all hope of having it now, and looked for the Golden Age to come. Probably this is part of the reason why these groups failed to survive the cataclysm that came upon the Jewish nation. The Pharisees, whatever else might be said of them, were sufficiently adaptable that they could continue some form of religious life no matter what the national status was.

The organic relation of the Qumranians and the Zealots is quite possible; the identification of the groups, however, is impossible.[4b]

The *Ebionites* were a Jewish-Christian sect known also as Nazarenes. Teicher has attempted to prove that the Qumran sect was Ebionite, but the peculiar way in which he has insisted on his view has perhaps discouraged other scholars from following out certain lines of thought that need further study. To attempt to identify Qumran with the Ebionites, in the light of the archaeological and other evidence, is impossible, for the Ebionites must be dated in the late first or early second century A.D. However, there were various Ebionite sects, one of which, at least, as described in the Patristic writings, has points of similarity with the Qumran group. It would be an attractive theory that they grew out of the Qumran group after it disappeared from the Qumran region (c. A.D. 67). This, however, would require much careful study before it could be presented as anything more than just a vague speculation.[5]

The *Dositheans*, followers of a self-styled messiah, Dositheus, appeared about the time of Jesus and continued into

---

[4b]The most thoroughgoing effort to identify the Qumranians with the Zealots is by C. Roth, *The Historical Background of the Dead Sea Scrolls* (Oxford: Basil Blackwell, 1958). I found it unconvincing.

[5]Cf., e.g., O. Cullmann. "Die neuentdeckten Qumrantexte und das Judenchristum der Pseudoklementinen," *ZNW*, 21 (1954): 35-51.

the sixth century A.D. There are points of similarity with the Qumranians in the insistence upon the keeping of the Law, particularly the Sabbath laws, the thirty-day-month calendar, and other points. However, the identification of the two groups is made impossible by (1) the chronological difference in their appearance, and (2) by the fact that the Dositheans were Samaritans and as such rejected all but the Torah (Pentateuch), whereas the Qumranians freely used the entire Old Testament.

The *Therapeutae* were an Egyptian sect, with colonies scattered in other parts of the world. The discovery of the *Damascus Document* in a Cairo genizah probably gave impetus to efforts to identify the Qumranians with the Therapeutae. The latter met together only on Sabbaths and holy days (in which they differed essentially from the Qumranians), said prayers at sunrise and sunset, studied the Scriptures, wrote commentaries with emphasis upon allegorical interpretation, and composed hymns to God's praise (in all of which, as Brownlee notes, they are similar to the Qumran sect). However, these similarities are such that they could well have sprung up independently. Even so, we should not lightly dismiss the matter; and a thorough study of Judaism must seek to account for the cause of such similar movements.

JOHN THE BAPTIST GROUPS

We sometimes forget that John the Baptist is not the property of Christianity alone. Even the New Testament reminds us that there were disciples of John the Baptist who had penetrated as far as Ephesus who were not essentially Christian (Acts 19:1-7). Perhaps a similar group had formed at (or migrated to) Alexandria, for Apollos seems to have been a follower of John the Baptist when he came to Ephesus from Alexandria (Acts 18:24-25). "Christians of St. John" at Bosrah (now in southern Iraq) in the seventeenth century later came to be known as "Mandeans," "Nazareans," or "Sabians." The study of the baptist movements in general, and the Mandeans in particular is a task belonging to specialists, and much remains to be done.[6]

Without going into the details, I would incline to the view that the original home of the Mandeans was in the Jerusalem area. The connection with the John the Baptist groups in Asia Minor and Egypt would be an interesting subject for further study, especially in the light of the Qumran literature.[7] Some have attempted to identify John the Baptist with the Teacher of Righteousness. This once again raises the question of dating the Qumran documents, and the theory must be rejected in the light of the archaeological evidence. To say this, however, is not to deny that there is still a very interesting area for study. John the Baptist did grow up in the wilderness. He did (willingly or not) give rise to a movement that had at its center a baptismal rite. There was a strong eschatological or Messianic note in his preaching. And his followers spread into other regions just about or prior to, the time of the disap-

---

[6]On the baptist movement, see Josèph Thomas, *Le mouvement baptiste en Palestine et Syrie (150 av. J.-C.–300 ap. J.-C.)*, (Gembloux, Belgium: J. Duculot, 1935), 455 pp. On the Mandeans, see Lady E. S. Drower, *The Mandeans of Iraq and Iran* (Oxford: Clarendon Press, 1937), and more recently (although some of his conclusions are, in my opinion, a retrogression), H. C. Puech, *Le Mandéisme* (Paris, 1945). T. Säve-Söderbergh, *Studies in the Coptic Manichaean Psalmbook* (Uppsala: Almqvist and Wiksells, 1949), p. 165, raises questions that need to be answered.

[7]It should be noted that all the standard works on the Mandeans' and related subjects are dated prior to the Qumran discoveries. Cullmann's suggestion is important: "A thorough comparison of the Qumran writings with the Mandean literature is still lacking. It would be very helpful."—"The Significance of the Qumran Texts," *JBL*, 74 (1955): 219. [We can now add at least one title: F. M. Braun, "Le Mandéism et le Secte Essénienne de Qumran," in *L'Ancien Testament et l'Orient* (Louvain, 1957), pp. 193-230.]

pearance of the Qumran Community. Some of his disciples, of course, became followers and later apostles of Jesus (John 1:35-39), but not all (Matt. 11:2). Could it be that John was a member of the Qumran sect, and that some of his followers failed to see the weakness of an asceticism that repudiates the world?

Before accepting such a view, however, we should study the whole baptist movement.[8] There were different types of baptism.

One was initiatory: a symbolic rite through which a candidate must pass in order to enter the group, but which does not have to be repeated. A second type was remedial: the washing produces a cure for diseases, and is repeated as needed. A third type was purificatory: the baptism washes away impurity, either physical or spiritual (or perhaps both), and is administered, often self-administered, rather frequently. Qumran baptism was certainly not initiatory, for the waters were forbidden to those who were unclean. There is no indication that it was considered remedial. To a certain degree it was purificatory, yet not mechanically so.

John's baptism, likewise, was not initiatory. It was for Israel, but there is no indication that John was establishing a "true Israel" with an initiatory rite. His baptism was not remedial. It was most closely related to the Qumran rite. But even here, there seems to be a difference. John's baptism seems to have symbolized a repentance of the Israelite, a desire to be a true Israelite in Israel. Qumran baptism, on the other hand, seems to be part of a system that denied that anyone could be a true Israelite unless he separated himself from Jerusalem Judaism and joined himself to Qumran Judaism. Qumran baptism was a symbol of a turn-

---

[8] Cf. Thomas, *op. cit.*, pp. 269-436.

ing away from sinful Israel. John's baptism was a symbol of a turning away from the sins of Israel.[9]

That John may have grown up in the Qumran group is a possibility that cannot at present be denied. But if he did, it seems to me that he must have parted company with them when he began to preach his Gospel of repentance. With true prophetic insight he placed the Messiah within Israel, and he left for the Messiah the task of separating the true Israel from the false (Matt. 3:11-12).[10]

---

[9]Josephus, however, says that John's baptism was ceremonial lustration like that of the Essenes (*Wars* ii 8:7). I am inclined to agree with R. P. Casey, who calls this "Josephus' forced misrepresentation of John's Baptism." *The Background of the New Testament and Its Eschatology*, edited by W. D. Davies and D. Daube (Cambridge: Cambridge University Press, 1956), p. 61.

[10]Modern separatist groups would do well to study this point carefully. The New Testament repeatedly insists that judgment be left in divine hands. What mere human being is wise enough to determine who shall be among the redeemed and who shall not?

CHAPTER SIXTEEN

The Relation of Christianity to Qumran

MANY THINGS HAVE BEEN WRITTEN concerning the relation of Christianity to the Qumran Community. Some of the statements are sweeping generalities that should never have gotten into print. Some of the studies have been very carefully made and are profitable, regardless of our opinion of the conclusions reached. The subject needs patient and painstaking work.

A survey of the literature shows a gradual development of the approach of scholarship. The early writers were attempting all sorts of conclusions; the later writers are working at specific problems. Graystone tells us that two scholars alone (Kuhn in 1950 and Grossouw in 1951) had found no less than 500 parallels between the New Testament and the scrolls. Such a vast number could not possibly have been critically studied in so few years. In 1950, Dupont-Sommer was writing:

> Thus, the revelation of the Jewish "New Covenant," which has just been brought to us in such detail by the Dead Sea discoveries, enriches very substantially our knowledge of Essenism. In the last two centuries B.C. and the first century A.D. this represented a movement in Judaism as widespread as it was deep, both inside and outside of Palestine. It is from the womb of this religious ferment

that Christianity, the Christian "New Covenant," emerged.[1]

Almost every clause in these three sentences presumes a settled conclusion instead of what was then, and in many cases is yet, only an area of scholarly controversy. As recently as the fall of 1955, Lankester Harding was writing:

> John the Baptist was almost certainly an Essene and must have studied and worked in this building [the monastery now Khirbet Qumran]: he undoubtedly derived the idea of ritual immersion, or baptism from them. Many authorities consider that Christ himself also studied with them for some time.[2]

But was John an Essene? Is it beyond question that the Qumran Community was Essene? Was John's baptism "ritual immersion"? Was it the same as either the Essene or the Qumran type of baptism? Is there indeed a large segment of scholarship that will accept the last sentence quoted?

Such generalizations, made sometimes by men whose names and official titles lend weight to whatever they write, have aroused many questions in the minds of laymen and clergy who do not have the time and opportunity for private research. Little wonder, then, that we are constantly bombarded with questions concerning the effect of the Dead Sea discoveries on the Christian faith![2a]

---

[1]*Dead Sea Scrolls*, p. 98. The date is that of the original French edition.

[2]"Where Christ Himself May Have Studied: An Essene Monastery at Khirbet Qumrân," *Illustrated London News*, 227 (Sept. 3, 1955), pp. 379-381.

[2a]More recently we have seen the appearance of pulp works that seek to ridicule Christian ministers and belittle Jesus Christ—all in the name of the Dead Sea Scrolls. I refer to the works by A. P. Davies and C. F. Potter. If it were not for the fact that tens of thousands of persons, chiefly young people, are taking these seriously, I would take no notice of them. They have no claim to Dead Sea Scrolls scholarship whatever, and their arguments against New Testament Christianity are at least forty years old and have been answered many times. In fact, their old-line Liberalism has been repudiated by most of the new generation of Liberals.

It was to try to answer some of these questions by putting the material into the hands of such interested (and sometimes confused) persons that this book was written. Many points have been suggested along the way. In this concluding chapter I shall try to bring the pertinent material together. If at times I seem to be not positive enough, it is because I am trying to avoid the generalizations that I have criticized in others.

QUMRAN AND THE JERUSALEM CHURCH

We sometimes forget that the Church existed before the New Testament.[3] For perhaps twenty years, there was no New Testament book, and for nearly a century the New Testament was incomplete. Its official canonization came still later. What was the Church like in its formative years? Most critics have been willing to admit that the early chapters of Acts are essentially historical. Hence, we must begin our comparison at this point. The best study that has appeared to date is Sherman Johnson's article, "The Dead Sea Manual of Discipline and the Jerusalem Church of Acts."[4]

The Jerusalem Church started with an experience of the Holy Spirit. It stressed the need of baptism for repentance. It insisted that baptism alone was not the ultimate, but spiritual regeneration was more important. Parallels with Qumran are apparent—yet, so are differences at significant points, not the least of which is the absence of any hint of repudiation of the Temple service by the Jerusalem Church.

The Jerusalem Church practiced some kind of community

---

[3]The Liberals and Neo-orthodox have used this fact to dispute the accuracy of the New Testament, and the Roman Catholic Church, through paid advertisements of the Knights of Columbus, has used it to argue for the importance of tradition and ecclesiastical authority.

[4]*ZAW*, 66 (1954): 106-120. The work should be continued to include all of the Qumran materials, although most of the significant material is in 1QS.

of goods (Acts 2:44, 45; 4:34-37). Punishment was meted out to those who lied about their wealth (Acts 5:1-6). Poverty was a prominent element of the early Church. Again, parallels with Qumran are obvious (e.g., 1QS 1:12; 6:16-20; and 1QS 6:25). But what community is without its poor? And what religious group has not attempted to work some amelioration? These things alone do not prove interdependence. As for enforced community property, a study of Acts 5:4 will clearly indicate that the early Church and the Qumran Community were diametrically opposed (cf. 1QS 6:22).

The Qumran group was ruled by twelve laymen and three priests (1QS 8:1). Johnson sees here a parallel with the early Church, which had its twelve apostles (Acts 6:2) and its three pillars (Gal. 2:9). Johnson does not explain how it is that the same three appear in both groups, or how to equate laymen in Qumran with apostles in Acts.[4a]

Both groups had some kind of communal meal (Acts 2: 42-47; 1QS 6:2-3; 1QSa 2:11-22). But, as we have seen, there is a basic difference between the two groups at this point, in that the common meal of the Church was linked to the death of its Master.[5]

Both groups had some antipathy toward the Temple cultus. Yet even this point has to be modified, as Johnson recognizes, for Stephen's speech, which somewhat represents the viewpoint of repudiation, must be placed over against the attitude of James and the non-Hellenist Jewish

---

[4a]In a curious work by a Mormon, in which he seeks to find substantiation for some of his church's claims, O. P. Robinson says that after the crucifixion, Jesus appointed Peter, James, and John as the First Presidency of the church and instructed them to select additional apostles to make up the number to twelve; *The Dead Sea Scrolls and Original Christianity* (Salt Lake City: Deseret Book Co., 1958), p. 77. But where is the evidence for this?

[5]Although this is not definitely stated in the early part of Acts, the presence of the statement in both Mark and I Corinthians, in my opinion, testifies to its early character.

Christians in Jerusalem (cf. Acts 7 with 2:46; 3:1-11; 21: 18-26).

The parallels in this early period, where we should expect to find the closest relationship if Christianity and Qumran are from a common source (e.g., if John the Baptist, or some of the apostles, or Jesus had been former Qumranians), are not convincing. To suggest a more remote connection between the two sects,[6] is to suggest the obvious.

QUMRAN AND THE JOHANNINE LITERATURE

Several scholars have written at length on the comparison of the Qumran literature with the Johannine writings, and others have noted similarities in passing. Lucetta Mowry published an article that contains many important points.[7] The dualism in the fourth Gospel is traced to its possible sources, and Miss Mowry suggests that Iranian influence came through Qumran into the Gospel. However, she finds basic differences. John avoided the speculations over origins; his concern over the calendar became merely a pulpit for his more important message. Ritual washing was of far less importance than spiritual change (the significance, to her, of the changing of water into wine). The Temple cultus was subtly put in the background by the story of the cleansing of the Temple and by the conversation with the woman of Samaria. The Law itself was secondary, as is brought out by the story of Nicodemus, the "teacher of Israel," who could not find the solution to his theological problems in the Law, but had to come to Jesus with them. Not all of Miss Mowry's interpretations of John are satisfactory to me. Yet I think we can use them as a basis for discussion in the present instance.

---

[6]The word is used in the New Testament of Christianity, cf. Acts 24:5, 14; 28:22.
[7]"The Dead Sea Scrolls and the Gospel of John," *BA*, 17 (1954): 78-97.

Cullman discusses some of the same points.[8] He finds a Jewish Gnosticism prior to Christian Gnosticism, and a Jewish Hellenism prior to Christian Hellenism. Then he concludes that there is a relationship between the fourth Gospel and the Hellenists, as well as between the fourth Gospel and the Qumran sect. The essential and characteristic point common to all three is the opposition to Temple worship. However, it is to be seriously questioned whether a common front on this point is indeed a distinctive that demonstrates relationship. On this basis, we should have to include some of the Old Testament prophets, or for that matter, anyone who is opposed to abuses in the priesthood. Cullmann further finds in John 10 a polemic against the Teacher of Righteousness, particularly in verses 8 and 11.[9] But how can such a generalized statement be made specific? One could as readily make out a case for a polemic against Socrates or Lao-tze. Cullmann's statement concerning another point is noteworthy: "Instead of the Spirit, the Qumran movement had an organization." Whether his next observation is valid is open to question: "This driving impulse [the Spirit] is lacking in the Qumran sect, and that is the reason that the Essenes ceased to exist after the Jewish wars in A.D. 70." One could probably suggest a number of groups that have thrived on organization in lieu of the Spirit.

---

[8] O. Cullmann, "The Significance of the Qumrân Texts," *JBL*, 74 (1955), pp. 213-226.

[9] There is a tendency in Cullmann to jump easily from the actual to the hypothetical. Having become convinced that the Qumranians were Essenes, he goes on to say, "Is it not significant that Josephus and Philo can both describe the Essenes in detail without once mentioning the Teacher of Righteousness?" Somehow, he fails to see that the significance of this *could be* in an entirely different direction: the Teacher of Righteousness, and indeed the entire Qumran sect, may not have been Essene.

Grossouw, who was not trying to prove interdependence, but rather merely demonstrating parallels, feels that in the Qumran texts we may have an important "possible *Vorstufe*" of John. One point of similarity he stresses is the emphasis upon brotherly love.

In a fully documented article, F.-M. Braun discusses the Jewish background of the fourth Gospel and the Qumran sect.[10] He discusses verbal affinities, doctrinal similarities, and similarities in eschatology and apocalyptic. In brief, he suggests that John the Baptist was influenced by the sect; through him John the author picked up vocabulary, while later John picked up similar ideas and terminology from Jesus; still later John came into contact with members or friends of the Qumran Community who had reached Ephesus. In my opinion, his thesis does not hold together well, because he has to weave together material from too widely scattered portions in order to make the case. Many of his individual points, however, are interesting, and some are quite important.

Raymond Brown discusses the similarities between the Qumran writings and Johannine literature.[11] First, he considers the dualistic concept in Qumran with reference to Creation, the two spirits, the struggle, man's role, and the sons of light. Then he takes up the ideas of truth and perversity, brotherly love, the fountain of living waters, apostasy, seasons and feasts, purifications and baptisms, and messianism. It would seem that he has made as good a case for parallelism as could be made. The most striking paral-

---

[10]"L'arrière-fond judaïque du quatrième évangile et la Communauté de l'Alliance," *RB*, 62 (1955): 5-44. His references to 1QH on p. 15, notes 1-5, should all be corrected to read 1QS.

[11]"The Qumran Scrolls and the Johannine Gospel and Epistles," *CBQ*, 17 (1955): 403-419; 559-574.

lels are in the teachings of truth and perversity. Yet, when he has finished, he states the conclusion:

> There remains a tremendous chasm between Qumran thought and Christianity. No matter how impressive the terminological and ideological similarities are, the difference that Jesus Christ makes between the two cannot be minimized (p. 571).

One cannot help but notice, by way of contrast, the almost complete lack of eschatology in John, the subordination of ethical teaching, and the lack of asceticism. In all of these points, QL stands closer to Paul than to John.

At the same time, we should also note that more and more scholars are recognizing the Jewish background of the fourth Gospel. Both Braun and Brown, cited above, come to conclusions that affect the date and authorship of John, while the general trend seems to be to lower the date. It is still too early to pronounce a final verdict, but continued scholarly investigation of the Johannine literature in the light of Qumran is making it increasingly less difficult to accept the traditional view, namely that John was a Palestinian, an apostle, and that he wrote his works within the first century.

Qumran and the Pauline Writings

Many writers have noted numerous similarities between the writings of Paul and the Qumran writings. Sherman Johnson has published a study that can serve as an introduction to this subject.[12] Obvious similarities are: Baptism, the Communion or Lord's Supper, the idea of the New Covenant, elements in Biblical interpretation, and the ethical imperative. Some of the more pointed parallels,

---

[12]S. E. Johnson, "Paul and the Manual of Discipline," *HTR*, 48 (1955): 157-165.

such as the need of two or three witnesses (II Cor. 13:1; CD 9:17-23[13]), giving room to the wrath of God (Rom. 12:19; 1QS 10:18), and singing with understanding (I Cor. 14:15; 1QS 10:9), Johnson traces to a common Old Testament background.

Regarding the New Covenant, Johnson thinks it was a common point between the Jerusalem and Pauline churches, and that it became more marked in Paul's successive writings. By the time of the writing of Colossians, Paul seems to be speaking against the central interests of the Qumran sect: the rules pertaining to food, drink, new moons, sabbaths, and asceticism.[14] The most important parallels are found in Cols. 10 and 11 of the *Manual of Discipline,* and have to do with righteousness and justification. Without going into the intricacies of Johnson's article, we simply say that the evidence leads to the conclusion that Paul was neither deriving his ideas from Hellenism, nor using *ad hoc* creations for Galatian and Roman readers. Rather, he was discussing real issues about which Jewish people, and probably others who had come into contact with the same currents of thought, were actually and deeply concerned. Brownlee also found marked parallels in the doctrines of grace and justification.

Even before the discovery of the Dead Sea materials, Bo Reicke had made a similar study of the *Damascus Document.*[15] Some of the more interesting comparisons are: the caution against keeping wrath over night (CD 7:2-3; Eph. 4:26); the taking over of the New Covenant by the sect (CD 19:30; Rom. 4:11 ff.; 9:4 ff.; 11:17 ff.; Gal. 3:15);

---

[13]Johnson fails to supply a parallel in 1QS, and I have found none.
[14]*Op. cit.,* p. 159; cf. Col. 2:16-23.
[15]*The Jewish "Damascus Documents" and the New Testament* (Uppsala: Wretmans, 1946) 24 pp.

the Angel Mastema (CD 16:5) and the Angel Satan (II Cor. 12:7); the long-suffering nature of God (CD 2:4-5; Rom. 2:7-9); and the view of purpose (CD 6:15; II Cor. 6:17).

Once again we note two things: (1) there is definitely a relationship, even if somewhat removed, between the two bodies of writing; and (2) this relationship is not such that either must be looked upon as dependent upon the other.

QUMRAN AND OTHER CHRISTIAN WRITINGS

There is little to be gained by continuing to analyze the parallels that various writers have pointed out. By now it must have become clear to the reader that there are doubtless points of contact.

Several writers have discussed parallels with the Epistle to the Hebrews.[15a] Since there is admittedly a remarkable similarity between the Johannine writings and Hebrews, this is to be expected.

Others have noted the parallels with the more eschatological portions of the New Testament (such as II Peter, Jude, and portions of the Thessalonian letters). But again, since there is a marked similarity with, if not even dependence upon the apocalyptic writings (Enoch, Jubilees, and the like) on the part of the Qumran writings, and since these same apocalyptic writings have often been compared with the portions of the New Testament here under consideration, this is to be expected. The most that can be claimed, however, is that both the New Testament writers and the Qumran writers drew from common sources.

Braun attempted a comparison of QL with the Apocalypse, with no significant results.[16]

[15a] A stimulating discussion by Y. Yadin, "The Dead Sea Scrolls and the Epistle to the Hebrews," has been published in *Aspects of the Dead Sea Scrolls (Scripta Hierosolymitana* IV [Jerusalem, 1957]), pp. 36-45.

[16] F.-M. Braun, *art. cit., RB*, 62: 31-32.

J.-P. Audet made a study of the literary and doctrinal affinities of the *Manual of Discipline* with the "Two Ways" (which is a portion of the Epistle of Barnabas considered by some to have been originally an independent writing; also a portion of the Didachê, the relationship of which to the "Two Ways" he discusses briefly),[17] and the Shepherd of Hermas.[18] Most of my readers will probably recall that these works are found in some manuscripts, and there has been debate on occasion, as to their right to inclusion in the New Testament Canon. I cannot here go into the reasons why they were finally rejected by the Church. But the very fact the subject could even have been discussed seriously is sufficient reason to recognize the close connection between these writings and the New Testament. Audet's conclusion is, briefly: it was not the author of the Shepherd of Hermas who knew the *Damascus Document* and the *Manual of Discipline,* but rather it was his family from whom he got a secondary knowledge. Once again we see that Judaism was a complex woven of threads that were spread over a wide geographical area. It is almost impossible to draw straight lines of relationship.

QUMRAN AND REVEALED TRUTH

A question that will continue to disturb many Christians is, What does all this have to do with revelation? On the one hand, if the Scriptures of the Old Testament are, as we believe they are, the Word of God, why should we care what the Qumran writings say? On the other hand, if we admit the interrelationship of the Qumran writings and the New Testament, does this not deny the revealed nature of the New Testament?

---

[17]J.-P. Audet, "Affinités littéraires et doctrinales du 'Manuel de Discipline,'" *RB,* 59 (1952): 219-238.
[18]*Ibid.,* 60 (1953): 41-82.

To ask such questions, in my opinion, is to stop short of understanding what is meant by revelation, and to stop short of understanding God's work in history.

Revelation is *in history*. We must ever insist upon this point. We cannot accept the "suprahistorical." Revelation is *not only* history. We cannot simply read the newspapers and history books and discover God. But revelation is *in* history. God entered into the history of the human race on this planet, whether it was by holy men of old, or later by His Son. The events of the Bible are history, and through historical events God gave His revelation.

The incarnation took place at a particular juncture of history. The more we study history, the more we realize what is meant when the moment of the incarnation is called *the fullness of time* (Gal. 4:4).

Two thousand years before the incarnation, God called out Abraham, and established with him and his seed the well-known Covenant. For about 1,000 years the people of that Covenant lived in the tiny land of Palestine. I cannot here enlarge upon the purpose as I see it of that splendid isolation. Only the period of Egyptian bondage was outside of the land. (Even that, I am convinced, has its significance.) But God did not move immediately into the incarnation when the Old Testament period ended. The fullness of time had not yet come.

About 600 years before the incarnation, God sent His people into Exile. It was impossible that they could have lived through that period without absorbing some of the life and thought of the East. The influence of the Persian period on the Old Testament is not a figment of scholars. It is a providential fact of history.

After the return to Palestine, the Hellenization of the world began. Again, it was impossible that the people of the land could have lived through that experience without being affected by it. Think what happened, for example, when the Old Testament was translated into the Greek language! Not only did Greek take on new shades of meaning, so that theological terms and concepts required the formation of new words and lent new meanings to old words, but at the same time, the Old Testament ideas burst open like flowers. Paul's theological terminology is not limited to the Old Testament. One of the major differences between Christianity and Judaism is in the extent to which Christianity became a world religion. No longer was it bound to Palestine. It was for the uttermost part of the world!

The *fullness of time* means all of this—and probably a great deal more.

Judaism, after the Exile, was undergoing a process of expansion. Eastern and western thought had entered into the Jewish mind, and various lines of development began to emerge. Who dares to deny that this was as much a part of the divine plan as was the sojourn in Egypt? Could the Gospel ever have reached the world if its thought and expression had been limited by narrow confines of space and experience?

Qumran was one, perhaps very small, part of the development. Pharisaism was another. Christianity was still another. All of them, as well as other movements in Palestine, had many common strands. Each of them had distinctive strands. To understand the fullness of time better is to understand God's activity in history better. And to understand God's activity better is to understand God's revelation in history better.

After all, the Lord Jesus Christ not only died on Calvary—much as that wonderful redemptive act means to us!—He also lived among men and taught them. Let us never forget His teachings! But it would have been of little value if He had spoken to them outside their own context. We must use every possible means, then, to understand exactly what He was trying to tell them.

It is here that the Qumran material, like all other pertinent historical material, is of value to the man of faith. Through historical materials we come to understand the revealed word better. The more similarities we find (if they are indeed true similarities), the better we understand the Scriptures.

But does this not destroy the distinctives of Christianity? Not at all! Christianity still has Christ. Qumran may have its Teacher of Righteousness, and Pharisaism may have its Hillel. But only Christianity has Jesus Christ, who is God come in the flesh.

CONCLUSION

The Qumran sect was a closed sect. It believed itself to be the remnant that was to be redeemed. But there is no evidence that it considered itself to be the redemptive remnant. Its major emphasis was to re-establish a purified Law-ritual. Its Teacher had come and had died: it was still looking for the Messianic deliverer. Its Messianic hope, however, lost its point of focus, for it had three anointed personalities: one a prophet, another of the priestly line, the third of the Davidic line.

Christianity, on the other hand, quickly set its sights on the world. It was composed of "the being-saved ones" (Acts 2:47), but their part in the redemptive work was made crystal clear. They were to be the recipients of the divine power and by that power they were to go into all the world with the Gospel (Acts 1:8). For a few years there was tension over the Temple, but within forty years the beggarly elements were replaced by the better things.[19] Christianity's Teacher had come and died—but He was alive forevermore. He was to return, it is true, but He was also present in the Spirit, and His presence was manifest by mighty works. The danger of fragmentation under a plurality of ideal anointed ones was overcome by the realization that the Anointed One was at once Prophet and Priest and King.

Perhaps even here is a lesson for us today. We can become so engrossed in our own redemption that we can go off into some mental or spiritual Qumran and tell ourselves that we are the only ones that God loves. Or we can set up our elaborate ritual of legalism to try to prove to God that we deserve to be saved out of this sinful world. Or we can realize the truth of God's revelation: that we are the source by which God's redemptive power flows out to the world that God has so mysteriously loved and at such awful cost.

But we must remember our Teacher's words. If we seek to save our life, we shall only lose it in the end. Witness Qumran! Only the grain of wheat that is willing to give up its own life in the ground—the world: this dirty, sinful earth! —can produce the fruit for which God intended it (John 12:24-25).[20]

---

[19] Cf. the entire Epistle to the Hebrews, Gal. 3:1-3, etc.

[20] The results of a thorough restudy of the relationship between Qumran and the New Testament will soon appear in a book which I am now completing for the Crowell-Collier Publishing Co., with the provisional title, *The Dead Sea Scrolls and the New Testament*.

Appendix

QUMRAN AND A RECONSTRUCTION OF JUDAISM

IT IS STILL much too early to attempt to rewrite the history of Judaism during the early centuries. However, the materials that have been made available by the Qumran discoveries should be organized into a body, so far as possible, that will some day be useful in a new study of such a history. This I have attempted to do, and I wish here simply to make some of the details available to other interested students. At present, the materials have the appearance more of a mosaic, or rather parts of a mosaic, some of which have been reconstructed more or less completely, while others have little or no apparent form at present. Perhaps others can see traces of the outline in some of the fragments which have not yet begun to take form in my own mind. Probably, however, we shall have to wait for further discoveries to bring to light other material. I am, however, convinced that only confusion and distortion can result if we try to complete the mosaic without having all the parts.

THE HISTORICAL FRAMEWORK

Certain fixed points can be set out, and the facts can be fit, so far as possible, into the outline thus established.

The Founding of the Second Temple

With the return of some of the Jews from Babylonia in

539 B.C., plans were made for the rebuilding of the Temple. The work was begun by Zerubbabel and Joshua the following year (Ezra 3:8), but the work languished. It was not until 515 B.C. that the Temple was completed (Ezra 6:15).

The Persian Period

Little is known of the Persian period of the Jews. Ezra and the Great Synagogue form an important landmark (c. 410 B.C.), and according to Jewish tradition, they were responsible for the writing of the Scriptures. This possibly means the writing in the "square" or Aramaic characters, which is more familiar to most of us than the older "Phoenician" type of writing. According to Old Testament Criticism, the Priestly Code was formulated some time before this. However, critical viewpoints have been somewhat in flux in recent years, and elements previously attributed to the priestly movement have in some instances been discovered in the Ugaritic writings of the fourteenth century B.C., discovered a quarter of a century ago at Ras Shamra.[1] This lies beyond our subject, but it is one of the parts of the mosaic still to be pieced together.

Palestinian Judaism was, however, only one part of the Judaism of that time. Both Babylonian Judaism (which developed from the numbers of Jews who did not return from the Exile) and Egyptian Judaism (which probably began with the emigration in the closing days of Judah's history or slightly earlier) should be carefully studied. We must leave this to scholars qualified for the task.

---

[1] For a brief review, see the chapter by C. R. North on "Pentateuchal Criticism," *The Old Testament and Modern Study*, ed. H. H. Rowley (Oxford: Clarendon Press, 1951), pp. 48-83. For a more detailed study, cf. H. F. Hahn, *The Old Testament in Modern Research* (Philadelphia: Muhlenberg Press, 1954).

The Hellenistic Period

With the conquest of the Persians by the Macedonians (333 B.C.) and the subsequent break-up of the empire into the dominions of the Ptolemies and the Seleucids (to limit ourselves to the pertinent area) the Hellenistic period came upon Judaism.

The Great Synagogue continued, according to tradition, until c. 270 B.C., and then gave way to the Sanhedrin. The scribes were active in this period, and the Greek version of the Pentateuch (the Septuagint) was produced. Some state of canonization appears to have been reached, but the extent of it is not agreed upon by scholars.

These elements might suggest an active religious life, but actually it was in many respects at a low ebb. The participation of the priests in the gymnasia, the attempted removal of circumcision, and the growing Hellenization of the nation were strong factors. Finally, Antiochus IV (Epiphanes) came to the throne in 175 B.C. and made an effort to do away with Judaism entirely. His proscription of Judaism, however, instead of being the death-blow he intended, was the cause of the rejuvenation, for it led to revolt.

Onias III had been the high priest from 185 to 174 B.C., and from all reports he was a pious man. Through intrigue, his brother Jason had him deposed and succeeded him with the declared purpose of completing the Hellenization of the Jews (II Macc. 4:7-26). His brother Menelaus was to help him, but instead Menelaus succeeded in getting the high priesthood away from Jason in 171 B.C.[2] Menelaus in turn was put to death in the days of Judas Maccabeus, and Jakim was put in the office by Demetrius in 161 B.C. He

---

[2] So Josephus; others hold that Menelaus was the brother of a different Simon, cf. II Macc. 3:4.

took the name Alcimus, and either he or Menelaus (depending on the relationship of the latter to the Oniad line) was the first high priest not in the line of succession.

Many scholars locate the origin of the Qumran sect in this period. The 390 years of the *Damascus Document* (CD 1:5), figured from the Exile (586 B.C.), would place the raising up of the "root" (the Community) about 196 B.C., and the "twenty years" (CD 1:10) would put the Teacher of Righteousness at 176 B.C.—which is close enough to be Onias III. I have tried to point out, however, that such mathematical calculation is precarious.

The Hasmonean Period

The background of the Maccabean revolt can be sketched somewhat as follows:[3] Antiochus was on a campaign against Egypt in 168 B.C. A rumor that he was dead swept Jerusalem, and Jason seized the opportunity to capture the city with a small force. Because of his tyrannical acts, he was soon driven out. Antiochus was not dead, however, and he used the situation as an occasion to take horrible vengeance on the city. In 167 B.C., he defiled the Temple and proscribed Judaism. Menelaus ceased to officiate, and the Temple cultus came to an end.

The Asideans (or *Hasidim*, pious ones) refused to obey the edict, some choosing martyrdom and others, under the leadership of Judas Maccabeus, openly rebelling. The rebellion, perhaps partly because it was so unexpected, was successful, after bloody battles. In 165 B.C. the Temple was cleansed and dedicated again with the inauguration of the Feast of Lights (*Hanukkah*).

The tide reversed two or three times in the next few years, but through political intrigue, Jonathan (of the Mac-

---

[3]The only source is II Macc. 5:5-8.

cabean, or more properly Hasmonean line) was made priest-king by Alexander Balas in 162 B.C. (I Macc. 10: 18-21). Jonathan was succeeded by his brother Simon in 143 B.C., and the next year Simon took the Acra in Jerusalem and made the Jews independent from the Seleucids. He was succeeded by his son John Hyrcanus (135-104 B.C.), who brought the Jewish state to the height of its power. For the first time a Jewish prince had his name stamped on the coinage.

The Hasmonean line continued after Hyrcanus for about seventy years. The warlike character of some of the priest-kings, particularly Alexander Jannaeus (103-76 B.C.), led to dissatisfaction and open rebellion. The Hasmoneans were able to maintain their power, however, notably by the expedient of Alexandra (the widow of Jannaeus) admitting the Pharisees to the Sanhedrin for the first time. Alexandra, we might note, was the sister of Shime'on ben-Shattach, a famous Pharisee. According to reports that are not confirmed, the Pharisees, who were never too sympathetic to the Hasmonean rule, were responsible for stirring up popular feeling on one or more occasions.

The Herodian Period

The Roman forces under Pompey intervened in a war that had broken out between Aristobulus II (the Jewish ruler, 67-63 B.C.) and Hyrcanus II (the legitimate high priest and eldest son of Alexandra). The Jewish people made it plan to Pompey that they would rather abolish the monarchy than have either Aristobulus or Hyrcanus as their ruler. As it turned out, the Romans laid siege to Jerusalem, captured it with horrible butchery, entered the Temple and the Holy of Holies, but permitted worship to be continued. Hyrcanus II was made ethnarch.

The years that followed were filled with strife and bloodshed, while the Roman nation was passing through its civil war. Antigonus (Mattathias) was the last of the Hasmoneans (40-37 B.C.). Herod captured Jerusalem in 37 B.C., and the cruel Herodian period had begun. Six years later, 31 B.C., occurred the great earthquake that killed 10,000 or 30,000 persons.[4] The birth of Jesus is dated just prior to the death of Herod. Herod was a patron of Rome, and encouraged Romanization, as others had encouraged Hellenization.

There was popular dissatisfaction with the fact that the nation was under Roman rule; this was increased when Roman procurators were placed over the ethnarchy of Archelaus (Judea, Samaria, and Idumea). During this period the Zealots came into being, possibly through the efforts of Judas the Galilean and a Pharisee named Zadok. Pfeiffer says:

> In any case, we may say that as the Pharisees are the heirs of the Hasidim so the Zealots are the heirs of the Maccabees: intolerant of foreign rule, they did not expect, like Daniel and the Pharisees, the kingdom of God miraculously from heaven, but endeavored to achieve it by fighting the Romans.[5]

In the days of Caligula, anti-Semitic feelings flared up in Palestine, and the statue of Caligula was ordered to be erected in each synagogue. Later Caligula ordered a statue of himself to be placed in the Temple. This order was countermanded, and Caligula died before further damage could be done to the rapidly deteriorating relations. When

---

[4] Both figures are from Josephus, cf. *Antiquities* xv 5:2 and *Wars* i 19:3.

[5] R. H. Pfeiffer, *History of New Testament Times* (New York: Harper and Brothers, 1949), p. 36.

Felix became governor (A.D. 51), the tension began to mount. This ultimately led to the *First Jewish Revolt* (A.D. 66-73).

During the Herodian period there had been twenty-eight high priests. The succession was usually occasioned by the removal of the incumbent through political action.

The Jewish Wars

The First Jewish Revolt came about through minor events which in normal times would have passed with little notice. Insults, local acts, then refusal to offer the sacrifice which Nero had commanded, plus the leadership of Eleazar, son of a former high priest, brought on the war which the Romans apparently did not want. The fanatical opposition of the Jews brought down on their heads the full force of the Roman legions. Jerusalem was utterly destroyed in A.D. 70, although small forces held out until A.D. 73.[6] Agrippa II had been on the Roman side in the struggle, and was rewarded with the addition of territory after the war. With his death in A.D. 100, the Herodian line came to an end.

The destruction of the Temple meant the end of the sacrificial system—which would have meant the end of Judaism but for two factors. First, there was the development of the synagogue, with Diaspora Judaism. This provided for worship without Temple sacrifices (although the ideal of the Temple sacrifices was always kept alive). Then Jonathan ben-Zakkai had escaped from Jerusalem during the siege of the city, and had somehow obtained permission to reopen his school at Jamnia in Galilee. This school (the Beth Din) preserved the teachings of Judaism with a zeal that was almost fanaticism. Every detail of the

---

[6]Josephus, *Wars*, Books 3—7.

Temple service was scrupulously preserved against the day when the Temple would be built again. Every detail of the Law was treasured up. Since the school was entirely Pharisean, it is obvious that the Pharisaic slant would dominate all the work of the school. It became the successor of the Sanhedrin, and the Sadducees, who had dominated the Sanhedrin, passed out of the picture entirely and forever.

A Jewish revolt flared up in A.D. 115-116 in Egypt and Cyrene, under Trajan, resulting in the death of many Jews. Other revolts broke out in Mesopotamia and Cyprus.

Then in the days of Hadrian, the *Second Jewish Revolt* was led by Simon, who came to be known as bar-Cocheba. He was widely accepted as the Messiah. When his revolt failed, the Romans built a temple to Jupiter on the site of the Temple, and the adoration which had been given to bar-Cocheba turned to disillusionment. He was forthwith called bar-Kozibah, "the liar." The state which he had established, that even minted its own coinage, was short-lived (A.D. 132-135).

THE RELIGIOUS SCENE

It is obvious to all who have worked in this period of Jewish history that the picture is confused. There were many strains, many cross currents, many similar or nearly similar situations, each of which would or could account for movements that developed. Emotions aroused by the violation of the Temple could be traced to the time of Antiochus IV or Pompey or Caligula. Religious leadership might refer to the Great Synagogue, the Sanhedrin, or the Beth Dîn—and we should add that the leadership would not be the same in constituency or theology. A great deliverer might be one of the Maccabees, or Judas of Galilee, or bar-Cocheba. There were doubtless other figures.

Pharisees and Sadducees

It was approximately in the time of John Hyrcanus that the names *Pharisees* and *Sadducees* first occur in Josephus. The Pharisees generally have been taken to be the descendants of the Asideans. Now it begins to appear that the Pharisees were not merely a lay group of religious enthusiasts, but included as well some priests (or Sadducees)—for Josephus was both a priest and a Pharisee, and so was Jozar. Perhaps we should look upon the Pharisees as a group distinguished by religious zeal, rather than attempt to draw the line any finer.

John/Hyrcanus broke away from the Pharisees, possibly joining the Sadducees. The Sadducees are often identified with the priestly line. They were closely associated with the reigning group. Later, they developed doctrinal distinctives that set them over against the Pharisees. But are we justified in reading these distinctives back to the time of John Hyrcanus? If the Sadducean distinctives were developed to maintain a position against the progressive attitude of the Pharisees, does it not follow that the innovations of the Pharisees—traditions of the Fathers, Halakah, and the like—would have had to develop first? This would take time. The Mishnah developed slowly. Diverging lines should converge if we work backward. Perhaps we should look for greater similarity between the two groups in the second century B.C.

The suggestion has been made that the name *Sadducees* may be related to the name Ṣadôq. The name Ṣadôq is also connected with the Qumran group, for they were the "sons of Zadok." The juxtaposition of the religious revival following the abominable act of Antiochus Epiphanes, the passing of the high priesthood out of the legitimate line (the line of Zadok), and the appearance of the zealous Pharisees alongside the aristocratic Sadducees—all within the space of thirty or forty years—strongly suggests that there was a connection.

Piecing the parts together, we begin to get the following picture, which in my opinion should be given careful scrutiny.

The religious deterioration of the Jewish nation had been opposed by a small but vital group of enthusiasts, pious ones (*Ḥâsîdîm*) or separatists (*pᵉrûšîyîm* or Pharisees), who were the heirs of the religious activities of the great Synagogue and the scribes. If this small group had a name at that time, it was probably "Ḥasidim." The Great Synagogue had yielded to the Sanhedrin, and the control of the latter body came more and more into the hands of the formalists. The time was the second half of the third century B.C.

Any innovations in the religious thought and life of the Jews would be able to penetrate only the Ḥasidim (using the term for the sake of convenience), simply because the formalists would not be interested. Later, this disinterest would be rationalized by a doctrinal position—but that had not yet taken place. The innovations that may have entered at that time would include dualistic trends (probably not uniform), possibly some concepts that would stress the spiritual nature of religion as over against ritual and temple sacrifice, and probably some developments of the idea of election. The elements of apocalyptic and eschatology probably were also present at that time, but it would take a crisis to bring them into prominence. The study of Scripture and its interpretation was almost certainly present, while the translation of it, possibly with interpretation, was an innovation of the period.

With the Maccabean revolt, the picture suddenly became

more complicated. Some of the Ḥasidim were so faithful
to the Law that they were willing to die rather than defend
themselves on the Sabbath. Others found that they could
conscientiously modify the Sabbath Law. Some took a
more permanent interest in the religious life of the nation.
Others returned to the purely religious life as soon as the
threat to it had been removed. It is almost certain that the
same division was taking place in the priestly class. Some
certainly continued in their formalism. Others almost beyond doubt were shaken from their lethargy and "got religion." In fact, we can almost hear one group saying
vehemently to the other, "We are the sons of Zadok—the
priests who keep the covenant!" (1QS 5:2).

Then, with the end of the Zadokite line of high priests
(see p. 226), another element entered the picture. In the
Habakkuk Commentary the "House of Absalom" is mentioned (1QpHab. 5:9). Scholars have attempted to identify this with some person or family in the contemporary
scene. It may be better to look upon the expression as part
of the Biblical portrayal of Zadok.

There were two lines of high priests descended from
Aaron: the one through Eleazar to Zadok, the other through
Ithamar and Eli to Abiathar. In the days of David, both
Zadok and Abiathar were his priests (II Sam. 15:24-29, 35).
Both lines were united in service at that point. Then the
question of David's successor came into prominence. There
were two attempted revolts: the first was that of David's
son Absalom; the second that of David's son Adonijah.
Abiathar cast his lot in with Adonijah, and Zadok remained
loyal to David (I Kings 1:7, 8). Accordingly, Zadok's line
was established and the "house of Eli" (Abiathar's line)

fell (I Kings 2:27). The revolting house might well be called the "House of Absalom," since Absalom was the first and therefore the representative rebel in David's line.

The entire statement in the *Habakkuk Commentary* reads:

> The house of Absalom and the men of their counsel who were silent at the reproof of the Teacher of Righteousness and did not help him against the Man of the Lie, who had rejected the Law among all peoples (1QpHab. 5:9-10).

If the suggestion that has just been advanced is valid, we could conclude that the origin of the Qumran group, or its ancestor, is to be found shortly after the end of the Zadokite high priesthood. The "House of Absalom," then, would be the priests who remained in the formalist group (the Sanhedrin), and who, by refusing to speak out against the outrage, had conspired against the House of David. The men who had spoken out, on the other hand, were the "true sons of Zadok," who had moved out of the formalist group in protest.

It will be noticed that this would establish a common origin for both Sadducees and the Qumran group, which would, of course, account for similarities we have noted between the two groups. However, the details as presented would require the later development of each group sufficiently to account for the known differences between them.

This theory would also account for the presence of priests among the Pharisees (namely, some of those who had broken with the continuing line) as well as in the Qumran group (namely, others of the separatists). It would also account for Pharisaic elements among the Qumran group, for there would have been, according to this reconstruction, a period of time during which they were all thrown together and before a secondary schism caused the Qumranians to leave Jerusalem for the wilderness.[7]

Is there any indication of a cause for a second schism? I believe there is.

Apocalyptic and Apocalyptists

At some time during the period we have just tried to reconstruct, and from some place that we cannot identify more specifically than "probably Babylonia through Persian influence," certain ideas began to penetrate Jewish thought. The ideas are probably interrelated, although they are usually treated separately: dualism and eschatology.[8]

As man tries to solve the problem of the end of the world he knows, he also has to introduce his idea of God and the extent that God participates in the consummation. Does man solve all problems by himself? Eschatology, in that case, is the sum of human progress. On the other hand, if he cannot solve them, and God must intervene, an apocalyptic system is set up.

But another question must at the same time be answered. Why can man not solve his problems? Perhaps it is because there are unseen forces, "demons," working against him. Then God will also have to destroy those demons. But suppose the demons, too, have a "god," or a super demon? Then, God will have to destroy him. But can God do that? And where did that demon come from: did God create him? So the questions develop.

----

[7] J. C. G. Greig, by a somewhat different approach, came to the same general period for the rise of the Qumran group. Cf. "The Teacher of Righteousness," *New Testament Studies*, 2 (1955): 119-126. I cannot go along with him in identifying the Teacher of Righteousness with Mattathias. Nor am I convinced that the wicked priest was Menelaus—although he fills the qualifications well.

[8] See pp. 94-103.

The process, of course, would take decades, perhaps generations. Not all would be satisfied with the same answers. Some would put more stress on "lot" or "fate," or some other form of determinism. Others would be inclined to see man's part as the more significant. Some would enjoy drawing lurid pictures of demonic and angelic combat. Others would be more prosaic. Gradually, schools of thought would develop.

In my opinion, that which would send men into the wilderness would be a conviction that the whole situation had become so tragic, and man was so impotent, that all he could do was get his own house in order and wait for God to take over and win the battle.

Was there any particular historical situation to precipitate such a decision? As a matter of fact, there were several. Two stand out more prominently. The first would be the culmination of the warlike nature of the Hasmoneans in Alexander Jannaeus (p. 227). The second would be in the days of Herod the Great, when he moved against certain religious groups in the land.[9] The second is too late for the evidence of the coins found at Khirbet Qumran. The first harmonizes well with that evidence (pp. 35-37).

Sufficient remains of the Zealot attitude in the days of the Maccabees would filter down to account for the few similarities to the Zealots found in the Qumran sect. The same attitude would be preserved in the main stream of Judaism, so that it would be unnecessary to seek the origin of the Zealots in the Qumran Community.

With the apocalyptic attitude there is generally associated

---

[9] C. T. Fritsch thinks this is the most likely time for the flight to Damascus by the Qumran group; cf. "Herod the Great and the Qumrân Community," *JBL*, 74 (1955): 173-181.

a type of individual who enjoys delving into the esoteric, working with numerology, or portraying the grotesque. This is not necessarily a part of apocalyptic, but it is often found in apocalyptic writings or groups. It is found in Qumran. It does not seem to be part of Pharisaism (although it may have been eliminated after the end of the Second Temple).

As for the Pharisees and Sadducees and the idea of eschatology, we can conclude that it had some effect on the Pharisees, to judge from their belief in angels and the resurrection. But the Sadducees, by the time the "penitents of the desert" (4QpPs37 2:7) had emigrated, were securely established in their position and had no need for, or theory of, the end.

Out of this same period came apocalyptic literature, some of which is markedly similar to QL.[10] As we might anticipate, the Sadducees had nothing to do with it. The Pharisees had little reason to need it. But the schismatic groups could be expected to make extensive use of it; and the Qumran discoveries confirm this. We must remember, however, that other schismatic groups would be similarly inclined, hence the fact that a group used apocalyptic writings would not necessarily indicate that it was identical with, or even closely related to, the Qumran Community.

Baptism and Baptists

Whether the idea of baptism came into Israel from without or was indigenous is to me not clear. The idea is common enough that there is no great significance in trying to answer this question. However, it would appear to be rea-

---

[10] Particularly Jubilees, 1 Enoch, Testaments of the Twelve Patriarchs, and part of Psalms of Solomon. Cf. H. H. Rowley, *The Relevance of Apocalyptic* (London: Lutterworth, 1947) for a description of this literature.

sonable to suppose that baptism, particularly ritual lustra-tions, would be present in a sect when ritual sacrifice is absent. The two acts are attempts to accomplish removal of sin or guilt.

If the reconstruction of the beginnings of the Qumran as I have presented it is valid, we can well understand the attitude toward the Jerusalem priesthood which is expressed in the Qumran writings. The "sons of Zadok, the ones who keep the covenant" want nothing to do with the illegitimate priests who have defiled the sanctuary. But no Jew would think of building a rival Temple. (That is what made the Samaritans so despicable!) Accordingly, ritual bathing, which was already provided for in the Law, passed over approximately to the sacramental concept.

It is this sectarian character which Cullmann has put his finger upon, and which he calls "Hellenism."[11] The name is not well chosen. That which the Hellenists and the Qum-ranians had in common was a religious concept that was emancipated from the Temple. In the Qumran group, the Temple remained the ideal and they could look forward to its purification. The Hellenists, however, moved on to com-plete rejection of animal sacrifice.

What about John the Baptist? Coming from a priestly family, as the New Testament indicates, he would hardly have had a propensity toward baptism in lieu of Temple sacrifices. In the light of the evidence as presented by Braun, Brownlee, and others, it seems reasonable to admit that there had been some influence of the Qumran Com-munity upon John. He seems to have broken with them, however, in his view of baptism, and particularly in his view of the world as composed of men not to be shunned,

[11] *Art. cit., JBL,* 74:220.

but to be summoned to repentance in order to enter into the kingdom of God.

The influence of this movement, as Thomas has shown, was widespread. Much of it went beyond the bounds of Judaism, and Judaism in turn tended to circumscribe its legalism so as to drive baptists and apocalyptists into non-Judaic groups.

What of the Essenes?

In view of Josephus' testimony and the time of his writing, it is impossible to say either that he misunderstood the Essenes, or that his sect was sufficiently separated from the Qumran Community to account for the difference between the two groups. On the other hand, there are differences between the two sects that cannot be overlooked.

There are two possibilities that seem to me to be worth consideration. (1) Josephus went to live with the Essenes about A.D. 50. The Community was destroyed in A.D. 68. Its literature had probably been produced a century or more before that time. We should not overlook the possibility that the group had in that interval undergone sufficient development in relevant points to account for the differences. (2) Or it is possible that there were a number of small communities scattered around Palestine, all of them originating in much the same way that the Qumran group did, therefore all having a basic similarity. Each group may have developed its own individuality, and Josephus may not have known of the various shades other than the two he mentions: the marrying and the nonmarrying Essenes.[12] His total of 4,000 may be a reasonably reliable

---

[12]It would not be difficult to make out a case for two (or more) subgroups in the Qumran Community, on the basis of the documents. There is even a difference between 1QSa and 1QS, so that Barthélemy thinks he can label 1QS as Essene and 1QSa as Hasidim. Cf. *Discoveries in the Judean Desert*, I: 108.

figure for all the various groups; it is obviously too high for the Qumran group alone. However, these conjectures must await confirmation.

Christianity

Christianity existed as a Jewish sect in its formative years, possibly down to Hadrian's time. In fact, it was protected from the action of the Roman law against new religions specifically because it was considered to be a Jewish sect.

We have seen that Christianity drew on Judaism for much of its thought. Some elements which were formerly considered to be Greek are now seen as Jewish. Its attitude toward the Temple, its baptism, its concept of Community, its apocalyptic, and even its incipient Gnosticism, can be traced to normative, or more often sectarian Judaism.

A word of caution is not out of place, for the tendency will be to oversimplify, as before; but this time to neglect the Hellenistic contributions to Christianity.

MISCELLANEOUS ITEMS

There are a few heterogeneous items that should be set down, spare pieces of our mosaic that must not be lost, but which are yet too few to be fit into the larger pattern.

Language

It has long been held that Hebrew died out with the Exile, and thereafter the Jews used Aramaic. In the days of the Maccabees, to be sure, there was a feeble renaissance, but it did not succeed. Now, evidence from Qumran seems to prove otherwise. As a matter of fact, Qumran Hebrew fits into place between Biblical Hebrew and Mishnaic

Hebrew,[13] and proves what Segal had maintained twenty years before the discovery of the Dead Sea Scrolls, that Mishnaic Hebrew "had an independent existence as a natural, living speech."[14] Zeitlin has repeatedly branded Qumran Hebrew as "bad Hebrew." But who is to judge what is "good" and what is "bad" in a language or dialect that is not controlled? Is Nuzi "bad Babylonian," or simply good Nuzi? Apparently the people spoke the language, and the scribes wrote it. Who am I to attempt a value judgment of it? There is sufficient material from Qumran that we can say, "Apparently that is the way they wrote Hebrew."

At the same time, the presence of Aramaic documents from Qumran, particularly letters, guards us from jumping to the other extreme. Aramaic and Hebrew were both used. The recovery of a quantity of Aramaic fills a pressing need, for hitherto no Aramaic from Palestine of the period contemporary with Jesus had been found. Studies in the Aramaic backgrounds of the Gospels, which formerly had been reconstructed somewhat hypothetically, will in the future be based on a better knowledge of the subject.

Morphology

In the early writings, several scholars discussed unusual Qumran forms, and more than one concluded that the documents must be late on the basis of these word formations. Now that the date is controlled, it becomes obvious that these forms represent an earlier morphological development than that which is found in the Masoretic text.

I shall not here attempt to be specific or technical. However, the subject of the introduction and usage of the *matres*

---

[13]Four MSS from cave 4Q are reportedly in Mishnaic Hebrew.
[14]M. H. Segal, *Grammar of Mishnaic Hebrew* (Oxford: Clarendon Press, 1927), pp. 8-13.

lectionis, or vowel letters (the use of *'áleph, wáw,* and *hé* to represent vowels), now needs further study. It would appear that these letters represent consonants, rather than vowels, in more cases than previously recognized. As a matter of fact, it seems to me that the subject should also be reopened for Moabite and Phoenician.[15]

Text Families

Closely related to the subject of Judaism is the study of the Biblical texts used by the Jews.

Three text families seem to be established by the studies of the Biblical texts found at Qumran. (It is of course possible that still others will be isolated and identified.) One is the ancestor of the Masoretic text, or our present Hebrew Bible. Scholars now recognize that the Masoretic text is not a later recension, but has received considerable support from Qumran. At the same time, a non-Masoretic text, similar to the Septuagint text, is supported by many Qumran fragments, and a second non-Masoretic text, which is also non-Septuagint, is supported by still other fragments. It is of interest to note in passing that the fragments of Greek text in QL now positively demonstrate the use of the Greek text in Palestine by Jews.

Of course, the facts demonstrated by the Qumran materials have long been suspected on other grounds. It is known, for example, that quotations of the Old Testament found in the New Testament fall into three main types: those that agree substantially with the Septuagint, those that agree with the Masoretic Text, and those that refuse to fit

---

[15]In order that this may not be too vague, I would suggest that one area of study might be the use of these letters in word-end. My seminars in Moabite, Phoenician, and Qumran in recent years have convinced me that many of the so-called final vowels are in reality consonants introducing an extra syllable.

into either of these categories. It will take years of textual studies to work out the details of this problem.

It has been recognized in the past by some scholars that the Council of Jamnia, A.D. 90, was to a greater or lesser extent responsible for the establishment of a "received text" of the Hebrew Bible, and that all competing texts were thereafter destroyed. The presence of competing texts in QL adds substance to this theory. A text similar to the Masoretic text was, we now know, in existence before the Council of Jamnia, but it was not the only text. As of the year A.D. 68, when Khirbet Qumran was destroyed and probably the time of the hiding of the manuscripts, these competing texts were still in existence. After A.D. 90 a single text is found. Scholars will be occupied for years with the study of the details of this problem; but the main lines seem now to be clearly established.

Canon and Higher Criticism

It is too early to draw any conclusions concerning the Canon of the Old Testament on the basis of Qumran evidence. However, a number of important questions have been raised. The Canon of the Hebrew Bible contains seven less books than are found in the Greek Old Testament. The Roman Catholic Church accepts the Canon of the Latin Vulgate, which is the Canon of the Greek Old Testament, and the Protestant churches generally accept the Canon of the Hebrew Bible. One of the arguments that has been advanced by Protestant scholars in defense of the present Hebrew Canon is based on the supposition that no Hebrew texts of the Deuterocanonical books are in existence. It must now be recognized that three manuscripts of Tobit—one in Hebrew and two in Aramaic—all corresponding to the Greek text have been found in cave 4Q. It is my opinion that Protestant scholars must now reopen the question of the validity of this particular argument for the Canon which we as Protestants accept.

Along with this same matter, we might mention the absence (so far) of any fragment of Esther. Does this indicate that the Qumran sect did not include Esther in its Canon? The matter needs careful study, particularly as to its implications.

The question of an Aramaic original for Ecclesiastes (Qoheleth) has often been debated. The discovery of a number of Hebrew texts of Qoheleth among the Qumran fragments seems to make the theory of an Aramaic original more difficult to maintain.

The date of the composition of Daniel may need to be reconsidered as a result of the Qumran discoveries. Driver recognized promptly that a date of about 150 B.C. for the Qumran materials, which included fragments of Daniel (at that time, only one manuscript; since then, others have been identified), would require a date prior to 167 B.C. for the composition of the work.[16] This, of course, would be quite a revolution in critical studies, for the date of Daniel, according to the critics, is firmly established by the profaning of the Temple by Antiochus Epiphanes (p. 225). New studies in Aramaic, based on the Qumran materials may shed light on the same problem.[17] Once

[16]G. R. Driver, *The Hebrew Scrolls, from the Neighbourhood of Jericho and the Dead Sea* (London: Oxford University Press, 1951), p. 9, n. 5.

[17]J. A. Montgomery, in his *Commentary on the Book of Daniel* (*The International Critical Commentary* [New York: Scribner's 1927], pp. 14-20), points out that the language of Daniel is that of the fifth to third centuries B.C.—although he dates chs. 1-6 in the third and chs. 7-12 in the second century. Interestingly enough, Montgomery, speaking of the Hebrew of Daniel, says, "For a document which reads most akin to the diction of Daniel, attention must be called to the so-called Zadokite Fragments . . . ." (p. 15).

again, the complications of the problem suggest caution, and scholarship will be required to handle each of the problems individually before attempting a synthesis of the findings.

Similarly, the problem of the Maccabean Psalms is probably brought into new light, although this point can hardly be discussed until there is a catalogue of the individual Psalms represented in the Qumran fragments.

Of one thing we can be certain: the discovery of the Dead Sea Scrolls has opened up vast areas of study, some of them new, some of them old, but all of them important for the study of the Holy Scriptures.

Abbreviations

art. cit.	in the article cited
ASV	American Standard Version
BA	*Biblical Archaeologist*
BASOR	*Bulletin of the American Schools of Oriental Research*
CBQ	*Catholic Biblical Quarterly*
CD	*Damascus Document*
Deut. Rab.	*Deuteronomy Rabbah*
ed.	editor, edited by
11QPsa	Scroll of Psalms from Cave 11Q
11QLev	Scroll of Leviticus from Cave 11Q
EstBib	*Estudios Biblicos*
f., ff.	following page, following pages
4QDᵇ	Fragments of *Damascus Document* from Cave 4Q
4QFlor	Fragment of *Florilegium* from Cave 4Q
4QJerᵇ	Second exemplar of Jeremiah from Cave 4Q
4QTest	Fragment of *Testimonia* from Cave 4Q
4QPBless	Fragment of *Patriarchal Blessings* from Cave 4Q (previously identified as 4QpGen 49)
4QpPs37	*Commentary on Ps. 37* from Cave 4Q
HTR	*Harvard Theological Review*
HUCA	*Hebrew Union College Annual*
ibid.	in the same place
ILN	*Illustrated London News*
JBL	*Journal of Biblical Literature*
JJS	*Journal of Jewish Studies*
JQR	*Jewish Quarterly Review*
KJV	King James Version
loc. cit.	in the place cited
LXX	Septuagint (Greek Old Testament)
I Macc.	I Maccabees
II Macc.	II Maccabees
MGJW	*Monatsschrift für Geschichte und Wissenschaft des Judentums*

MS, MSS	Manuscript, Manuscripts
MT	Masoretic Text (Hebrew Old Testament)
n.	note
NS	New Series
NTS	*New Testament Studies*
1QH	*Thanksgiving Psalms*
1QIs^a	First Exemplar of Isaiah from Cave 1Q
1QIs^b	Second Exemplar of Isaiah from Cave 1Q
1QM	*Order of Warfare*
1QpHab	*Habakkuk Commentary*
1QS	*Manual of Discipline*
1QSa	"Two Columns" of *Manual of Discipline,* or *Rule of the Congregation* (=1Q 28a)
1Q28a	Fragments of MS 28a from Cave 1Q (=1QSa)
1Q28b	Fragments of MS 28b from Cave 1Q (=1QSb)
1Q30	Fragments of MS 30 from Cave 1Q
op. cit.	in the work cited
p., pp.	page, pages
PEQ	*Palestine Exploration Quarterly*
Ps. Sol.	Psalms of Solomon
QL	Qumran Literature
RB	*Revue Biblique*
RHR	*Revue de l'Histoire des Religions*
RSV	Revised Standard Version
st. cstr.	construct state
TZ	*Theologische Zeitschrift*
vol.	volume
VT	*Vetus Testamentum*
ZAW	*Zeitschrift für Alttestamentliche Wissenschaft*
ZNW	*Zeitschrift für Neutestamentliche Wissenschaft*
ZTK	*Zeitschrift für Theologie und Kirche*

Index

247